D0541296

THE
HIDDEN PLACES

of

Southern &
Central Scotland

Written by **JOY DAVID**
Foreword by **ANGELA RIPPON**

Acknowledgements

This book would not have been compiled without the dedicated help of a number of people, especially Zoë, Jayne and Anne, to whom the editor offers sincere thanks.

OTHER TITLES IN THIS SERIES

The Hidden Places of North Yorkshire
The Hidden Places of Devon and Cornwall
The Hidden Places of Somerset, Avon and Dorset
The Hidden Places of Norfolk and Suffolk
The Hidden Places of Sussex
The Hidden Places of Cumbria
The Hidden Places of Yorkshire, South, East and West
The Hidden Places of Hampshire and The Isle of Wight

AVAILABLE SHORTLY

The Hidden Places of Surrey and Berkshire
The Hidden Places of Gloucestershire and Wiltshire
The Hidden Places of Kent
The Hidden Places of Wales
The Hidden Places of Northumberland and Durham

ISBN 1-871815-25-8
First published in 1990
© M & M PUBLISHING LTD.
Northern Office: Hammerain House, Hookstone Avenue, Harrogate HG2 8ER.
Southern Office: Dolphin House, Sutton Harbour, Plymouth, Devon PL4 ODW.
All information is included by the editors in good faith and is believed to be correct at the time of going to press.
No responsibility can be accepted for error.

Printed and bound in Great Britain by Troutbeck Press
a subsidiary of R. Booth (Bookbinder) Limited
Antron Hill, Mabe, Penryn, Cornwall

THE HIDDEN PLACES
OF
Southern and Central Scotland

Contents

Warworth Castle

Foreword

How many times have you heard someone say "I don't know why we keep going abroad on holiday every year when we haven't begun to explore or get to know our own country?"

It's true that Britain, as a whole, is full of the most wonderful countryside and coastline and whether it is in the far west peninsular of Devon and Cornwall or in the Orkneys, we have some of the world's finest natural treasures. It's the hidden nooks and crannies, the quiet places and the unexpected that hold much of the true charm of any region.

Being a local helps, they have known about such places for generations. The visitor may pass them by and so miss many of the real pleasures.

These books are by way of a privilege, giving access to places, county by county, you may never have seen. So enjoy and perhaps understand why those of us fortunate to have been born here think of it as being God's own Kingdom.

ANGELA RIPPON

Berwickshire and East Lothian

Manderston House

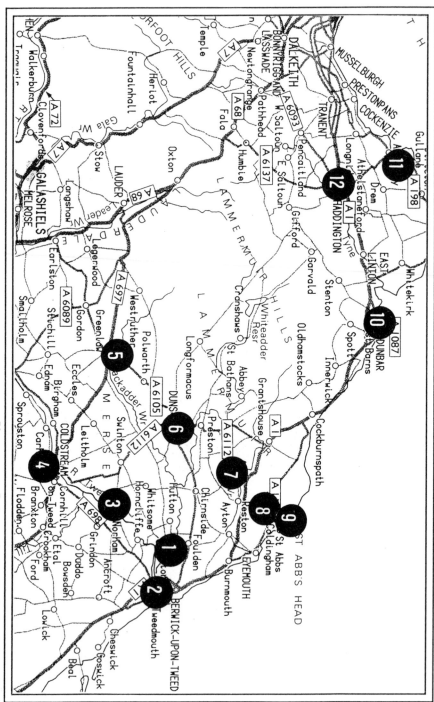

Please turn to Reference Section for further information.

CHAPTER ONE

Berwickshire &East Lothian

We begin our journey in this border country with its noble heritage and sometimes bloody history, alive today with the names of the people and places that have played a vital role in the shaping of this proud and ancient area. We were pleased to have a chance to travel in this beautiful land with such a rich history of kings and queens, heroic legends and, above all, its fiercely independent and majestic character.

There can be no more fitting place to begin our journey than **Berwick Upon Tweed**, ideally situated on the edge of the border with a history stretching back to Roman times. There are beautiful and awesome medieval fortifications here and even today the Elizabethan walls are regarded as the best preserved in Europe.

Although, strictly speaking, Berwick now lies in England, we found that it has changed hands no less than fourteen times in the continual tug of war that existed for so many years in the conflicts between the English and the Scots.

Today the old and the new mingle in this lovely town and we are sure that you will delight in its many contrasts of customs and buildings, where Elizabethan architecture is joined by elegant Georgian buildings. We have always loved the pretty houses, with their grey stone walls and red roofs, and, if you follow the old walls, you will have a fascinating journey for nearly two miles as they wind and twist around the narrow streets and small alleyways that almost gave us the impression of being in a Cornish town.

Whatever you find here, it will certainly have a distinctive flavour of its own. In more turbulent times the pride of Berwick was its castle, which managed to withstand centuries of sieges only to be sadly destroyed to make way for the railway just over a century ago.

Part of the Great Hall still stands by the platform, and it was here that Edward I decided between Balliol and Bruce for the succession to the throne of Scotland in 1291. Edward decided in favour of Balliol only to seize the throne himself in 1296. You can almost imagine the fearful ghost of Edward Plantagenet stalking the remains of the Great Hall after dark.

Berwick should not however be considered primarily as a museum. It has lovely parks and gardens to walk in, plus wide sandy beaches in a resort of **Spittal**, a stone's throw away across the Tweed. We have already mentioned the independent character of the town, and so we were not surprised to hear that at one time it was customary in Acts of Parliament for Berwick to be mentioned separately after Wales, as it was considered to be a territory of its own, the borders of which were known as the 'Berwick Bounds'.

The symbolic marking of this area is a custom that is still carried out each year, accompanied by festivities on the first of May. There is much to do and see in Berwick and we were interested in visiting the 'Barracks', which are in fact the oldest purpose-built barracks in the country, and now house a fascinating museum complex and art gallery. The town itself has many interesting shops and its narrow streets come alive on market day, which is traditionally held each Wednesday and Saturday. Have you got a sweet tooth? Then you might try Berwick's cockles, not as you might expect a shellfish, but a peppermint sweet in the shape of a cockle.

Berwick Barracks

Berwick is dominated by the sea and the magnificent River Tweed that sweeps in through the town. The livelihood of the town was based on the sea, and Berwick's most famous industries were in salmon and sea fishing, which have survived here despite the decline suffered in many coastal towns.

The River Tweed is spanned at no less than three points by historic bridges: Berwick Bridge, which dates from the 17th century, The Royal Tweed Bridge, built in 1928 and The Royal Border Railway Bridge, which was designed by Robert Stephenson and has twenty eight arches, this was opened by Queen Victoria in 1850.

From a point nearly four miles above Berwick Bridge, the Tweed follows the border for some eighteen miles. The Tweed is really one of the most enchanting and distinctive border rivers, and if you are feeling up to a walk it is well worth taking the time to explore it by foot by way of a bankside path that starts from Tweedmouth.

Travelling along the Berwick bypass out of town, you may well find yourself in need of refreshments. Well, we have the answer. Keep your eyes open for the B6461. A short drive along there will bring you to **Canty's Brig**, a superb country pub sitting on the banks of the River Whiteadder.

This is a welcoming little pub, even more so for families for proprietor

Peter Mailer makes a special point of catering for children. Let them romp around in the garden where there is a slide, swing and collection of animals including rabbits and ducks. When the weather doesn't suit, however, you'll want to bring them inside to the family room, liberally stocked with toys and leading onto a lovely sun lounge overlooking the river.

Going up from this room is a spiral staircase which leads you to the large split level, L-shaped main bar. Now here you will see a splendid example of best mahogany, the bar no less, which has been installed here and originally came from the Theatre Royal in Newcastle.

Canty's Brig is open from 11am to 3pm and 6pm to 11pm daily. Bar food is available at both lunch times and in the evenings. The menu changes daily and there is always a wide range of traditional meals available. Of course there is a special children's menu too, and another thoughtful touch from Peter is the availability of half portions which he feels are very popular with older visitors.

A visit to the Tweed Valley would not be complete without a riverside lunch and whether you choose to eat inside, or take advantage of the sun and sit on the patio, Canty's Brig is an obvious choice for a break in the journey.

Canty's Brig

Twenty miles along the Tweed at **Norham** we were pleased to come across **Norham Castle**, which was apparently the inspiration for several landscapes by Turner, and certainly worthy of our attention, set as it has been for some three hundred years in this lovely setting.

Norham village itself thoroughly charmed us. We found it a very pleasant place, with its cottages lining each side of a lovely green. The church dates from 830AD, and we were surprised to find that it had more than once been occupied as a base from which to besiege the castle.

We had heard the name **Coldstream**, and wanted to know a little more. This place name is given of course to that most famous regiment The Coldstream Guards, which was founded here in 1639 by General Monck, a

5

supporter of Charles II. A plaque on the Guards' House, rebuilt in 1865, at the east end of the market place, indicates their original headquarters.

We also knew Coldstream because of a man we greatly admire, Alec Douglas Home, Lord Home of the Hirsel. His family home is here at Coldstream and as we wandered in this pleasant place we thought about him. In our view he was one of Britain's finest Prime Minsters who but for the advent of television would have been Prime Minister for a long time. This was a man who gave up his Earldom in order to become Prime Minister and then his ungrateful party deposed him because he did not come over well on television. We wonder what would have happened to Gladstone in his time if there had been TV!.

A few miles from Coldstream lies the site of the Battle of Flodden, 1513, where ten thousand Scotsmen, including their king, James IV, perished at the hands of the English, despite outnumbering the enemy. It was one of the most fearful days in Scotish history where the flower of nobility was slain, a simple and popular version of the traditional lament for this day sums the loss:

'I've heard them lilting, at the ewe milking.
Lasses a'lilting, before dawn of day;
But now they are moaning, on ilka green loaning;
The flowers of the forest are a'wede away.'

The disastrous defeat was a result of some bad tactical decisions by the king, who at one stage dismounted his horse and fought hand to hand surrounded by his soldiers in a valiant attempt to turn the tide. This great loss is still remembered each year in Coldstream.

Like Gretna Green, Coldstream, being on the border, has had its fair share of runaway marriages. Although not as well known as Gretna, eloping couples used to cross at Smeaton's Bridge and make for the old marriage house that can still be seen.

Talking about being on the border by mistake we found ourselves in Northumbria and just six miles of Alnwick and on the road to Wooler we came to **Eglingham** village.

This picturesque place village boasts a beautiful Norman church, and is the perfect base for walking, touring and just enjoying the peace and tranquility of this area.

Visitors to Eglingham seeking quality accommodation in comfortable surroundings need look no further than **Ogle House Guest House And Restaurant**.

Built around 1790 as a coaching inn, this stone built grade two listed building has been tastefully renovated to provide a high standard of comfort. For their efforts, proprietors Norman and Carol Ann McRoberts hold a three coronet award from the English Tourist Board.

There are three guest rooms available, all comfortably furnished and with full ensuite facilities. Parents with young children will be pleased to know that baby listening services are also provided.

Norman and Carol Ann strive to provide their guests with only the best in fresh local produce, served in their cosy restaurant which is also open to non-residents. A typical menu may include home made soup, fresh locally caught salmon with vegetables, and fresh cream gateau with coffee to follow. A table license is pending, for those of you who enjoy a drink with your meal.

If you're looking for a special gift to take home, or simply wish to treat yourself, you'll discover a marvellous selection of original gifts available in the McRoberts' adjoining Ogle House Craft Shop.

All in all, you will find that this charming couple will do all they can to make your stay in Eglingham as pleasant as possible. We will come back to Eglingham in our Hidden Places of Northumbria.

Rather reluctantly, we left the Tweed and the borderline behind us, and decided to head towards the Lammermuir Hills and the ancient town of **Greenlaw**, which originated in 1147.

Set against wooded country, and on the Blackadder Water, the present town dates from the 17th century, replacing the older village that stood on a nearby hill. The church here was built in 1675 and has an interesting tower that adjoins it. We found that it was originally used as a prison.

Greenlaw was of importance for two main reasons. It was the market town of Berwickshire for over one hundred and fifty years until Duns took over this role, as a larger and more important town. Secondly, Greenlaw became a convenient stopping place for weary stage coach travellers between Edinburgh and Newcastle in the days of horse-drawn transport. A fire in 1545 destroyed much of the village, although it was subsequently rebuilt, and by 1698 had become the chief burgh of the shire.

Here you will find **The Castle Inn Hotel**, an impressive Georgian style coaching inn situated on the A697 in the heart of the village. The original Castle Inn was a coaching establishment with massive stables to the rear, and sited behind the old village green. In 1831, however, a new County building was completed on the site of the green and the old inn was demolished and rebuilt on the site of the old stables.

The Castle Inn's proprietors Paul Worthington and Chris Cochran offer excellent accommodation with good food and personal service at very reasonable prices. Each elegant and spacious bedroom has direct dial telephones and private facilities.

The Castle Inn and the surrounding Berwickshire countryside is a haven for fishing fans, golfers, outdoor sports people and nature lovers. Equally popular with locals, the hotel serves morning coffee, lunches, high teas, dinners and bar suppers daily and the a la carte restaurant is open each evening. The hotel has a fully equipped gym, sauna and solarium.

Castle Inn Hotel

Commended by the Scottish Tourist Board, and carrying a two crowns award, The Castle Inn is a shining example of Messrs Worthington and Cochran's policy of continuous expansion and improvement.

Are you keen on fishing? If so, you will not be disappointed as there is trout fishing on the Blackadder from March to early October. Permits are available from the post office or from hotels in Greenlaw.

Until we came to Greenlaw we had not realised that there was really a Blackadder. We thought the name had been invented by Rowan Atkinson and his team of merry men.

Much refreshed, we continued our journey, thankfully not by stagecoach, heading for Duns, situated right in the heart of Berwickshire. **Polwarth** is three miles from Greenlaw, on the A6105, and is a place of rural quiet but with a charming tale to tell. Whenever a marriage was celebrated in the village, all the villagers would dance around the two holly trees on the green. The trees are still there, though the dancing has now ceased; a pity.

Duns itself is still essentially a market town, though set away from main traffic routes and, like Greenlaw, against the backdrop of the Lammermuir Hills. The name Duns we thought was a strange one, and we found that it derives from an old word for hill fort, the original settlement being situated on the slopes of Duns Law, a word for hill.

In Newton Street we took a look at the **Jim Clark Memorial Room**, which is a rather unusual museum. It commemorates the life and career of the racing driver who lived in Duns and was world champion in 1963 and again in 1965, before his tragic death in Munich in 1968. The museum is open from Easter to October and contains many of his trophies and memorabilia.

If you are feeling in the mood for a little sport, not far away on the other side of the square is a public park where you can enjoy bowls, tennis and putting.

A mile or so to the east of Duns, it is worth paying a visit to Manderston House. This is one of the finest examples of Edwardian country houses in Britain. There is much to see here, and we were fascinated by the 'downstairs', the domestic quarters which have been preserved to give one a real flavour of life in such a house eighty or ninety years ago. The house itself is a wonderful example of extravagance, and has a staircase which is a replica of the Petite Trianon at Versailles, the rails being plated in silver.

Manderston House

We passed through **Chirnside** which, we were delighted to be told, has a plant that makes the paper for the teabags that we use so often.

We had heard that **The Craw Inn** at **Auchencrow** would offer us an ideal place in which to unwind and refresh ourselves, and we had not been misinformed. Set in beautiful rolling farmland, Auchencrow is a haven of peace and tranquillity, situated only two miles from the busy A1 trunk road, twelve miles north of Berwick upon Tweed.

The Craw Inn

In a relaxed and friendly atmosphere, The Craw Inn restaurant offers char-grilled steaks, bistro-style Scottish and French country cooking and superb local seafood, complemented by a good quality wine list and some specialist malt whiskies. All dishes are prepared from only the freshest of basic ingredients, so there is no whiff of 'boil in the bag' cooking here.

Dine in comfort here in the restaurant, or take advantage of the extensive bar menu also available. Should you prefer real ale, then enjoy it in the hurly burly of the public bar, with its exposed beams and bar billiard table.

Families with children are welcome in the children's room, the eighteen hole putting green with its beer garden, and the children's play area.

In summer the inn is open all day Saturday and Sunday, Sundays only in winter.

From Auchencrow we joined the A1 and then joined the B6355 to take us into **Eyemouth**, a picturesque fishing town, which retains not only its cobbled streets but also a distinct old world charm. The harbour has a breakwater that dates from 1770, and is protected by the 'Hurkars' rocks. Overlooking the harbour is Gunsgreen House, an 18th century mansion, and an old haunt of smugglers. The coast here is rich in smuggling legend, with numerous cliffs hiding caves and passages.

Eyemouth harbour is still a busy place, and proved to be fascinating as we watched the fish being landed and auctioned here. The fishing is mainly for white fish, prawns, lobster and crab. It is always possible for you to charter a boat and do some sea fishing of your own, if you are feeling adventurous.

During a great storm in 1881, Eyemouth endured a terrible tragedy when half of the fishing fleet was sunk and over one hundred men lost. A marvellous tapestry depicting the disaster was sewn by local women in 1981 to mark the centenary. It is fifteen feet long, containing one million stitches, and all of the women involved in the work were descendants of the men who were drowned. The tapestry can be seen in the Eyemouth museum, together with the story of the storm and other exhibits, showing how both fishing and Eyemouth have changed over the years.

Not far away, a scenic clifftop walk will take you from Eyemouth to St. Abbs via **Coldingham**. Coldingham itself is an 18th century town, though the priory here dates back to 1098 and now serves as a chapel. It was once in possession of a tower nine hundred feet high until it was destroyed by Cromwell in 1648.

There are a wide range of activities available in Coldingham and, apart from numerous walks, there is a small art studio in the village where classes are held each summer. If you like diving, then this is just the place to put it into practice. The waters here are ideal and there are facilities for this sport that has become so very popular. Both sailing and sea angling are also available.

While we were exploring Coldingham, we discovered **The Spirit Level**.

It is always refreshing to come across an inn with a difference; and that's precisely what John and Christine Ross have here in The Spirit Level in Coldingham.

The inn is over two hundred years old, although inside it offers all the modern comforts and facilities that we come to expect today. The split level lounge bar has a cosy open fire, and a newly refurbished family room means that you can bring the children in when the weather outside is not as accommodating as we would like it to be. If however you are lucky enough to visit Coldingham during one of the finer days of a Scottish summer, you will undoubtedly prefer to relax in The Spirit Level's beer garden.

In the lounge you will see a fascinating collection of old carpenters' tools on display; some, like the inn itself, dating back over two hundred years to the 18th century.

The Spirit Level

The Spirit Level is justifiably proud of its selection of real ales, and there certainly is something to suit everyone's taste. For those who prefer bottled beers, John has introduced a range of around sixty different beers from all over the world, including Russian lager and Green lager from Denmark.

Traditional meals and snacks are available all day but one look at the menu will tell you that John and Christine specialise in the unusual. They do in fact claim to be the first inn in Britain to serve buffalo steaks! Alongside this on their 'Off The Level' menu you will find swordfish, kingfish, alligator steaks and even rattlesnake and beaver sausages! It's also worth trying out their mouthwatering oak smoked chicken.

There are three letting rooms available at The Spirit Level, which means visitors can also use the inn as a base for touring the local area.

On the whole, whether your tastes are as adventurous as the menu here, or if you are simply looking for traditional food from a varied menu, then John and Christine have certainly achieved this objective; with the added bonus of value for money and friendly service throughout.

There is much to see on this beautiful coast, and we decided to take a closer look at **St. Abbs**, a picturesque fishing village which nestles around a tiny harbour. The harbour is still used by a small fleet of crab and lobster boats. Here we saw a row of tiny buildings which were apparently used by the fishermen to store their gear. If you are feeling fit, do walk on further towards St. Abb's Head as the view off the three hundred feet high red sandstone cliffs is truly spectacular.

Do you enjoy painting and sketching? The landscapes and seabirds of St. Abb's Head National Nature Reserve offer superb opportunities for the budding artist. Apart from being an important area for seabirds, many species can be seen here, especially between April and July, and these include guillemots, razorbills, kittiwakes, fulmars and even puffins. Birds on land include wheatears, meadow pipits and stonechats.

The nature reserve is an ideal stopping-off place for the birds travelling south from the Arctic winter in the British Isles. We were enthralled as we watched the artists trying to capture the entrancing scenes on paper.

Three miles to the west of St. Abb's Head is one of the most extraordinary ruined castles that we have ever come across. Fast Castle is perched precariously on a stack of rock, and is barely accessible by the steep cliff footpath. The ruin is best viewed from above; we did not dare to attempt a closer look. Fast Castle was used by Sir Walter Scott as the model for Wolf's Crag in 'The Bride of Lammermuir'. It is also fascinating to think that the fourteen year old princess, Margaret Tudor, used the castle as a resting place on her way to marry James IV of Scotland, Flodden's tragic monarch.

We followed the coast road from Coldingham, the A1107, which took us across the moor and, following the coast, gave us some splendid views of the sea as we approached **Dunbar**.

Here, we were pleased to learn, is a town which boasts more sunshine hours than any other location in Scotland. It is also a popular holiday resort, with Belhaven Beach to the west and White Sands to the east. Dunbar has a history of brewing which goes back to the Middle Ages, and today boasts a number of brewing firms renowned for their real ales, still brewed in the original manner.

Dunbar was at one time a prosperous fishing centre, and in 1879 could boast a fishing fleet of over three hundred boats. The wide high street and big solid sandstone buildings are evidence of the prosperity that was brought to the town through the industry. Indeed, a walk around Dunbar will be a rewarding experience.

Many visitors to Scotland will go home with a suitcase containing perhaps a kilt, suit or other item of traditional clothing purchased after a lengthy trek up and down the crowded streets of Edinburgh. Well, we have some advice for you. Forget about the rigours of Princes Street, and opt instead for a leisurely stroll down Dunbar's uncrowded High Street.

Here, for three generations and more, the firm of **Daniel Smith** has provided a high class tailoring service and earned an enviable reputation among those who appreciate quality, selection and service. In 1981, when Daniel Smith retired, he entrusted this high class business to another son of East Lothian, Mr Dan Cairney.

Daniel Smith

Mr Cairney claims he is the only real 'tailor' left in the East Lothian area and, having been in the business for forty six years, he offers an impeccable degree of knowledge and personal service to all visitors.

Today Mr Cairney continues to satisfy customers nationwide by maintaining the firm's first class service in tailoring and kilt making, and also operating a personal calling service for customers in and around Dunbar.

Perhaps Daniel Smith's most famous patron, however, was Queen Victoria, who is known to have shopped here during her stay at nearby Dunglass.

As well as a bespoke service, Dan Cairney also offers a wide range of ready to wear outfits for gents from his extensive stock. These include most of the leading makes, such as Pringle, Viyella, Grenfell and Magee suits.

Discerning visitors will note the 'tailor' logo depicted on the firm's stationery; an award given only to craftsmen of the very highest standard.

Dunbar Castle overlooks one of the town's two harbours. It was here that Mary Queen of Scots was brought by the Earl of Bothwell in April 1567, and where they remained for ten days prior to their marriage.

To the western side of the town and located on a beautiful stretch of coastline, we visited the **John Muir Country Park**. American patrons, will feel at home here for this park was named in honour of the man who himself emigrated to the States and founded America's first national park. Dunbar is his home town, and today the Sierra Club of America regularly visit the town in memory of the man who provided them with perhaps one of the most important elements of their national heritage. The park is some one thousand, six hundred and sixty seven acres and actually extends into Dunbar and includes the castle.

We thought it to be a spectacular outing, taking in a vast area of countryside and coastline, and it is a haven for the family and the naturalist. The park contains a wide variety of birds and plants and there is ample opportunity for walking and exploring with marked routes of interest and nature trails. There are also facilities for a range of activities including horse riding, golf and sea fishing. Be prepared to take along your own sausages and charcoal as there are even facilities for setting up your own barbecue. All in all, we think that the park makes for a perfect day out.

North Berwick can be reached by taking the A198 after leaving Dunbar, and here you will find a popular yachting resort and centre for tourism. Offshore is the fascinating Bass Rock, rising some three hundred and twelve feet from the sea, now a famous bird sanctuary, providing one of the few nesting colonies for the gannet, a bird with legendary diving abilities and, we were surprised to learn, once a sought after dish. We thought it would be rather too salty for most people's taste.

Many other birds nest on the rocky edges, and even puffins nest on the grassy slopes. Boat trips can be made by arrangement from North Berwick, and we think that you will be amazed at the sights and sounds of the birds on this spectacular rock.

Inland, the country rises to North Berwick Law which is six hundred and thirteen feet above sea level and can be seen from as far away as Edinburgh and Fife. On the top of this ancient volcano, from which the view on a clear day is stunning, have been placed the jaws of a whale.

If you are in need of somewhere to stay whilst soaking up this glorious countryside and coastline, then we would recommend you to head for **Gullane**, which is only a few miles outside the town of North Berwick. The coastal town of Gullane, with its beautiful beach, is a popular spot for visitors and locals alike. The town itself is fortunate enough to be fairly well served with moderately priced hotels, one of these being personally run by Mrs Ann Robertson, **The Queens Hotel** is a firm favourite among the golfing fraternity. The surrounding countryside is an undoubted haven for golfers, with several first rate courses to play, including the internationally famous Muirfield, used previously as a stage for the British Open Championship.

Mrs Robertson can trace the origins of her hotel back to the early 1800s, and is always keen to find out more about its early history. Today, however, we are sure you will agree that The Queens offers modern comfort in a family atmosphere enjoying the best of both worlds, countryside and coastal.

There are thirty five rooms here, of which sixteen offer en-suite facilities. All rooms have tea and coffee-making facilities and there is a colour TV in

14

the residents' lounge.

Fully licensed, the hotel has two bars, and non-residents are always welcome.

The Queens Hotel

The restaurant at The Queens offers a relaxed, airy atmosphere in which to enjoy the best of traditional fayre. As with many of East Lothian's coastal towns and villages, you will find that fresh fish is the speciality here, and well worth sampling. A moderately priced wine list provides the ideal partner for the menu, and complements the dishes well. So whether or not you intend to take advantage of the fabulous golfing facilities on offer here, or simply wish to relax and enjoy the best of East Lothian's coast and countryside, The Queens is an ideal base for you, the family and the golf clubs!

St. Mary's, Haddington

We were also keen to visit **Haddington**, as we had heard it was one of those rare towns that has come into the twentieth century with its elegance and character intact. We were delighted to find that it was indeed a

15

magnificent town, with many lovingly restored houses and shops, a mixture of both Georgian and Victorian buildings.

Unfortunately, the town lay directly in the path of invading English armies and was repeatedly destroyed before reaching more prosperous days in the 18th century. Since then, its biggest threat came from the river Tyne that runs around it, flooding it in 1775 when it rose to a height of seventeen feet above its normal level. As recently as 1948 the Tyne rose above all recorded levels, forming a torrent some eight hundred yards across.

The Waterside Bistro

One of the most popular restaurants in East Lothian is **The Waterside Bistro** at Haddington. The proprietor of the restaurant, Jim Findlay, previously ran The Horse Shoe at Eddleston, and since that was an equally popular restaurant in its time, it would appear that Mr Findlay obviously has found his own recipe for success. The Waterside has a snug downstairs bar which has a convivial atmosphere all of its own. Here you will find a full range of beers, lagers, wines and cocktails to choose from.

Go upstairs to the restaurant and you enter a much grander room, surrounded by wood panelling and housing a pleasant selection of potted plants. The a la carte menu here offers intercontinental cuisine, specialising in a varied selection of classic French dishes. Variety certainly seems to be the norm at The Waterside though, for fresh dishes are introduced on a daily basis.

Choose from a good selection of fresh seafood or go for a vegetarian meal; you will be well catered for. The food here is admirably complemented by a comprehensive wine list which will undoubtedly make it a pleasure for you to choose a drink to suit your choice from the impressive range of dishes available.

When you know that Jim Findlay's Waterside Bistro is the current holder of a Best Restaurant - East Lothian award and also holds a Bollinger Best Restaurant award, you will perhaps understand why this place is so

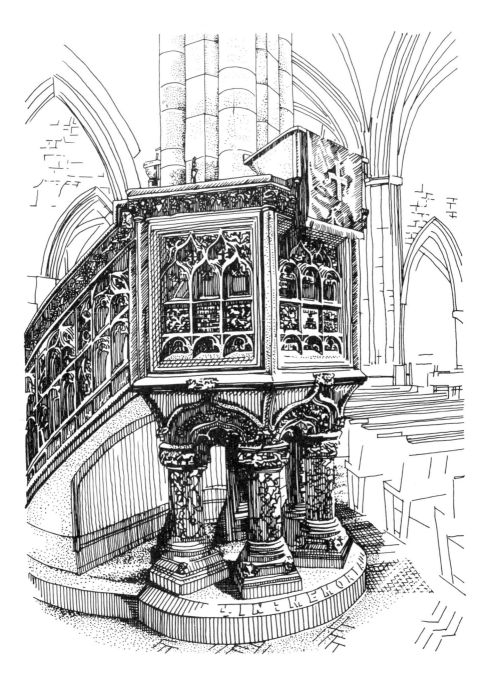

Pulpit, St. Mary's Church, Haddington

and avoid disappointment. This is a busy place and trade is no doubt boosted by the fact that Jim can arrange for a courtesy bus to be made available for parties of six or more.

Take our advice, book up now and treat yourself to a meal in one of this area's most historic towns; you won't be disappointed.

Roxburghshire

Melrose Abbey

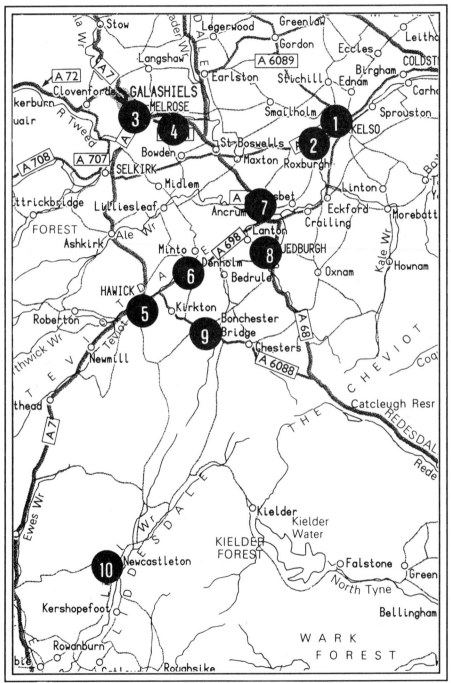

CHAPTER TWO

Roxburghshire

Once described by the writer, Sir Walter Scott, as the "most beautiful town in England", **Kelso**, set majestically at the junction of two rivers, the Tweed and the Teviot, must certainly be a contender for this coveted title.

A busy market town with a population of just five thousand, Kelso has a lovely elegant square which is surrounded by fine buildings. The roofs, pinnacles and small streets of the town look strangely continental, with its shop windows peering through arches, and the grey and brown houses which front the market square. It really was hard to believe, on the summer evening when we visited, that we were not in the Pyrenees.

There is still a bullring in the centre of the square, which is the point where bulls were once tethered during markets. Today markets and shows are no longer held here, but in Springwood Park, which is across the river.

We were told that the arched bridge spanning the river was built in 1800, and was in fact the model for the old Waterloo Bridge across the Thames. There are two lamp posts here which were retrieved from London Bridge when it was demolished in 1930.

During World War II, Polish troops were stationed in Kelso, and there is a plaque in the town which was presented by the visitors in gratitude for their stay. They must surely have enjoyed being here, as indeed we did. The surrounding countryside is very beautiful, and there is so much to be explored.

Kelso Abbey

The magnificent Kelso Abbey was built on the instructions of King David I, and was started around 1128. Vatican records show that it was one of the largest of the Border abbeys. In 1545 it was used as a stronghold against the

English invasion and sadly the defendants, including the monks, were ruthlessly slaughtered.

If ever there was a jewel in the crown, then **Floors Castle** must be a prime example. This magnificent mansion overlooking the River Tweed and the town of Kelso is the home of the tenth Duke and Duchess of Roxburghe. Some visitors may feel that the castle looks familiar. In fact it provided the setting for the celebrated Tarzan movie 'Greystoke'.

Built in 1721 by the builder/architect William Adam, Floors Castle became the Scottish seat of the First Duke of Roxburghe, an eminent gentleman who was bestowed with many titles by Queen Anne and became the first Secretary of State for Scotland following the Union of 1707.

The castle occupies the site of the previous home of the Earls of Roxburghe, 'Auld Floors', which had been their home since 1650 when they abandoned the now ruined Cessford Castle, this had been the principal seat of the Kers for four centuries. It is interesting to note that 'Auld Floors' was sometimes known as 'Floris' which in Scots tongue means 'Flowers'. Could it be that this was The Flower of the Borderlands, which in Sir Walter Scott's words was the "Kingdom of Oberon and Titania"?

Floors Castle is rich in history, for 'Auld Floors' was known to be a refuge for the Royalists in the days of 'Habbie' Ker, the first Earl. Another story tells us of the present castle being used as a temporary lodging for Prince Charles' men during the 1745 rebellion. At this time however, the castle was still under construction.

Romance is not far away either; romance connected with drama, a drama that interrupted the family line. The third Duke of Roxburghe, a man known for his great intellect, became deeply attached to Christina, the elder daughter of the Duke of Mecklenberg-Strelitze. Unfortunately for him, her younger sister, Charlotte, became George IV's Queen and court etiquette decreed that an elder sister could not become a subject of a younger sister. Their love was thwarted and in their despair both undertook a life of celibacy. The Duke sublimated his affections by becoming the most discerning book collector of his century. Amongst his collection are such books as Caxton's 'Recuyell of the History of Troy' and a first edition of 'Decameron'.

The hiccough in the family line in the early 1800s, caused partly through Duke John's lack of issue, was the subject of a lengthy lawsuit which continued for seven years. As the fifth Duke took his rightful place, the lawsuit had to be funded from the sale of the Roxburghe library. Irony, but not total disaster, for the main components of the library were saved by a handful of peers who founded the Roxburghe Club. They each held originals and undertook to produce facsimiles until they all had a complete collection consisting of originals and facsimiles.

It is however almost impossible to give but the barest of details here, for to do Floors Castle justice you must visit yourself, and, wandering from room to room, you will see how each tells its own story.

As you look from the windows, part of Scotland's heritage lies before you. There are the mounds of the old city of **Roxburgh** and of Roxburgh Castle; in its day one of Scotland's principal fortresses and home to many monarchs. Alas, all that remains now are the ruins of a postern gate. In 1460, King James II was killed when one of his own cannons exploded; a holly tree marks the spot in the parkland before the Castle.

Floors Castle

The roofscape at Floors has often been compared to Chambord, and this is not where the French connection ends, for as you enter the drawing room you will see a room typical of 18th century France. Modelled in the style of Louis XV, the eighth Duchess of Roxburghe adorned the walls with Brussels tapestries, and furnished the room with 18th century French furniture of high provenance, one piece coming from the apartments of the Comtesse D'Artois at Versailles. These came from her own collection which she brought from her Rhode Island home after her marriage to the eighth Duke of Roxburghe in 1903. A small ante-room which she styled in the Versailles manner has been lifted into a later century by the inclusion of paintings by Matisse, Bonnard and Redon.

The romantically inclined among you will be glad to know that it was here at Floors that Prince Andrew made his proposal of marriage to Miss Sarah Ferguson; now his bride and Duchess of York.

Following your wander through the castle you may well require a cup of tea, or perhaps a meal. You can enjoy either in the castle's restaurant which offers food from the estate and river, and is cooked in the castle kitchen. Within the courtyard you will find a pleasant little gift shop, for that special something to take home.

If you have the time to spare, there is a regular minibus from the castle to the Garden Centre, which is enclosed within the Walled Garden, and where

23

you can choose from the varied selection of plants and shrubs on sale.

Three miles out of Kelso on the A698 road to Carlisle stands another superb building owned by the Duke and Duchess of Roxburghe. **Sunlaws House Hotel** is set in two hundred acres of gardens and mature parkland, on the banks of the river Teviot. Carefully converted by the Duke and Duchess, Sunlaws is a small friendly hotel, offering only the best in comfort and character.

There are twenty two bedrooms, all with private bathroom or shower, colour television, radio and direct dial telephones. Disabled guests are thoughtfully provided for, with all the amenities available that they require.

Sunlaws is ideally situated to take full advantage of the fresh fish, meat and game from the Duke's estate. Head Chef Peter Chevin and the team always ensure that the menu, changed daily, reflects true Scottish country house cooking at its best. This is certainly true, even of breakfast at Sunlaws. Guaranteed to set you up for the day, the hotel's morning menu will be of great benefit to those wishing to take advantage of the many sporting activities on offer.

Choose from fishing on the Duke's own waters, shooting, including clay pigeon, and riding. Horse lovers of all levels are extremely well catered for, with pony trekking, riding tuition and livery stables readily available.

Golfers have a splendid choice of local courses on which to try their swing, and internationally famous Muirfield and Gullane are only an hour's drive away.

The whole team at Sunlaws obviously take great pleasure in striving to make this one of the best hotels in the Borders, and it undoubtedly is.

The road from Kelso to Melrose runs along the southern banks of the Tweed and is one of the loveliest routes in Scotland. We passed through the village of **St. Boswells**, which is situated on a common, with the main part of the village built mainly in the local red sandstone. It's hard to believe that in the 18th and early 19th centuries, this common was the setting of the largest annual fair in the south of Scotland, with lambs, cattle, horses and wool all being sold.

We took some time for a visit to **Merton House**, just two miles to the east of St. Boswells. Designed by Sir William Bruce in 1703, It became the home of the sixth Duke of Sutherland, and boasts twenty acres of beautiful grounds, with lovely walks and views of the river Tweed.

Melrose lies on the lowest slopes of the Eildon Hills, which are the three distinctive peaks dominating the scenery in this part of the Borders. Nearby is **Abbotsford**, the home of Sir Walter Scott, whose fame has ensured that Melrose is now a busy tourist centre. There are many tributes to this man throughout the whole of this area; he was a well-loved figure who, through his writings, is credited with the opening up and preserving of the stories and ballads of the Borders.

Although Sir Walter Scott was actually born in Edinburgh, the area which has always been most associated with the poet and story-teller, who was a collector of old tales and ballads, is the Scottish Borderlands where he made his home.

Scott had only spent the first two years of his life in Edinburgh, as he was afflicted by lameness and sent to live and recover on his grandfather's farm near Smailholm in Roxburghshire. The friendship he developed here with the countryside was to stay with him throughout his life.

His family history is not without its own characters and tales. One of Scott's ancestors was captured by a rival hostile clan, and offered a choice between marriage or hanging. He apparently took one look at the bride, who was the daughter of the clan's chief and not the most fortunate looking girl, and chose hanging! He was, though, persuaded to change his mind at a later date.

As Walter grew up and went to school, he became well-known as a teller of tales and a voracious reader of books, all the time developing the love of the beautiful countryside that surrounded him. As he went to university in Edinburgh and then to practise law, he always maintained the strongest links with the countryside, and especially the town of Kelso where he had an aunt and uncle living, whom he would visit often. He would sometimes take a gig and ride out into the countryside, staying at inns or farms, collecting tales and talking to the characters and countryfolk.

He made good progress in his position and was appointed Sheriff of Selkirk in 1799. With a good income and a stable position, he was able to work on his collection of ballads and poetry. In 1801 he published 'The Border Minstrelsy' which was very well received. His own romantic narrative poems followed, including 'The Lay of the Last Minstrel', 'Marmion' and 'The Lady of the Lake'. Scott became well respected and among his admirers were the Wordsworths, who visited him at his home in the Borders.

As a sheriff he was fair and often kind. When he needed a shepherd to help run his newly acquired land at Ashestiel, he hired a man who had appeared before him, accused of poaching, but whose defence was that he lived in poverty and had a family to feed. The man, Tam Purdie, became one of Scott's lifelong friends.

Scott would rise early and work for three hours before breakfast, after which he would return to his work for a further two hours, before lending himself to the day's official activities. He spent his leisure time with his friends and family, often riding into the hills or taking part in the spearing of salmon, which more often than not involved getting a soaking.

In 1812 Scott bought the farm that was later to develop into the extravagance of Abbotsford. The farm as it was then was unimpressive and was in fact known as 'Clartyhole', meaning 'Dirty hole'. The place was renamed 'Abbotsford' by Scott and he moved in with his family and began the series of alterations that would change the place beyond all recognition.

As Abbotsford grew, Scott worked as hard as always at his poetry and then turned his hand to novels. 'Waverley' was produced in 1814 and brought Scott instant acclaim, earning him the nickname 'The Great Unknown'.

Abbotsford

By 1825, Abbotsford was vastly expanded, taking in many surrounding farms and estates and it became Scott's pride and joy. However, the renovation severely drained Scott's finances and he was forced to work harder to pay the bills. His pace of work is said to have contributed to his death and on the twenty first of September, 1832, he died at the age of sixty-one.

Today the house is much as it was in Scott's day, with its remarkable collection of armour and historical relics, such as Rob Roy's sporran, Napoleon's cloak clasp, a lock of Bonnie Prince Charlie's hair and even a silver urn from Lord Byron. The library and study where Scott worked are fascinating to look at.

Melrose Abbey

The beautiful ruins of **Melrose Abbey**, dating largely from the 15th century, are best viewed, according to Scott, by moonlight. We visited the abbey during the day, however, we were certainly impressed by it. Although badly damaged, some of the surviving parts are considered to be amongst the most splendid and detailed work of the time, and include the famous jolly figure of a pig playing the bagpipes on the roof. The heart of Robert the Bruce is also reputedly buried near the high altar.

If you are in need of refreshment, then here in the heart of Melrose you will find **The Old Smiddy Bistro**. Tucked away in a delightful little alleyway, you can see instantly that an old smiddy is exactly what this unique little restaurant used to be.

The bistro is now run personally by Jacqueline and Allan Young who took over this charming place about eighteen months ago. The balcony of the restaurant was once the metal store, with a ground floor restaurant now taking the place of what was the smiddy itself.

Today it is a listed building, you will find The Old Smiddy is open from 9.30am until 11pm daily, and offers a choice of menus. Choose from an a la carte meal in the main restaurant; or, alternatively, try a bar lunch or bar supper in the lower bar, with its real log fire.

Vegetarian meals are available, as well as a full range of beers, wines and spirits, for this cosy little bistro also carries a full public house licence.

The Old Smiddy

Across the road from the bistro is the family run gift and coffee shop. The coffee shop is run by Mrs Young's daughters, although it was originally run by their grandfather, seventeen years ago, before being passed on to the younger members of the family. The gift shop is run by Mrs Young's brother-in-law; as you can see, this is a real family affair!

Melrose is a beautiful and intriguing border town, steeped in history and with lots to offer. You will be glad you came here, and the hospitality you receive at The Old Smiddy will tell you that your visit was well worthwhile.

We are always especially pleased to be able to tell you of achievements that have been attained through hard work and dedication. We had heard tell of **Melrose Station**, and wanted to find out more.

Once described as the "handsomest provincial station in Scotland", Melrose Station lay derelict from 1969 when the Waverley Route from Edinburgh to Carlisle was axed. Now this is the only town station still standing in the Borders region.

Melrose Station was saved from the same fate as its sister stations by the foresight of architect Dennis Rodwell who purchased the building in 1985. He recognised that the station had the potential to house a craft centre which would be the focal point for skilled craftsmen and women throughout the Borders to display their skills and products.

After two years of hard work and sympathetic restoration, this fine Jacobean style building now houses not only the craft centre itself, but also workshops where visitors can see hand crafted articles during manufacture. There is also an art gallery which provides a changing programme of art and craft exhibitions, mainly featuring the work of Borders artists and craftspeople.

For railway enthusiasts, **The Waverley Route Heritage Centre and Model Railway** provides a fascinating reminder of the old Waverley Route and Borders branch lines. The Heritage Centre displays a wide variety of photos, posters, signs, lamps, documents and tickets. There is also a large working model railway and you can purchase general and specialist books, posters, cards and railway souvenirs.

Additionally there is an exhibition mounted by The Trimontium Trust which offers those interested in archaeology colourful and informative displays related to the Roman fort at Newstead.

It is unlikely that visitors to Melrose Station will see all that they want to in less than two hours. Craft shop manageress Jean Walley therefore recommends that you split your visit and enjoy a break in the restaurant. Here you can enjoy coffee, home baking, lunches, afternoon teas, high teas and evening meals. A member of the Taste of Scotland scheme, and recommended by several food guides, the restaurant serves creative and traditional dishes, including vegetarian.

Melrose Station should certainly be on your itinerary, for here you will find that the skill of Dennis Rodwell and the enthusiasm of Jean Walley combine to ensure that your visit is enjoyed to the full.

Hawick is the largest of the Border burghs, with a population of around seventeen thousand. It also has a thriving reputation for the manufacture of quality knitwear, clothing and carpets. The town is the home of such names as Pringle of Scotland, Lyle and Scott, Peter Scott and many other smaller firms producing fully fashioned knitwear in cashmere, lambswool and Shetland yarns. Visits to local factories can sometimes be arranged on week days and the products can be purchased in many shops in the town, often at very competitive prices.

Melrose Station Craft Centre

The centre of a vibrant farming community, Hawick has an interest in animals both alive and dead, as it is the centre for the longest established auction mart in the whole of Britain.

The Scottish Borders was for centuries an area of turmoil and intrigue. To the English, it was the area of first and last encounter with a traditional enemy and the target for quick and often bloody retribution.

All of the Border towns were destroyed many times by raiders from England. Hawick was buried down no fewer than six times by the mid 1600's. On one occasion the natives of Hawick buried the town themselves to prevent the English from having the pleasure of extracting their vengeance.

Traffic in marauding was by no means confined to the Scottish side - many English towns suffered a similar fate when the 'Rievers' of the Borders, on their small ponies, appeared from nowhere to burn, kill and rob.

There is still a hint of bi-partisanship on either side of the Border - not least in the tradition of rugby football as the regional sport. Hawick having won the Scottish Cup ten times out of sixteen seasons. Modern forays across the Border still have a keen competitive edge!

Perhaps it is because Hawick was not 'stable' enough that few ancient buildings exist - no abbey or castle or magnificent building has survived. The Black Tower of Drumlanrig - perhaps the oldest building - has suffered partial destruction on numerous occasions (the latest being dry-rot and vermin.) Needle Street, in the town's West End, is the oldest remaining street. A dearth of ancient buildings does not mean a lack of ancient tradition and ceremony, however. Each year, in June, the town holds its colourful Common Riding Celebration, a legacy of the aftermath of Flodden in 1513.

Due to the turbulent nature of the Borders, houses were often built in strategic positions overlooking the approach route of possible marauders. **Hopehill House** is no exception. It is now a nice family run Guest House, off Mayfield Drive. The original building was called Rose Cottage and was situated on the Town's Rough Haugh. Recent renovations, necessary after an extensive outbreak of dry-rot, uncovered the whinstone structure of the cottage contained within the sandstone of the Victorian section of the building.

The yellow sandstone frontage of Hopehill dates from the mid 1870's, that being the most recent addition to the house. An interesting discovery was made some years ago - Kiri, the family pet collie was digging at the rear of the building, when the earth started to subside in front of her - a gaping hole appeared - this turned out to be an ancient well which had been partially filled in.

At present Hopehill is owned by the Borthwick family: Anne and Bill and children, Anna and Mark. It is a friendly house in which to stay, with a range of accommodation from master bedroom with en-suite bathrooms to a comfortable single room. All the rooms have colour T.V's and tea and coffee making facilities with commanding views of the surrounding countryside. There is ample parking and the prices are extremely reasonable.

Hopehill Guesthouse

The town provides an excellent range of facilities for the visitor, which include an eighteen hole golf course, a modern swimming pool and a leisure centre. In the nearby one hundred and seven acre Lodge Park you can enjoy tennis, bowls and putting, or if you are feeling exceptionally fit, how about a workout on the Jubilee Trim Track?

Alternatively, you can just take things easy, as we did, and enjoy the beautiful surroundings, strolling amongst the trees and sitting by the riverside. At the west end of the park, where Langlands Bridge crosses the river Teviot, there is a pleasant walk by the river that will lead you back to town.

It is likely that visitors to Hawick will eventually find themselves in the town's Buccleuch Street, situated on the A7 towards Carlisle. If by then you've decided you could do with some refreshments, then look no further than **Dames Bistro And Coffee Shop**. You will find this charming little bistro tucked behind a facade of colourful hanging baskets and floral displays. Proprietor Mandy Ballantyne opens her restaurant daily from nine to five, and can offer you anything from a snack to a three course lunch.

Mandy insists that here at Dames they do all their own cooking and specialise in fresh wholefood cooking, including special vegetarian meals. The menu is changed daily and all food is prepared from fresh ingredients; because of a little extra effort, Mandy succeeds in satisfying all tastes.

Half portions are available for the children, and with an eye on safe driving there are a number of non-alcoholic wines and lagers to complement your meal.

Dames has the type of cosy atmosphere that makes it popular with everyone from business people to those who wish to pop in for afternoon tea. Either way, a warm welcome is given to all who patronise this delightful bistro and coffee shop.

Dames Bistro and Coffee Shop

We were lucky enough to be in Hawick for the main events of the annual Common Ridings. Held on the first and second weekends of June, these are ceremonies commemorating the Hoshole raid of 1514, when Hawick youths routed a band of English raiders after the tragedy of Flodden. Many of the townsfolk become involved in the festivities, which usually last for over a month.

Are any of you seasoned riders? We are not, but riders visiting Hawick at the time of the festivities, or indeed at any other time of year, might like to try the 'Hawick Circular', which is a twenty seven mile ride running along minor roads, tracks and cross country sections. What a marvellous way to take in this glorious countryside.

Mansfield House Hotel

A real transformation has taken place over the years at Hawick's **Mansfield House Hotel**. Since 1985 the current owners Ian and Sheila MacKinnon have been working hard on restoring the hotel and grounds to their original splendour. The main transformation has already happened inside the hotel, where the public rooms, in particular the magnificent dining room, have been restored to their former glory. No expense has been spared in stripping the lovely timbers back to their natural state and in decorating the ornate plaster work and cornices.

You will delight in the splendour of the fine ceilings and Italian marble fireplaces which befit this imposing one hundred and twenty year old house of Italian design. The hotel has eleven rooms, of which eight are en-suite, and all with colour TV and tea/coffee making facilities.

Have a drink in the cocktail bar before or after you enjoy a meal in the splendid dining room where you will eat only the best of local and Scottish produce. Choose a wine to complement your meal from the extensive wine list available. We are sure you will enjoy an outstanding meal in the most memorable of surroundings.

With the added attraction of the marquee, the hotel is certainly one of the best establishments in the area for a special occasion such as a wedding or a garden party.

Ian and Sheila are keen to point out that the Mansfield is a family business. They are justifiably proud of their excellent reputation for friendliness and high standards of cuisine. The Mansfield House Hotel is without question one of the finest hotels in the Scottish borders.

Just one word of warning about Hawick - the local dialect is difficult to understand if you are unfamiliar with it. The reasons for its existence are both historical and industrial. An example of it may be 'Ir 'ee wi us or ir 'oo wi you yins?" See what we mean ?

How about an unusual activity that you're never likely to forget? The **Scottish Academy of Falconry and Related Studies**; sounds impressive, doesn't it? Leonard and Diana Durman-Walters started this holiday with a difference in 1986. Since then, the academy has grown in popularity and prestige because of its spectacular setting, and the quality of its internationally renowned tutors. This absorbing and exciting holiday offers the chance to be able to fly and hunt with a selection of some of the stunning array of birds of prey owned and trained by the academy.

At this wonderful place, we were treated to the the company of Harris Hawks, goshawks and falcons of all descriptions, including peregrines that will take you masterfully through your week. One of the delights of this holiday is the chance to spend virtually all your time flying these hunters. Its purely practical side is one of the things which make it so appealing.

Scottish Academy of Falconry & Related Studies

The academy is also host to a small number of owls, and these too enjoy a day out with you. All of them are capable of flying with you and indeed they provided us with another aspect of the behaviour of birds of prey.

The academy's delights can appeal to all age groups, from children of 12 year onwards to adults of all ages. We felt that the pleasure of walking through countryside uncluttered with buildings and crowded streets, made the art of learning falconry an unforgettable pleasure.

Leonard and Diana left no stone unturned in their efforts to provide us with the comfort we needed at the academy. Good food is part of the course, as well as good company. Leonard was instrumental in the building of the academy in the early Eighties and, as Senior Tutor, takes guests through their week with skill and good humour. Diana told us that she was a professional teacher in Scotland and has since used her skills and ability to become the additional tutor that the academy required. Despite the fact that they also have falconry and kennel staff, they are kept busy all year round.

The Scottish Academy of Falconry and Related Studies is the only centre of its kind in Scotland, and offers a first class holiday flying falcons and hawks. We thoroughly enjoyed our stay at this virtually unique centre.

On the road towards **Jedburgh** we were keen to sample some of the famous knitwear that we have heard so much about. In an era of uncertainty and closures in the Borders knitwear industry, **Tom Scott** of **Denholm** stands out as a shining example of success; a success borne of skill and an outstanding ability to give customers what they want. This is no ordinary wool shop, but a thriving family business, producing fashionable designer knitwear, popular from Hawick to London and the fashion houses of Europe.

Now established for fourteen years, the business was founded by Tom after he was made redundant by the knitwear company for whom he had worked for forty seven years. Starting with an old frame in his garden shed, Tom Scott has now expanded to become a knitwear factory employing twenty eight local people and all the family.

Tom Scott Knitware

The factory shop is run by Tom's neice, Eleanor, and her husband Jim, a former knitwear mechanic, now manages the factory itself.

Tom Scott's mill shop is patronised by members of the royal family in Britain and abroad.

Sitting in the centre of this lovely conservation village, you will find there is a welcome here for all who appreciate high quality goods; able bodied and disabled alike. The cashmere designs are a delight and you can see why Tom Scott supplies the major fashion houses in London and Europe so successfully.

Being surrounded by so much beautiful countryside, our thoughts were with those people who devote their time to keeping us in touch with all these wonderful things, for we are always keen to learn more about our habitat. A few miles north of Jedburgh on the A68, we found the perfect place for gaining a greater understanding of the woods that are so important to us. A visit to **The Woodland Centre** at **Ancrum** can best be described as a day out with a difference for people of all ages.

Situated just a couple of miles east of Ancrum on the B6400, The Woodland Centre, supervised by Dr. Rosemary Evans, is an integral part of Lothian Estates, and brainchild of the Estate Factor, David Bridges. His intention was to open up a beautiful area for public recreation available to the general public, as well as educational groups such as schools, nature and history societies. The purpose of the centre, therefore, is to show the importance of trees through their life cycle from seedlings to furniture.

Visitors to the centre are encouraged to become involved with their environment and hopefully to appreciate the role played by organisations such as Lothian Estates in caring for and conserving our countryside.

There are four woodland walks to enjoy, varying in length from one mile to three and a half miles, with a specially adapted walk for the disabled. The centre also houses a book and gift shop, as well as a tea room where home baking and light snacks are available. There is plenty to do here, even in wet weather, with a games room and adventure playground to keep the youngsters happy.

A warm welcome is extended here to all visitors, whether a family staying for the day, or a traveller dropping in for a quiet cup of coffee. The objective of paramount importance here, though, is that the visitor should enjoy the experience, and leave with an increased awareness of the richness of the countryside.

The Woodland Centre

And so at last we took the main A68 road to **Jedburgh**, which is just ten miles from the border, and presents a pleasant and striking blend of the old and the new.

In the middle of the High Street, now dressed in up to date modern garb, lies what is reputedly the oldest hotel in Scotland, and fourth oldest in the British Isles; **The Spread Eagle**. Considered 'fit for a queen', The Spread Eagle was the first lodging in Jedburgh of Mary, Queen of Scots, in 1566. However, hardly a mile outside the town there is a large British-American factory filled with the latest automatic machines whose products are exported to over fifty countries. In Jedburgh the old world charm pervades the town and relics of a storied past face us at every turn.

In October 1566, Mary, Queen of Scots, travelled to Jedburgh to hold a Justice Ayres, or Circuit Court, in the Tolbooth that stood in Canongate, and as the Spread Eagle Hotel had already been established, she naturally sought lodging there. She remained until driven out by a fire next door, when she moved to **Mary Queen of Scots' House**, which has beeen excellently preserved since its complete renovation in 1928 to 1929, a hundred yards away.

Another distinguished guest at the hotel was Sir Walter Scott, who lodged there when engaged in the local circuit court, where he made his first appearance as an advocate. Robert Burns also lived, for a short time, some hundred yards away and one can safely assume that he also had a knowledge of the 'Spread', as it is known locally, and of the fiery fluid purveyed therein.

The Spread Eagle

In the hotel itself, cheek by jowl with the modern conveniences provided for guests, you can see the window of Mary, Queen of Scots' bedroom, made of hand-made glass no less than four hundred years old by John Renilson, one of Jedburgh's antiquarians. So in this room with all 'mod cons' the old rubs shoulders with the new. If you are allocated this room you can look through the same window glass as was used by that charming and tragic Queen.

The Spread Eagle has ten rooms, all with tea and coffee making facilities.

For those who don't like to miss their favourite programmes, there is also a colour TV in the residents' lounge.

Proprietors Billy and Denise Spence offer traditional bar food, available from both lunchtime and evening menus; our tip, and best value for money, has to be their delicious T-bone steak with onions and mushrooms for around £8.00.

Leaving Jedburgh, we followed the B6357, which is a lovely scenic route leading through the Wauchope Forest. Do take some time to savour the beauty of this ancient area. You will eventually find yourself in the village of **Bonchester Bridge**. This, as you might gather from its name, is a place with former Roman connections, and there was once a fort on Bonchester Hill.

Those of you with an appetite for exploring will find this an excellent base for forays into the surrounding countryside, and we made a visit to one of the most splendid attractions in the area, the Kielder Reservoir, which has ample opportunity for walking and picnicking, with its magnificent scenery.

After our visit to Keilder Water, we decided to act on the recommendation that we spend some time at **Bonchester Bridge Caravan Park**. Located in this pretty little village on the banks of Rule Water, a tributary of the river Teviot, the park is ideal for restful camping, and makes an excellent base from which to enjoy the many attractions of the Borders.

Bonchester Bridge Caravan Park

Personally run by the owners, Margaret and Sandy Forbes, this delightful park can accommodate up to twenty five touring caravans. Tents and camper vans are also most welcome. Margaret and Sandy moved to Bonchester Bridge in 1968 from Aberdeen, where Sandy was a builder by trade. His skills have certainly been put to good use here as he has built this site from scratch.

From the beautifully kept grass to the spotless toilet areas, the whole site is meticulously clean, and particularly welcoming after an enjoyable but nonetheless tiring journey. The hand basins provide hot water, with coin operated showers also available as well as a washing machine and spin dryer. Electricity hook-ups and drains are all conveniently situated.

Outside entertainment includes a nine hole miniature golf course, and a children's play area. There is a shop on site, not open on Wednesday afternoons, which stocks most items, including calor gas, and also houses the village post office. The old post office building has been carefully converted by Sandy to provide self-catering accommodation and can sleep five to six people comfortably.

There is no bar on site, but those wishing to relax over a drink or even a meal are only a minute from **The Horse and Hound Inn**, adjacent to the site. This charming village inn dates back to the 18th century and is run by Robert Chrystie and his wife. An extremely friendly inn, The Horse and Hounds is ideal for visitors but also carries a strong local following. They will be the first to tell you that, while inside, you simply must take a look at the inn's painting of the 'Rule Water Foothunters'; an amusing caricature of some of the local Bonchester Bridge populace, painted back in the 1940's.

The bar is small and cosy with everyone's favourite; a real log fire to warm you up on those chillier days and evenings. In the comfy lounge bar and dining room you can choose to eat from a selection of local dishes, or take advantage of a daily 'special'; all are very moderately priced. Mr and Mrs Chrystie provide a different menu for lunch and dinner, both of which vary from day to day. Try home-made bacon and tomato soup with hunks of crusty bread; truly value for money at only 70p.

Families need not worry for children are made especially welcome and are catered for with a special menu. Mrs Chrystie will happily make up a vegetarian dish for you too; all you have to do is ask.

The Horse & Hound Inn
Should you wish to linger a little longer at Bonchester Bridge, you will be

happy to know that the inn has five bedrooms, all with tea and coffee making facilities. Don't worry about missing your favourite TV programme though; you can always put your feet up and relax in the residents' lounge.

Whatever the time of year, you are always assured a warm welcome at the Horse and Hound Inn.

Rather than taking the A7 through the Borders region, we preferred to take the B6357 from Bonchester Bridge. This road follows the Liddel Water through Liddesdale, and is altogether a more peaceful route. Once you reach **Newcastleton**, do keep an eye out for the **Copshaw Kitchen Licensed Restaurant**. Now this should be easy for you to find, because its eyecatching sign is made up of a real old copper kettle, hanging above the restaurant itself.

Here you will see that proprietor Jean Elliot has combined her interest in antiques and needlework with a third: cooking. Jean has transformed this former grocer's shop into a unique restaurant where you can browse over a selection of antique china, paintings, linen, books and furniture whilst you dine.

The Copshaw Kitchen is open every day except Tuesday from 9.30am to 6.30pm, with lunches being served from 12 o'clock onwards. We suggest you make a reservation for dinner, served from 7.30pm Wednesday to Saturday.

The Copshaw Kitchen

Dining here is recommended by all the major guides including Egon Ronay, and we can certainly agree that you will find it a delightful experience.

Newcastleton is the only planned village in Scotland, and it made an ideal base for us to tour the local area and visit local attractions. These include Kielder Water, Hermitage Castle and the Border abbeys. Visit Newcastleton, and the "small hotel with the big welcome" could be just the place for your stay. This is the proud boast of **The Liddesdale Hotel**.

The 18th century coaching inn is open all year around and has one double and three twin rooms, all with bath or shower facilities, tea and coffee making facilities and colour TV. Enjoy a relaxing drink by the hotel's open fires, or partake of lunch or an evening meal in either of the hotel's two dining rooms. The larger one is used for functions and coach parties and the small and intimate room for residents.

The Liddlesdale Hotel

A strong emphasis is placed here on home cooked food using fresh vegetables and meats.

Salmon and trout from the Liddel Water are on the menu whenever possible, as is game.

For the angling enthusiast who enjoys catching his own, Newcastleton offers excellent salmon and trout fishing. The village is surrounded by hills and woodland which makes it a walker's paradise.

Jedburgh Abbey

Peebleshire and Selkirkshire

Traquair Gates

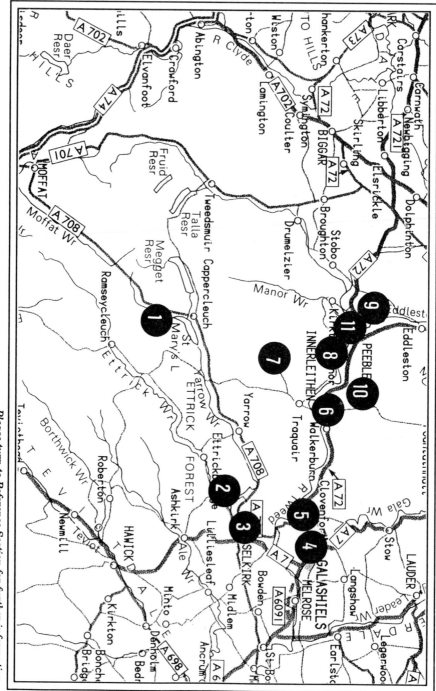

Please turn to Reference Section for further information.

CHAPTER THREE

Peebleshire and Selkirkshire

So far in our journey we have not had the chance to sample the renowned delights of those famous Scottish lochs, and so we were delighted to find ourselves on the shores of St. Mary's Loch at the edge of the Ettrick Forest. This truly is a beautiful spot, and made the perfect starting point for our journey around the areas once known as Peebleshire and Selkirkshire. **St. Mary's Loch** is set amongst some of the smoothest rolling green hills that we have had the pleasure to experience.

The loch is three miles long and these days it is commonly used for sailing, with a popular sailing club on the western end. The atmosphere is wonderfully peaceful here, and we lingered by the shores, skimming stones and generally letting time just pass us by. We were curious though to know more about a name that we had heard many mentions of in this part of the country, 'Tibbie Shiel' and we travelled to the neck of land that separates St. Mary's Loch from the smaller Loch of the Lowes, where we had been told that we would find an inn with the answer to our questions.

On the shores of St. Mary's Loch, in one of the most tranquil spots in Southern Scotland, is an inn with this intriguing name of **Tibbie Shiels**. The A708 from Moffat passes the door, as does the Southern Upland Way, and any traveller should visit the Tibbie Shiels Inn, if only to discover its historical past.

Tibbie Shiels Inn

Now personally run by proprietors Jack and Jill Brown, the inn was originally a cottage owned by Lord Napier and rented by Tibbie and Robert Richardson, a mole catcher. It was St. Mary's Cottage then, but, on the death of her husband, Tibbie reverted to her maiden name of Shiel and started to take in lodgers to support herself and her six children. Until her death in 1878, in her ninety sixth year, Tibbie played host to such famous names as Sir Walter Scott, Professor Wilson, alias Christopher North, the publisher Robert Chambers and local poet James Hogg, the Ettrick Shepherd.

Returning to the present day, Tibbie Shiels Inn now has five rooms available for guests, all with tea and coffee making facilities, and with en-suite facilities currently intended.

The inn's main restaurant overlooks St. Mary's Loch, a stunning panorama guaranteed to make any meal seem special. Meals are also served in the room which was originally Tibbie Shiel's own kitchen. Bar snacks are served in the bar, which is part of the original cottage. All menus include a selection of delicious vegetarian dishes. A first class wine list complements the menu and, although very comprehensive (French, German, Spanish, Italian, Bulgarian, Chilean and Portuguese wines are all there), it represents outstanding value for money.

To enjoy a meal with Jack and Jill Brown at the Tibbie Shiels conjures up images of days gone by and of James Hogg penning his verse in the candlelit inn with only the log fires for company. There are certainly many references to Tibbie Shiels in his poetry and his literature. Like ourselves, he obviously felt, as you will too, that the Tibbie Shiels Inn is worth writing home about.

Not wanting to hurry our journey, we followed the A708 towards Selkirk, catching brief glimpses of the Yarrow Water that runs beside. Some four miles before reaching Selkirk, you will come across **Bowhill**. We set a whole day aside for exploring this magnificent mansion and home of the Scotts of Buccleuch. Erected by the third Duke of Buccleuch in 1795, it is open to the public during the summer months.

The house contains many fine works of art, including paintings by Van Dyck, Reynolds, Raeburn and Claude Lorraine, and has the privilege of having the 'Madonna and the Yarnwinder' which is the only painting by Leonardo da Vinci still in private hands in this country. We also delighted in the many fine examples of 17th and 18th century furniture and clocks. One clock especially appealed to us, as it was able to play eight different Scottish airs, or tunes, though the mechanism was so set that the clock actually observes the Sabbath by not striking from twelve o' clock on Saturday until midnight on Sunday. How peaceful life must have been.

In the grounds there are some fine gardens, with nature trails and lovely woodland walks. For the children you will find that the adventure playground is ideal. If, after your walk, you have built up a thirst, then you can stay awhile and have a drink or a snack in the tea rooms.

From the delights of Bowhill it is a short distance to the town of **Selkirk** which, like so many of these Border towns, has a history linked to those fateful conflicts with the English. The town itself was actually destroyed by the English after the Battle of Flodden in 1513. Selkirk sent eighty men to fight in the battle for James IV, but only one of them survived to come back to this saddened and decimated community. The story goes that he returned, however, bearing a captured English flag and, unable to speak of his sorrow and of the loss of his countrymen, he simply waved the flag down towards the ground. This act is symbolically re-enacted each year in the Common Riding, in remembrance of all those who have fallen in battle.

Bowhill House

Sir Walter Scott was sheriff of the county in the early 18th century and his statue is in the market place, near to the courthouse where he dispensed his justice.

When you visit Selkirk, come to the heart of this royal burgh, to the town's market place, and here you will find **The Court House Coffee Shop and Licensed Restaurant**. This family run business is a hive of local knowledge where all staff are well versed on the sort of local information that visitors to the town find so useful.

The Court House Coffee Shop

Open from 9.00am until 6.00pm daily, The Court House serves tea, coffee and light meals all day, including breakfast, lunch and high tea. A restaurant licence enables you to enjoy a drink as you relax with your meal.

The building which houses The Court House Coffee Shop was, not surprisingly, originally part of the old Sheriff Court rooms, used on occasion by Sir Walter Scott.

Nowadays, however, the restaurant is patronised by many more up-to-date personalities, from pop stars to Members of Parliament. They, like many other visitors, come to enjoy what Selkirk has to offer, as a royal burgh steeped in history.

Another visit to make in Selkirk is to the Halliwells House Museum and Gallery. Located on the west side of the main square, it consists of a row of 18th century dwelling houses renovated to make a museum of Selkirk's colourful history. The buildings have links with the ironmongery trade and these have been renovated, providing a fascinating insight into the world of Edwardian shopping with a wonderful collection of domestic hardware from the period. In the adjoining Robson Gallery there is a range of touring exhibitions.

Nearby to the museum and next to the post office is **Robert Douglas' Bakery**, where the baker made the original Selkirk 'bannock', a fruit loaf which is said to have been much favoured by Queen Victoria.

Did you know that Selkirk natives were apparently known as 'souters'? This is as a result of the fact that the town has a long association with shoemaking and on one famous occasion supplied Bonnie Prince Charlie and his army with two thousand pairs of shoes for their ill-fated march to Derby in 1745.

Selkirk is still very much alive as a centre for tweed and woollen goods, and some of the mills are open to visitors. Let us tell you about another extremely interesting visit we made to **'Selkirk Glass'**. Here we were able to get a birds-eye view of the glass-making process, as we were made welcome to watch the craft in progress. We relaxed in the coffee shop and enjoyed some excellent home bakes as we watched the craftsmen at work producing the lovely glass products such as paperweights and perfume bottles that are exported all over the world. Selkirk will long stay with us as a fine and effective example of the blending of old and new crafts, which is never an easy task.

While we were staying in Selkirk, we decided to make our base at **Philipburn House Hotel**. Sincnce buying the hotel in 1972, Jim Hill, former architect, and his wife, Anne, have lovingly fashioned Philipburn into their idea of exactly what a country house hotel should be.

Philipburn, in former times the Dowager House to the Philiphaugh estate, was built in 1751 not long after the bloody Battle of Philiphaugh which took place a few yards from the now tranquil lawns, flowerbeds and woodlands amidst which this lovely old house stands. As the winner of numerous awards as a hotel and restaurant and as a member of the prestigious Scottish Heritage Hotels, Philipburn definitely enjoys a more friendly, what the Austrians might call "gemutlich", atmosphere.

From grandmother lovingly tending the flowers to youngest son Pelham, a Claridges trained chef, in the hotel kitchen, Philipburn is run with a passion by the Hill family. In the front line, Anne makes it her pleasure to give each and every guest her personal attention while husband Jim presides over the kitchen as chef patron.

Philipburn House Hotel

A dazzling array of dishes are produced here, embracing haute cuisine and classical Scottish dishes. They are produced from the bountiful supply of game from the surrounding hills, salmon from the nearby rivers and of course the finest Border lamb.

The Garden and Poolside restaurants provide a bright and leafy surrounding in which to enjoy this delicious fayre. Here, mellow pine panelling combines with delightful table settings, each of which has its own panoramic view of the pool, lawns or blazing heather on the rolling hills beyond. The wine list at Philipburn is a legend in its own right. It can also make intriguing bedtime reading, with its fascinating descriptions and humorous anecdotes.

Just as Philipburn is distinctly different from all other hotels, each of its bedrooms is markedly different from the other. There are charming country rooms, spacious family suites with solid pine bunks for the children, as well as some pretty cottages close to the hotel with breathtaking views of the hills and woodlands. There are also exclusive poolside suites with balconies, or you can try a stay in the Scandinavian Pine Lodge; straight out of Hans Christian Anderson with its own lounge and three sumptious bedrooms.

Naturally, all rooms are ensuite with tea and coffee making facilities, direct dial telephone, radio and TV. For business visitors there is a fax and photocopy service plus full laundry and dry cleaning facilities.

The Hill family have certainly overlooked nothing in their efforts to make your visit to Philipburn as special as possible. Here you will experience and never forget the incomparable harmony of wine, good food and ambience; the true definition of gastronomic pleasure.

This Borders area excels in producing one of Scotland's most famous products; tweed. Did you know that 'tweed' is actually a misnomer? The weave's name does not originate from the river Tweed at all, but is in fact the result of a mispelling of the word 'tweel' by, of course, an English clerk.

Manufacturing in our next stop, **Galashiels**, has been going on since as far back as 1622. The name Galashiels is an interesting one and it does have its roots in an associated trade, as it actually comes from the words 'gala' and 'sheiling' which mean 'huts of the shepherds'. The town is now famous for its woollens and textiles, and the Scottish College of Textiles was founded here in 1909. If you are interested in finding out more about the industry then do visit the Woollen Museum at Waverly Mills where, at Peter Andersons, there are guided tours showing the process of tartan weaving.

Galashiels is able to offer the visitor a superb choice of golf courses, both at Torwoodlee and at Ladhope. Fishing is also available on the Tweed and Gala waters, whilst horses can be hired for pony-trekking, if desired. Every year in July, the town hosts the Braw Lads' gathering which, amongst other things, celebrates the marriage in 1503 between James IV and Margaret Tudor, sister of Henry VIII. This union is commemorated by a symbolic mingling of a bouquet of red and white roses.

We spent a very pleasant time wandering around the town centre of Galashiels and delighted in the wonderful amount of flowers that seemed to abound. Leaving behind us the fragrance and splendour of Bank Street Gardens in full bloom, we made our way down High Street to Island Street, and **The Bridge Inn** for lunch. We had been told to expect a friendly welcome and value for money here, and we were not disappointed.

Bridge Inn

Proprietor Jim Maher and his wife Connie have carried out extensive refurbishments to the building, which is approximately two hundred and fifty years old. They also hope to introduce some old mill equipment for display shortly.

Currently there are several old pictures of Galashiels on the walls, some of which are sixty to eighty years old, and truly fascinating. They complement perfectly the surrounding 'old world' warmth and atmosphere of The Bridge.

Jim boasts a good local trade and, if you are a rugby enthusiast, it won't be long before you're drawn into conversation with local rugby followers as The Bridge has strong rugby connections.

After a pint of excellent beer, "We're very particular with our beer and like to be the best" says Jim, we played a game of pool in the games area and retired to the cosy lounge for lunch.

The Bridge does a good lunchtime trade in food, and it's easy to see why. Basic pub food is served quickly and cheerfully, and a choice of reasonably priced wines is available. Jim also provides a small selection of cocktails, which is changed weekly.

We couldn't believe how little our bill was when we came to leave, but as Jim says; "We provide an adequate amount at an extremely modest price". We would certainly agree with him!

Should you be here on Sunday lunchtime or a Friday and Saturday evening, an added bonus will be live entertainment which varies from jazz, Country and Western or traditional Scottish music.

Sometimes when we are travelling we find it excellent therapy to unwind in a quiet and peaceful setting, as it is all too easy to get caught up in the race to see everything and to forget that we are here to relax. A few miles from Galashiels on the A72 is such a place. The village of **Clovenfords** sits in the heart of the Borders in an area once known for its vineyards. In the past, the village has played host to a great many eminent figures, including Sir Walter Scott, obviously a well travelled man in Southern Scotland.

The Clovenfords Hotel

This great Scottish literary figure was one of many visitors to **The Clovenfords Hotel**, and today you can see his statue standing proudly in the hotel's forecourt. William Wordsworth also stayed here with his sister Dorothy when the two of them arrived Clovenfords on their way to meet Scott at Melrose, and Scott's friend, the poet and scholar John Leyden, lived and taught in this village for many years. It is not difficult to imagine this two hundred and sixty year old coaching inn providing lodging to these talented scholars while they swapped literary anecdotes.

Today, visitors to The Clovenfords Hotel are no less discerning than their predecessors, and host Maureen Corrie looks after all her patrons with the same care and attention that so long ago established this inn as such a popular meeting place.

All four of the comfortable guest rooms have en-suite bathrooms, and tea and coffee making facilities. Home cooked food offering excellent value for money is the order of the day in the restaurant where fresh local produce is the number one priority.

Clovenfords itself is perfectly situated for touring the Border towns of Melrose, Selkirk and Galashiels, all of which are only a few miles away. Sporting activities are naturally of the outdoor variety and this part of Scotland is ideal for its fishing, golfing, shooting, walking and pony trekking.

Tucked among the rolling hills of the Borders and sitting close to the famous river Tweed, the Clovenfords Hotel must surely enjoy one of the most beautiful settings in the Borders. Come and visit one of Sir Walter Scott's favourite haunts and sample for yourselves the traditional Border welcome of which he was so fond. We continued on our way towards the town of **Innerleithen**, which sits nicely between Peebles and Galashiels on the A72. The rivers Tweed and Leithen meet in this mill town which has a famous watering place known as St Ronan's Well. This was found in 1777 by local inhabitants who were drawn to it by the large number of pigeons sampling its benefits. The fame of the spa spread, and we were able to sample ourselves the waters that are supposedly health giving.

Another interesting visit to make in this town is to '**Robert Smail's Printing Works**', in the High Street. This is a vintage printing press and printworks, formerly driven by water wheels and now owned and displayed by the National Trust for Scotland as a museum. Innerleithen is a charming mill town in the heart of the Scottish borders, and it is here that you will find **Caddon View**, a quality guest house.

Caddon View, as its name suggests, enjoys excellent views over the hill of Caddon and the house itself, originally the local doctor's house, has beautiful wooden panelling and spacious comfortable rooms. All have colour television, tea and coffee making facilities, and pets are welcome.

Many of the Wrights' guests return again and again, and it is easy to see why. The personal attention paid to all visitors, and the quality and freshness of food offered, is of a high standard.

There are five bedrooms in all, two of which will have en-suite facilities for the 1990 season. The ground floor bedroom has a ground floor shower room, toilet and washhand basin. Small children are taken at reduced rates when sharing with parents.

There is so much to do in Innerleithen, from country sporting pursuits to hill walking or visits to the nearby Border Abbeys. You will probably be tempted to do what most of Will and Audrey's overseas guests do, and book up for next year before you leave.

There is also ample opportunity for fishing on the river Tweed and permits can be obtained locally.

Caddon View really is a rather special guest house.

Caddon View Guest House

Just outside the town you will find **Traquair House**. Formerly known as Traquair Castle, this famous house has played host to twenty-seven kings. The house as we see it has been virtually unchanged since the 17th century, and there is a fascinating story concerning the 'Steekit Yetts' or Bear Gates, which were formerly the main entrance to the house. The gates were last closed after the departure of Prince Charlie (Stuart), who had called on his cousins to enlist support for his march on England in 1745. They have remained unopened since then, and, according to legend, must remain so until a Stuart sits once again on the throne.

The current laird is a very industrious person, as he brews and sells worldwide his own brand of ale, and, be warned, it is to be savoured in small amounts, such is its strength. It proved to be a very worthwhile visit, as there is much to see in the house, and in its outbuildings are housed a number of craftworkers, including potters, weavers and woodworkers. There are many woodland and riverside walks to choose from, and afterwards you may be refreshed with a cup of tea in the cottage, which is in the garden dating from 1745. Before you leave this fascinating place, why not take a look around the maze?

Traquair Gates

If seeing the delights of living in such a grand place has enthralled you, the possibilities of doing so yourself may seem to be a million miles away, but this is not necessarily so. For a few days, or for a few weeks, you can be master of one of Scotland's best known country houses.

Glen House, situated a few miles south of Traquair House at Innerleithen, stands in over ten thousand acres of its own grounds in beautiful Scottish Border and hill country, some thirty miles from Edinburgh. In recent years it has been famous as the home of the Hon. Colin Tennent, whose numerous house guests have included many of the best known names in fashionable society.

You can now take over Glen House completely, and invite your guests to enjoy the privacy and comfort of a magnificent country house in surroundings of exceptional beauty.

This is the result of an initiative by Mr. Renwick, who has leased the house in order to make it available to individuals for discreet, top level business meetings, or simply to offer the opportunity to enjoy a relaxing break in luxurious surroundings, where you can be assured of total privacy.

The present building dates back to the 1850s, when Colin Tennent's great grandfather bought the estate, demolished most of the existing buildings and employed architect David Bryce. The house they created is one of the most notable examples of the Scottish baronial style and stands amid spacious terraces and splendidly landscaped gardens.

Glen House is yours for the duration of your stay, which can be for two days or longer. There is no double booking, and you can decide how many guests you wish to invite.

The price of your visit includes accommodation, breakfast, lunch and dinner. You can choose from a wide variety of traditional Scottish or international cooking, prepared to Cordon Bleu standard. Service at meals can be as formal or as discreet as you like, and you can request breakfast or lunch to be served outside in the garden or on the terrace.

The twenty two bedrooms have been individually designed so that each has its own particular character, although elegance and luxury are the two main features that they all have in common. Views from the windows are quite spectacular, and you may be lucky enough to have the added luxury of a traditional four poster bed.

The estate provides almost limitless space for walking and undisturbed exploration. There is a boating lake in the grounds and fishing, shooting and riding can be arranged by prior request. The outdoor swimming pool is heated and inside the house you can enjoy snooker and table tennis.

It would be hard to find an experience more rewarding than a stay here. For Glen House is in a world of its own. Once you enter this imposing estate, you leave the outside world behind and complete privacy is guaranteed for the duration of your stay.

Glen House

We are keen gardeners when we get the chance, though we must admit that sometimes it seems to be an endless task trying to keep the weeds at bay in those untidy corners. Imagine our delight when we had an opportunity to see seventeen acres of gardens that had been brought back from the wilderness by one Mrs Angela Richardson.

Her gardens at **Kailzie** have a wonderful reputation and we were not to be disappointed. The grounds are open to the public and surrounded by trees, containing many wonderful attractions such as vast lawns, shrubberies, a walled garden dating from 1812, a water garden, laburnum alley and lovely woodland and riverside walks. There is a pond stocked with various species of exotic fish, and the estate is populated with owls and several species of pheasant.

There is also an art gallery here where we spent some time looking around, and afterwards we relaxed with a cup of tea in the tea rooms.

If you are lucky enough to be travelling in style, you will notice that the gently rolling countryside of the Scottish Borders is perfect for those who enjoy a caravan holiday. This is an ideal part of the country for visitors who like to use their own touring caravans, or camper vans, as well as providing an excellent base for those who prefer to get away to a static van on a well-served caravan park.

Crossburn Caravan Park provides the answer to each one of these holiday requirements. The park is superbly sited as a base for touring the Borders, yet it is within forty minutes of the capital city, Edinburgh.

Crossburn is situated just outside Peebles, on the A703. Well signposted, the park is well deserving of its Scottish Tourist Board 'Thistle' award. Personally run by David and Marie Chisholm, you will find that they take great care to offer everything that will make your stay at Crossburn comfortable and pleasant.

All static homes are furnished and equipped to the highest standards and are connected to the mains services. There is a separate area for touring caravans, camper vans and tents, with hard standing available for most caravans, as well as electric hook-ups.

Crossburn Caravan Park

The British Caravan Parks Grading Scheme rates the facilities here as 'excellent', and it is certainly apparent that Crossburn Caravan Park offers unbeatable site facilities. The on-site shop holds a comprehensive selection of groceries as well as some essential caravan accessories. There is also a laundry room, recreational building and a delightful picnic and barbecue area.

Most facilities are housed in traditional log cabins. We're sure you'll agree that they lend a clean and tidy appearance to this charming caravan park, of which David and Marie are justifiably proud.

We were quickly becoming addicted to the glorious countryside in this area of the Borders known as Tweeddale. Its green hills and twisting country lanes, with glimpses of the river from time to time, are really quite beautiful. You may find yourself in an area of forest, and if you decide to walk you may well be lucky enough to catch a fleeting glance at a deer.

We were lucky enough before reaching Peebles to chance upon **The Countryside Inn**, at **Kirnlaw**. With its front raised garden and dazzling variety of low shrubs and heathers, it makes a pretty sight in the full bloom of summer.

Coming from Innerleithen, The Countryside is about two miles from Peebles on the A72. The inn enjoys panoramic views over the border countryside, sitting as it does at the foot of the beautiful Glentress Forest, popular for its forestry walks. Nearby is the river Tweed, for which the proprietors will be happy to arrange fishing permits.

Inside you will find the comfortable bar and restaurant where you can choose from a wide variety of dishes at prices that won't make a dent in your budget. House wine is available by the glass or carafe, and everything is served in a delightfully relaxing atmosphere.

Business and family accommodation is provided for those who wish to stay overnight at The Countryside Inn. There are eight rooms, two of which are en-suite. Families are always welcome as facilities are available for children.

In fact, you are assured of a warm welcome from everyone who works at The Countryside Inn.

The Countryside Inn

There are times when you come across a place that stays with you for many years, and we found **Peebles** to belong in that category. It epitomised for us everything that we have enjoyed so far in the Border country, being picturesque and historical, and yet with a thriving sense of its own character.

It is hard to imagine a more perfect setting for a town than the river Tweed, one of the most famous salmon rivers which runs through its centre. Peebles gives the impression of a place that was built for leisurely strolling, with its fine buildings and open parklands going down to the banks of the river. It has a wide shop-filled High Street, where we were able to browse amongst some of the best names in clothing, and looked at our leisure in the many small craft shops and cafes here. We delighted in the cobbled streets that run from the High Street to the Tweed.

It really is a must to spend some time in the elegant town and we can recommend that if you do, you should make a point of visiting or staying in the **Tweedbridge House Hotel**. As you turn into Port Brae from the High Street, Tweedbridge House beckons you from the banks of the river Tweed. Perhaps because of where it lies, tucked away from the hustle and bustle of the town itself, this has proved to be one of the most popular and elegant of hotels in Peebles.

Set on a hillside, Tweedbridge House enjoys splendid views of the town, the Tweed Valley and the Meldon Hills. Built in 1896, this imposing building has recently been upgraded and refurbished to offer the highest standards of accommodation and service.

Tweedbridge House Hotel

All five bedrooms are beautifully furnished in antique style with full en-suite facilities, colour television and direct dial telephones.

The Laurel Wood Restaurant is extremely popular with local residents and visitors alike. Taking its name from the superb laurel wood panelling encasing it, dining here is undoubtedly an experience not to be missed, for you will find the occasion both enjoyable and memorable. Whether you choose the a la carte menu or the set lunch menu, you are assured of a delicious meal with discreet but attentive service.

The outstanding beauty of the restaurant panelling is renowned and is considered to be such a fine example of architectural interest that it was removed from the building to be put on show at the 1920 British Empire

Exhibition at Wembley.

On arrival, visitors will enter their rooms to find that fresh flowers and a basket of fruit await them. This attention to detail is reflected throughout every aspect of the hotel and its service, and ensures that your stay at Tweedbridge House is that little bit more enjoyable and really rather special

Do you play scrabble? Or have you ever become frustrated at a crossword puzzle? The chances are that if you have done either of these things then you have at some time reached for your faithful dictionary. You might be interested to know that the Chamber brothers were born in Peebles. They were of course famous for their publications of encyclopaedias and dictionaries. William Chambers donated the Chambers Institute to Peebles, and it is now a museum and civic centre. Thriller fans amongst you will be intrigued to know that a writer associated with Peebles was John Buchan, who was the author of, amongst other things, 'The Thirty Nine Steps', made into a celebrated film by Alfred Hitchcock.

Peebles can boast a splendid eighteen hole golf course, which will give you panoramic views of the town and countryside beyond. There is also a swimming pool and boating. Tennis, putting and bowls are available.

Depending on when you visit Peebles, you may be able to see the agricultural show which is held each year in August, and if you go in September there are not only the Highland Games to look forward to, but also Peebles Arts Festival that has been running now for some five years, and is proving to be a wonderful myriad of drama, music, dance and exhibitions.

We decided to take a final walk down by the banks of the Tweed before we said farewell to Peebles, and we walked following the river out of town, so enchanted were we by it. Continuing upstream we soon came across **Neidpath Castle**. This fortress of a palace reputedly has walls that are as thick as ten feet. Cromwell was at considerable pains to destroy it on account of this, though it is now fortunately restored.

If you think that the surrounding area is not as thickly wooded as it might be, you might be interested to hear the story of the Queensbury family who once owned the castle. They incurred the wrath of the poet Wordsworth as a result of cutting down every tree on the estate to pay off their gambling debts in 1795.

We sat down and rested and took in the view looking back at Peebles. It truly is magical country, but we must turn our sights northward now, for twenty four miles away stands Edinburgh, one of the greatest cities in Europe.

Mid and West Lothian

Borthwick Castle

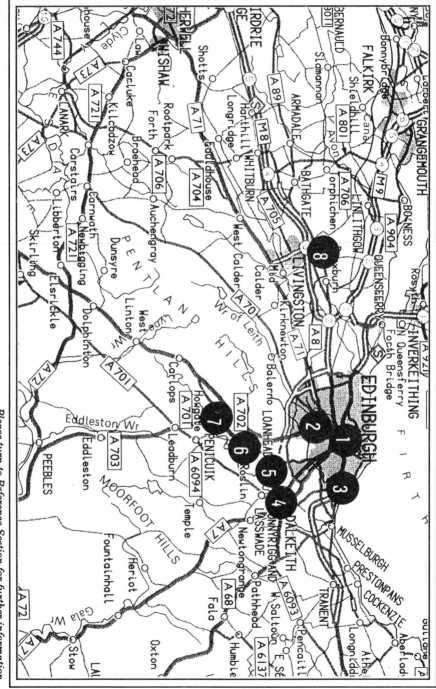

Please turn to Reference Section for further information.

CHAPTER FOUR

Mid and West Lothian

It is surely an impossible task to contain in just one chapter of a book a complete list of everything to see and do in a city with the wealth of history of **Edinburgh**. Whole books have been written on the subject, for the story of Edinburgh is almost the story of Scotland itself, and on every corner there is a tale to be told.

To us, Edinburgh is a truly lovely city, full of beauty and character, and there is much to be gained from its vast range of attractions which draw visitors each year from all around the world.

We will not attempt to cover every aspect of this city, but hope to show you some of its hidden places and to tell you a few of the stories that lie behind this dramatic place once referred to as the 'Athens of the North', in the hope that this will not only inspire you, but will give you a feeling for a city that we have come to love very much.

Edinburgh, like Rome, is built on seven hills and at the centre of these is the Castle Rock. This, together with the other main promontory, Arthur's Seat, helps to give a unique and splendid skyscape which has acted as a backdrop for some of the most poignant events in history.

At the centre of the city lie the Royal Mile and Princes Street. These divide the city into the Old Town and the New. The most dominant feature in Edinburgh is of course the famous castle. Perched high as it is, this great defender of the city features in every view. There has been a castle here for over a thousand years, and its dominance and important position has never been lost.

The name 'Edinburgh' stems from an encampment created by a former King of Northumbria called Edwin, whose building on top of the rock became known as Edwin's Burgh. In the years that followed, the town developed, clinging at first to the Castle Rock and stretching to the site of the palace and former abbey at Holyrood.

The name 'Holyrood' stretches back to when King David I of Scotland was reputedly charged by a stag while on a hunting trip in the forest that once stood here. He grabbed the stag's antlers but found himself holding onto a crucifix set between its horns which remained in his hands as the animal disappeared. That night in a dream, the king was told to build an abbey devoted to the Cross; the Abbey of Holyrood, or cross, was the result.

The castle has much of interest, and it is an ideal place to begin our look at Edinburgh. It was here that Mary Queen of Scots gave birth to her young son, James VI of Scotland, who was eventually to become James I of England.

There were many who were not happy at the birth of a Catholic king and stories abound of his early life. One that we found fascinating was that the infant James did in fact die when he was on a tour of the Borders with his mother and that the Countess of Mar, who had charge of the young prince, substituted her own child in his place.

Some say that if you look at a portrait of James he bears little resemblance to the facial characteristics of the Stuarts, but shows a startling likeness to the Earl of Mar. This theory was revived in 1830 when rumour has it that a small oak coffin was found in the wall of Mary's apartments in the castle. It contained the body of a small infant, wrapped in an embroidered silk covering bearing the initial 'J'.

Holyrood Abbey

Queen Mary's apartments can be seen in the castle, and her story is one that is linked vividly to the castles and abbeys of Edinburgh and the Borders. Indeed she seems to us to have been an unfortunate victim of circumstances and events who led a life doomed to be tragic.

At eighteen Mary was already a legend. When still a child, she was taken to France for safe keeping whilst quarrels erupted around her and there she was married to the heir of the throne and at seventeen Mary Stuart was Queen of France. A year later however her husband died and she was taken home to Edinburgh as the 'Queen of Scots', taking up residence in Holyrood Palace.

She was reputedly a great beauty, and with all the power of Scotland in her hand, she was victim to the struggles and scheming of all those who meant to take advantage of her position. She met and fell in love with Lord Darnley and they married in 1565. This proved to be a disastrous mistake, as Darnley was a callous and vain person, and on a fateful night murdered Mary's Italian secretary, a cultured and elegant man called Riccio in whom she confided, and who was accused of using these confidences to further his own ends.

Darnley plotted and had Riccio stabbed to death after he was dragged screaming from the queen. Mary was vulnerable and fell in love again, this time with the Earl of Bothwell. Again, tragedy struck when Darnley was killed in Kirk o'Field in 1567. Bothwell was blamed for the death of Darnley, and although he married Mary in secret in her own council chamber, he had many enemies who were powerful people. Mary was taken away to Holyrood and from there to a tiny island on the shores of Lochleven, where she was kept prisoner, locked away from any sort of communication with the outside world. Eventually, her followers managed to break her free and in 1568 she escaped.

However fate was not on her side and her supporters were defeated at the battle of Langside, and, though she escaped, it was only to England where she was to face nineteen years of captivity and finally death at the hands of the axeman. The story of the Queen of Scots is a truly fascinating tale, is it not?

Edinburgh Castle

In the crown room of the castle you will be able to see the 'Honours of Scotland' which are the equivalent of the crown jewels and include the Crown worn by Robert the Bruce, the Sceptre and the Sword of State. Many attempts have been made to have these precious items removed to London. Even a request by Charles I was turned down and he was forced to come to Edinburgh to be crowned King of Scotland. Cromwell was determined to get his hands on these symbols of royalty, but they were smuggled away from him to Dunhotter Castle for safe-keeping. After being buried in a church-yard they were eventually returned to Edinburgh Castle and sealed up in a room until Sir Walter Scott made a search and rediscovered them in 1818.

Of the large iron cannons that sit in the castle, the most famous was 'Mons Meg' and, though it now sits indoors, this cannon was renowned for its use at the siege of Norham, and it could blast a five hundredweight stone at a target more than a mile away.

The broad esplanade fronting the castle has always been used as a drilling ground. These days, the Edinburgh Military Tattoo revives some of its former glories for three weeks in the autumn. This military spectacle is world famous, and the massed pipes and drums, with tartans and kilts swinging, conjures up the majesty of years gone by. It really is a spectacle not to be missed.

Robert the Bruce

The castle is linked to the palace at Holyrood by a road known as the Royal Mile. This road, along with the area surrounding it, contains some of the most fascinating tales and the character of the old town. Across the street is Cannonball House with its two cannonballs lodged in the wall. These were supposedly fired from the castle at the time of the 1745 uprising, when Prince Charles Stuart was about to enter the city.

Castlehill has many tales to tell, and some of them are quite unnerving. It is here that a bronze plaque fixed to the wall tells us that witches were burned on this spot. Between 1479 and 1722 more than three hundred terrified women were branded as witches and cruelly put to death.

Did you know that in the early days the supply of water to Edinburgh was a serious problem? Most families owned a pair of 'stoups' for collecting water. These were two wooden vessels about two feet high which narrowed towards the top. They were popular wedding presents at the time. Queues would form around the various wells in the city at around six in the evening and the wait for water might last until as late as three in the morning, with the possibility of nothing to show for it if the wells ran dry.

If you had been in the Lawnmarket area two hundred years ago you might have been privileged enough to watch the local gentry and nobility displaying their finery whilst taking the air.

Nearby, Brodies Close was the home of the original 'Jekyll and Hyde' character. Deacon William Brodie was a respected member of the town council by day, and an extremely clever house burglar by night. However, unfortunately for him, he ventured out once too often and was recognised, arrested and hung. We thought that, if his ghost ever passes, he might be amused to see the inn that bears his name, standing by the site of the gallows from which he hung.

In nearby Tanners Close there once lived two rogues, much beloved by the makers of horror films. They were Burke and Hare, and these two enterprising gentlemen found that there was a trade in the supply of dead bodies for the purposes of medical research. The infamous duo took to grave robbing and then ultimately murder to meet the demand.

As you pass through Lawnmarket into High Street you will come to the High Kirk of Saint Giles. In the early days of Edinburgh there was little room for shops and traders would set up stalls wherever they could find room around Saint Giles. This is where both rich and poor would do their shopping for meat, bread, fish and other groceries.

When the congestion reached the point of chaos around St Giles, the magistrates decided to act and allocated various places where the traders could do business. It can be fascinating today to spot the old places of these traders with such names as Grassmarket, Lawnmarket, Flesher's Close, Candlemaker Row etc.

The Royal Mile is so full of history that at every turn it is possible to pick up a story about a king or queen or some turn of events. It eventually leads us to Holyrood Palace, and the ruins of the abbey. Across the road at intervals the letter "S" can be seen. This marks the sanctuary line of Holyrood Abbey, and we were intrigued to learn that many a debtor has been chased across the line by pursuing bailiffs.

The abbey was destroyed by the English under orders from Henry VIII when his demand for the return of the infant Mary Queen of Scots was refused. Also destroyed were the palace and the abbeys of Melrose, Kelso and Jedburgh on the Borders. The palace was eventually restored and you can visit the chambers lived in by Mary here, along with the spot where Riccio was murdered in the outer chambers. Queen Victoria visited here in 1842, and today the Queen stays here when she visits Edinburgh.

The palace and abbey remains sit in the perfect setting of Holyrood Park, and are well worth a visit, especially to see Arthur's Seat, rising up to some eight hundred and twenty two feet at the summit and providing views of a wonderful panorama of the city.

The exposed rocks on the west side are known as 'Samson's Ribs', and below this point is a road that runs to **Duddingston**, a pretty village on a loch in the shadow of Arthur's Seat. Nearby, we were lucky enough to find **The Sheep Heid Inn**.

The inn sits in the Causeway at Duddingston, on the south east corner of Holyrood Park, adjacent to the old kirk and the bird sanctuary on Duddingston Loch. The loch is a favourite spot for families, local and visiting, and is especially popular with children.

As you enter the inn's Horseshoe Bar you experience an eerie but intriguing feeling that you have stepped back in time, for the Sheep Heid is the oldest and most historic of Edinburgh's inns, dating back as it does to

1360. Patronised by Bonnie Prince Charlie when he lodged in Duddingston village, you can still see the house where he stayed. Mary, Queen of Scots, is another of the Sheep Heid's historical customers, known to have stopped here for refreshments on her way to Craigmillar Castle.

The inn's present name comes from an ornate snuff box in the shape of a ram's head, which was presented to the pub by James VI in 1580. He considered the Sheep Heid to be one of his favourite hostelries, and although the snuff box was proudly displayed in the bar for many years, its whereabouts are now unknown.

If today's fare is anything to go by, it's easy to see why the Sheep Heid has enjoyed such royal patronage. Those wishing to eat can do so in the Jacobean restaurant where an a la carte menu is available from Monday to Saturday, or in the lounge bar for tasty bar meals.

The secret of this old inn's success, we feel, is that patrons can choose to dine as simply or as grandly as they wish. On this occasion we ourselves chose the haggis starter made to the Sheep Heid's own recipe, which includes cream, turnip and Drambuie. We intend to return for a second chance at the menu, and some traditional Scottish afters! To complement your meal there is a full range of Tennent's quality beers and lagers, including the inn's own 80 shilling ale.

Sheep Heid Inn

Across the centuries, many a tale has been told about this hostelry. The most infamous of these concerns relationships between the Sheep Heid and the local kirk at Duddingston. These were strained to say the least, and one particular dispute is still recorded on the Kirk session minutes. Mrs Hamilton, one of the Sheep Heid's more enterprising landladies, actually cut the church bell ropes in order to prevent her patrons from leaving the inn to worship at the sound of those bells. As a consequence, the inn was never allowed to open on Sundays. Thankfully relations have greatly improved since then, although it wasn't until 1985 that the Sheep Heid was finally granted a Sunday licence.

When the weather is fine you can take advantage of the beer garden; a bonus if you've brought a young family along for lunch. The inn also boasts a super skittle alley which is available for morning, afternoon and evening sessions.

Visitors to the Sheep Heid are encouraged to look round and ask questions of the staff and management; just one of those little touches to ensure that a visit here makes for a relaxing and satisfying start or finish to a special day out.

The second half of our journey takes us to what is referred to as the New Town of Edinburgh. In 1752 steps were taken to oversee the development of Edinburgh in a style in keeping with the city's status. Designers and architects were employed to ensure the quality of the work and they began to construct the spacious and elegant streets that make Edinburgh famous throughout the world today.

As the New Town began to take shape, they were lucky to have a ready supply of a light coloured sandstone from local quarries. Craiglieth stone was particularly attractive, and indeed we were interested to learn that much of it was sent south to provide building materials for Buckingham Palace and the British Museum.

The area was planned and laid out by a young architect, the winner of a competition for the submission of the best design. This is made remarkable by the fact that the winner, James Craig, was only twenty three at the time.

Princes Street is of course one of the most famous shopping streets anywhere in the world and, with its buildings on one side of the street, it must surely rank as one of the most picturesque.

At the Mound, off Princes Street, are The Royal Scottish Academy and the National Gallery of Scotland. Held at the Academy, of painting, sculpture and architecture, are exhibitions running from May to August and a special show for the Edinburgh Festival. The Gallery houses an important collection of painting by Scottish artists as well as work by many famous European masters from the fourteenth century to Cezanne, including works by Degas, Turner, Monet, Renoir and Goya.

Another main feature of Princes Street is the Scott monument which began in 1840, eight years after the death of Edinburgh's most famous son. We were surprised to discover that it was designed by an untrained joiner called George Kemp, who was unfortunately drowned before he had a chance to see the finished result. If you are feeling fit you might like to attempt the two hundred and eighty seven steps climbing to the top.

You will be rewarded with lovely views over Princes Street and the Castle. The monument itself has much of interest to look at, including over sixty small statues of the figures in Scott's books.

You might like to take a walk or even rest in Princes Street Gardens. Here you will find fine floral displays, as well as what is reputed to be the oldest floral clock in the world, dating from 1903. There are more than twenty thousand plants used in the display on the clock, which are changed several times a year.

Cannongate Tolbooth

While you are in Edinburgh, why not take advantage of the zoo? It is open all year round and is a favourite with children of all ages. The zoo covers eighty acres and has a very comprehensive collection, all in all making for a wonderful day out. For younger children there is the Children's Zoo, which is almost a miniature farm with ponies, calves, goats and lambs.

Of course wherever we are in this city we are never very far from the sea, and we followed Leith Walk from Princes Street which eventually took us to Leith. Here there was a village that marked the point where the water of Leith entered the Firth of Forth. There is a very pleasant walk to be had along the waterway which stretches for some four miles back into the city.

Travelling eastwards from Leith we came across the once famous resort of **Portobello**, and if you are seeking the sort of activities you would not associate with a capital city then you need look no further. Spectacular seaviews, exciting watersports and comfortable modern accommodation; that's what you'll find at **The Hamilton Lodge Hotel**. This small, family run hotel is run by resident proprietors Ian and Marion Ferguson, and sits on the seafront at Joppa Promenade, Portobello.

Although its seaside location means Hamilton Lodge can offer the sort of peaceful and relaxing atmosphere many people enjoy, the fact that the hotel is just several miles outside Edinburgh city centre will no doubt please the shoppers, nightclubbers and hardened sightseers among you. Should you be arriving from Edinburgh, call the hotel before you arrive and they will arrange a free pick up by bus from the city's Waverley Station.

Hamilton Lodge Hotel has ten rooms, seven of which have en-suite facilities. All have colour television, tea and coffee making facilities and are comfortably furnished.

There are two bars plus a separate dining room and all are situated well away from the guest rooms. Enjoy traditional home cooked food at modest prices, eating in the dining room of the lounge bar if you prefer. The hotel's extensive gardens are an added bonus and are ideal for an after dinner stroll.

If you prefer something a little more adventurous, however, then why not try a little water and jet skiing, or even parascending, all activities available on the waterfront.

Hamilton Lodge Hotel

And of course there's a ghost. The ghostly figure of Lady Hamilton has been seen on numerous occasions, wandering the hotel, dressed in white. Ian and Marion, however, are keen to point out that their particular ghost is of the friendly variety!

Of course, no visit to Edinburgh would be complete without reference to the spectacular Edinburgh Arts Festival that takes place every summer. What can we say about one of the most renowned and famous arts events staged anywhere in the world? The festival includes music, opera, ballet, theatre, dance, poetry and of course the fringe events that take place on every corner. All in all Edinburgh is a wonderful melting pot, rich in character and charm. The city is an experience not to be missed.

Almost adjoining Portobello is the small town of **Musselburgh**, which was once known as Eskmouth, and is situated on the mouth of the River Esk. The modern name derives from a profitable mussel-bank in the river's estuary. Musselburgh is a place of very independent character. The tolbooth dates from 1590 and has an interesting story behind it, as it was built from the ruins of the Chapel of our Lady of Loretto which was destroyed by the English in 1544. Unfortunately the act of building the tolbooth from the sacred ruins was considered to be a sacrilege and brought the citizens under sentence of Papal excommunication for two hundred years.

There is a race course and golf course here, on which King James IV is said to have played in 1504. The actual golf club was founded in 1774 and used to offer a prize for the best fish-wife golfer. If it was unusual to find women on a golf course in the eighteenth century, it was not considered so in Musselburgh as the womenfolk had a tough reputation. We enjoyed the story of one such woman who was hanged at the Grassmarket in Edinburgh in 1728, only to be taken down to be buried in Musselburgh. The jolting of the wagon on her last journey however revived the spirit of this indomitable woman and we are told that she lived to get married and produce many children.

To the south east of Musselburgh is a rather charming village called **Inveresk** and you will find here a fine selection of buildings and houses dating from the seventeenth and eighteenth centuries.

We followed the B6415 which took us to **Dalkieth**, a town that once stood on a Roman road as it stands today on one of the main routes coming out of Edinburgh, situated on the River Esk. There are interesting houses here to look at, most notably the Palace which, although not open to visitors, has had celebrated guests such as James IV, George IV and Queen Victoria.

Nearby is a pleasant walk through Dalkieth Park and along the river. It is here at **Lothianbridge** that you will find **The Sun Inn**. Originally built as a house for the local blacksmith, it became a pub at the turn of the century and was used to serve the then thriving mining community.

The Sun Inn

Proprietors Roy and Sheila Tyldesley bought the pub in 1985. Both had been living in Germany until a management reshuffle at the chemical company Roy worked for meant a contractual payout and a return to the UK. Roy and Sheila decided they would like to buy a pub/restaurant and finally settled here at The Sun Inn, Midlothian.

Four years after taking over, the quality and choice of foods available here has meant that Roy and Sheila's client base has more than trebled. All food served is fresh and made on the premises. The menu offers everything from fish and steak dishes to vegetarian and spicy meals. The chef's sauces are his speciality, so you will find that dishes such as Rob Roy Steak, Trout Montrose and Chicken Suva are especially superb. Prices vary from #3 to #10 for a main course, with plenty of choice in between and a daily 'specials' menu, particularly popular with the locals.

Roy and Sheila intend to provide hotel accommodation in 1990, with probably around five bedrooms with en-suite facilities. There are plenty of facilities here for children too, with a play area for the younger ones. Enjoy a drink on the patio overlooking the River Esk; trout fishing permits for the river are for sale behind the bar.

Although Roy and Sheila openly admit to having no previous experience of this type of business, they have obviously found the secret of success: looking at the business from the customers' point of view, and giving them exactly what they want

A few miles from Dalkieth on the A6094 lie the towns of **Bonnyrigg** and **Lasswade**. Sir Walter Scott lived at Lasswade Cottage for the first six years of his married life, and during this time Scott began to establish himself as a poet and was in turn visited by William and Dorothy Wordsworth. Yet another noted literary figure, Thomas de Quincey, came to live at a cottage a mile away at Polton Station, from 1840 until his death in 1859. Lasswade is said to be the location of Gandercleugh in Scott's 'Tales of my Landlord'.

While Dorothy Wordsworth stayed here she recorded in her diary her impressions of this part of the Esk Valley, and in particular the Glen of Roslin that is a mile downstream from Polton. She noted that she had "never passed through a more pleasant dell", and remarked upon the ruins of **Rosslyn Castle and the Chapel**. Roslin Glen is now a public park and we suggest you visit this lovely area. After all, what better recommendation could you have than that of a Wordsworth?

The castle is believed to have been founded by Sir William St Clair, having reputedly won the lands in a wager he made, betting his head against the lands, that two of his hounds would bring down a deer by the time it reached a certain spot. Fortunately for Sir William the deer was killed and he was awarded the estate. Sir William seems to have been one of those rich characters, as we discovered that not only was he waited on by a number of lesser lords, but that his wife was attended by some seventy five gentlewomen. The Lady Chapel was the beginning of a much larger project that Sir William had intended as a monument of himself. Unfortunately he died when the project was only partially completed.

The remains are somewhat dilapidated, though what is left gives indications that, had it been finished, the church would have been one of the most remarkable medieval buildings in Europe.

Anyone visiting Rosslyn Chapel around three hundred years ago may well have lingered at the cottage adjacent to this old Midlothian church. Built around 1660, it was then The Old Roslin Inn. Famous patrons included King Edward VII when he was Prince of Wales, Sir Walter Scott, Robert Burns and William and Dorothy Wordsworth. The inn is thought to have closed its doors for the last time in 1866. Today's travellers, however, need only retrace their steps about a quarter of a mile back into Roslin village to find **The Original Rosslyn Inn.**

Dating back to around 1827, it may well have been this inn which accounted for the demise of the earlier chapelside hostelry. Family owned and run, Mr Graham Harris and his staff maintain that they are always keen to offer a warm welcome to visitors to their small hotel.

All six bedrooms are prettily furnished and have en-suite bathrooms, colour television and tea and coffee making facilities. A baby listening service is provided too

The Original Rosslyn Inn

The inn's candlelit restaurant is popular with old and young, visitors and locals alike. Serving mainly grills, there are naturally some excellent Scottish steaks on the menu. The wine list provides the perfect accompaniment to the food and Mr Harris has obviously given a lot of thought to its selection. Bar lunches and suppers are available at some very modest prices too, and are served with the same friendly efficiency that you will find in the restaurant.

The Original Rosslyn Inn is only seven miles from Edinburgh at Roslin Village, which is well signposted on the A701. This charming country inn is full of rural character and is the natural choice for all who come here to see the chapel, Rosslyn Castle, which is about two hundred yards away, and the peaceful Roslin Glen on the banks of the river Esk.

Also in the glen is **Hawthornden Castle**, which dates from the fifteenth century. It was the birth place of William Drummond the poet, 1585-1649, and remained in the Drummond family until the 1970s. It is now a retreat for poets and writers.

The small Midlothian town of **Penicuik** has its fair share of visitors, many of them attracted to the **Edinburgh Crystal Visitor Centre** on the edge of the town. If you are among them, and are looking for a truly satisfying value-for-money lunch, then make sure you pay a visit to **The Railway Tavern** in the town's High Street.

The tavern was originally situated on the other side of the High Street, but when the great fire of Penicuik engulfed most of that part of the town in flames around 1904, it was moved to higher and safer ground on its present site.

Mr and Mrs Faichney have owned the tavern now for seven years after Glenn made the move from manager to owner. This is a family run pub with a real family atmosphere. Father-in-law helps behind the bar, as do the Faichney's three children. We suspect, however, that Mr and Mrs Faichney's idea of 'helping' differs quite substantially from that of the children; they're all under five!

The Railway Tavern

Penicuik is a small town and The Railway Tavern looks after much of the local trade. You will find there is a good local atmosphere in both the refurbished lounge bar and the old style public bar with its cosy open fire.

Choose from a wide variety of bar lunches, or try the house speciality; jacket potatoes with various tasty fillings to suit every palette. We think you'll agree that any pub where you can enjoy such a deliciously satisfying lunch in such welcoming surroundings and still come out with change from a five pound note has to be worth a visit.

Penicuik is an excellent centre for the Pentland Hills, which are a long stretch of uplands that run south from the edge of Edinburgh. If you would like a rest from the enjoyable but tiring rigours of the cities and towns then why not abandon yourself to this nearby haven? You will find the grazing lands and the numerous reservoirs a picturesque and refreshing tonic. As many of the hills are over five hundred metres in height, you will of course be rewarded with many lovely views.

If, like us, you are tempted by the thought of being spoilt for a while then you will be glad of a chance to indulge yourself. Following the A8 out of Edinburgh to the east and driving to the West Lothian area you will find the very place near the town of Uphall.

Houstoun House Hotel at West Lothian is based around an early 17th century tower house built by Sir John Shairp, a man whose family have been lairds here for almost four centuries. Additions and improvements have been made over the centuries but have always respected the architectural integrity and elegance of the building. A hotel now since 1969, Houstoun House was purchased in 1987 by the owners of the celebrated Gleddoch House Hotel near Glasgow.

Houstoun House

Over the years, Houstoun House has won many awards and an international reputation for the quality and novelty of its cuisine. The hotel's three dining rooms are on the first floor of the tower, in the old drawing room, the library and the great hall, and are among the most attractive rooms in the hotel. Any one of them can be booked separately for a special occasion or function.

Each room features floor to ceiling wooden panelling, fine plaster mouldings, elegant paintings, magnificent polished mahogany furniture and is dressed with the garden's harvest of freshly cut flowers.

The menu here changes daily and the award winning culinary team continually strive to serve dishes which are at once innovative and deliciously satisfying. An extensive wine list of over four hundred bins will guarantee you a tipple to complement any dish you choose.

Houstoun House's thirty bedrooms are all furnished to an exceptionally

St. Giles Kirk

high standard on a variety of antique and modern themes. All rooms have their own bathroom or shower, colour television, radio, direct dial telephone, trouser press, hair dryer and tea and coffee making facilities. Nine of these rooms offer the added luxury of a four poster bed.

The rural tranquillity of Houstoun House belies its proximity to the country's motorway network. Two minutes away is the M8, the Glasgow to Edinburgh road, which means that the whole of Scotland is literally on your doorstep. Edinburgh airport is only ten minutes away.

Come to Houstoun House to relax, do business or use the hotel as a base for exploring the surrounding area; Edinburgh and its castle, Hopetoun and Dalmeny house, Linlithgow Palace and the Forth Bridges are all nearby. Whatever the reason for your stay, you are assured of the very highest standards of service.

Certainly those who come here come to enjoy good food and wine in magnificent surroundings at the hands of a hotel team which is second to none.

Lanarkshire and Renfrewshire

Craignethan Castle

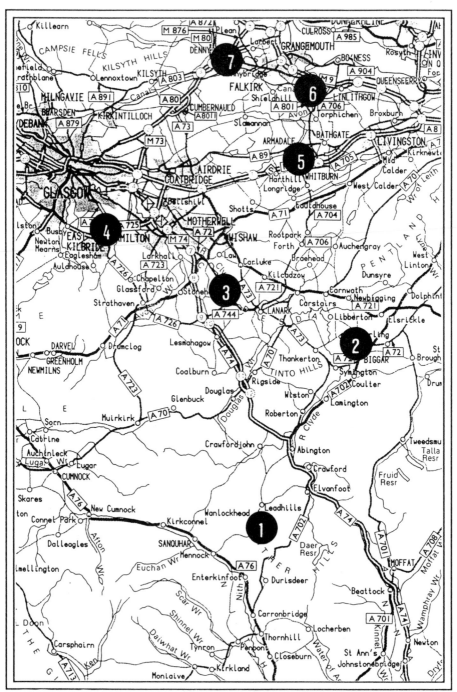

CHAPTER FIVE

Lanarkshire and Renfrewshire

"There's gold in them hills". Well at least there used to be. Not only gold but both silver and lead were first discovered in **Wanlockhead** and the aptly named Leadhills as far back as Roman times.

Wanlockhead is in fact the highest village in the Lowlands of Scotland, standing at 1,500 feet above sea level, and is almost completely isolated in its setting amongst the Lowther Hills.

The mines were closed in the 1930s, after some four hundred years of production, and there is a splendid museum in Goldscaur Road dedicated to the history of mining in the area, including a replica tin mine. A few miles away is **Leadmills**, which you may not be surprised to learn is the second highest village, and was also the birthplace of Allan Ramsay, 1686-1758, who was an important poet in the eighteenth century revival.

Wanlockhead Lead Mining Museum

Gold from the area was used to make parts of the crown of Scotland, which is kept of course in Edinburgh Castle.

The B7040 took us to **Elvanfoot**, which is close to the source of two of Scotland's greatest rivers, the Forth and the Clyde, standing in some of the wildest lowland country in Scotland.

There is a lovely red sandstone church here, with a stained glass window commemorating the actor-manager Wilton Barrat, whose drama productions would not have been seen by those of us who are more accustomed these days to watching television. We took a left turn at the A702 which enabled us to drive through the Dalvern Pass, our purpose being to sample some of the magnificent hillside scenery in this area.

We were certainly not disappointed, as the pass was one of the most beautiful and daunting places we have ever seen. On the steep, smooth hills were many sheep. What hardy beasts they are, grazing outside in all weathers. We were fascinated to learn that it takes over two thousand acres, and some eight hundred sheep, to support the livelihood of just one shepherd.

Did you know that red grouse is unique to Scotland and Northern England, and is widely encouraged to exist here amongst the more heathery areas?

The A74 is the main road leading to Glasgow and the north, but if you travel for some ten miles from Elvanfoot and turn off at the A70 you will come across the village of **Douglas**. The castle here was destroyed in the 1940s because mining works were found to have damaged its foundations. The chapel however can still be seen, and it contains the tombs of the famous Douglas chiefs including Good Sir James, 'the Black Douglas', who took King Robert I's heart on the Crusade against the Moors in Spain. Sir James' story is an interesting one, as he was Bruce's friend and the greatest of his lieutenants, so feared by the English that mothers would hush their children to sleep with the words,

> "Hush ye, hush ye, do not fret ye,
> The Black Douglas will not get ye".

How did this feared man end up taking Bruce's heart to the Holy Land? Well, apparently, on his death bed Bruce charged him with the task of removing his heart from his dead body and taking it on the crusade. Sir James obeyed his king's command and got as far as Spain, whereupon he was engaged in a battle in 1330 against the Moors.

Finding himself alone and cut off, Sir James threw the royal heart, in a silver casket, at the enemy, vowing to follow it. He was however killed in doing so, though his body and the king's heart were retrieved and brought back to Scotland. The heart, as you may remember from our previous chapter, is reputedly buried in Melrose Abbey. Since that time the Douglas coat of arms has carried a red heart beneath the three stars on blue.

Another Douglas buried here of whom we were fascinated to learn is Archibald 'Bell the Cat' Douglas. He earned his unusual nickname as the leader of a group of Scottish nobles who hated the favourites with whom James III had surrounded himself. Spurred on by Lord Grey and his telling of the fable of some mice, who agreed it would be a good idea to 'bell', or hang, the cat, although they couldn't decide who was to do it. Archibald took the lead, and in front of the King at Lauder, they seized these disliked favourites and hung them.

We followed the A70 northwards through the hamlets of Uddington and Rigside, whereupon we decided to drive along the B7055 across the Tinto

Hills. The name 'tinto' derives from the Gaelic 'tienteach' or 'place of fire' and there are ancient rhymes and stories which connect this place with fire raising powers.

Rejoining the A702 we made our way leisurely towards the town of **Biggar**, with its broad main street which livens up considerably on market day. The town itself has wide, tree lined main streets, and we were quite taken by the lovely colours of the shops and hotels. The family of the British prime minister Gladstone came from Biggar, and the **Gladstone Court Museum**, open from Easter to October, features an interesting 19th century town with shops, a library and a schoolroom.

We were also interested to see a museum of 17th century local life at the **Greenhill Covenanter's House**, and the fine 16th century church of Saint Mary, which still contains parts of the 12th century church dedicated to Saint Nicholas. Nearby Biggar Water, when in flood, reputedly flows in two directions at once.

Biggar's other main attraction is the **Moat Park Heritage Centre**, opened by Her Royal Highness the Princess Royal in June 1988. Other popular attractions include the **Biggar Gasworks Museum** and the town's **Puppet Theatre**, a must for the children.

Whatever you decide to do in Biggar, take a look in at **Whitehart Gallery and Crafts**. Jess Archibald's unique little craft centre is easy to find, sitting as it does in the town's main car park.

Whitehart Gallery and Crafts

Housed in what was formerly an inn dating back to 1836, Whitehart Gallery is an outlet for some of the finest quality paintings and crafts available in Scotland. All items on sale here have one very important thing in common; they are the work of artists and craftspeople from all over Scotland, and nothing here is imported. If what you are looking for is a high quality, hand-made Scottish gift, then you have come to the right place.

Jess is always keen to explain to visitors the history and background behind the paintings and crafts on display. Whitehart Gallery is proud of its 'made in Scotland only' policy, and rightly so.

We were in no great hurry, and elected to take the B7106 which took us gently up towards the village of **Carnwath**. Carnwath House, where Prince Charlie supposedly slept at one time, is now a golf course clubhouse. Nearby **Cowthally Castle** was originally the stronghold of the Sommerville family, and is known for providing James V with a mistress, Katherine Carmichael, whom he first met at a wedding party here.

It is but a short distance from here to the town of **Lanark**, and we were quite keen to see the famous falls which start on the Clyde where it becomes swollen with the waters of the Douglas. There are three falls, the first being **Bonnington** which surges over a drop of thirty feet. The river presses on for half a mile further before coming to **Corra Linn**, the middle fall.

Although the waters of Corra Linn fall ninety feet they do not seem as impressive as those of Bonnington, as the drop is not quite so sheer, but is a series of very beautiful cascades. Looking from the bottom, we were held for some time by the wonderful spectacle. Two miles further down are the broadest of the falls at **Stonebryes**. It is a magical feeling watching the water running through these falls, and such a wonderful way to have spent our time.

You will not be here for long before you hear the name **New Lanark**. It is, as you might suppose, a new town, but its origins are fascinating. It was built in the 18th century as an experimental cotton-spinning village by an entrepreneur called David Dale, working in partnership with Richard Arkwright. Although there is nothing particularly uncommon in this, when the partners fell out allegedly over the hanging of a bell on the belfry of the church, Robert Owen took over the project and it became an experiment in community living with work, housing and education organized on socialist principles.

It is well worth visiting today, as it has become a conservation project with craft industries and a famous heritage trail. As the site is so well preserved in the style of the Industrial Revolution, New Lanark has been used many times as the background for films and television programmes.

Close by you will find it easy to get to the **Falls of Clyde**, and surrounding them is a nature reserve run by the Scottish Wildlife Trust, where if you are lucky you might see red squirrels, kingfishers, otters and badgers.

In Lanark itself there is much of interest to be seen, as it was one of the original four royal burghs of Scotland created by David I, who built a castle here in the 12th century.

Known for its traditional ceremonies, there is a fascinating one called 'Whuppity Scoorie' which takes place on the first day of March each year. This ceremony is believed to drive the harsh winter away. A crowd gathers at the parish church of Saint Nicholas, and the children of the crowd are each given a tightly wadded paper ball on the end of a piece of string. At the sounding of the six o'clock bell, the children run around the church three times hitting each other with the paper balls on the way.

Five miles to the north west of Lanark from the A72 is **Crossford**, and here you will find **Craignethan Castle**, a Hamilton stronghold of the 16th century. It was once a refuge of Mary Queen of Scots and is said to be haunted by the Queen, minus her head, of course.

Craignethan Castle

From the castle you might like to take advantage of a small country track road that crosses the M74 and brings you out at Glassford. From here it is but a short distance to the small town of Strathaven, and the Calderglen Country Park. This park consists of three hundred acres of wooded gorge and parkland, and makes for a very enjoyable day's outing. There are many lovely marked routes around the park, as well as the woodlands and river with waterfalls, which are very picturesque. If you would like to spend some time in the park then why not do as we did, and take a picnic? There is also a children's zoo for the young ones, an ornamental garden and an adventure playground.

A short trip northwards on the A723 will take us to the town of **Hamilton**. You may have heard of its famous racecourse, which is situated close to the banks of the Clyde. **The Strathclyde Country Park**, which lies on both sides of the Clyde, has a man-made loch complete with sandy beaches and a nature reserve.

There once stood here one of the largest palaces ever to have been built in Scotland. Hamilton Palace was originally started in 1591 and substantially added to throughout the centuries, but not however to everyone's taste. Dorothy Wordsworth called it a "heavy lumpish mass". However she need not have worried, as underground mineworks caused the foundations to start sinking and it was eventually demolished in 1927.

The **Hamilton Mausoleum** that can be seen in the park was built by the tenth Duke of Hamilton, who was considered to be an eccentric. The building dates back to the mid-19th century and took four years to complete, costing over one hundred and fifty thousand pounds. A large portion of this sum was spent on the floor alone, which we thought was fascinating; a wheel mosaic containing almost all the known varieties of marble, many of them rare. The building has huge bronze doors and is famous for its echo.

Hamilton, of course, is not far from **Glasgow** and you may choose to take advantage of its proximity for exploring this historic and splendid city. We were keen however to cross the River Clyde, and to take in the area known as **Midlothian**. A visit to Glasgow was left for a later date and you will find out about it in Chapter 10. We crossed the river and joined the M74 which took us to Motherwell. The name of this town is an interesting one, and comes from an old healing well which was situated on Ladywell road. The A71 took us through adjoining **Wishaw** and out towards **Shotts**. Situated high on the moors, Shotts is some nine hundred feet above sea level. If you are lucky enough to be here in the month of July you will be able to see the Shotts Highland Games and enjoy the world famous sounds of the Shotts and Dykehead Pipe Band.

Crossing the M8 again, it is not far to the town of **Armadale**. The Dale, as it is better known to most of its inhabitants, is situated in an area once famous for its wild pig hunting.

Until 1790 there was nothing much here, however, Lord Armadale purchased a house here as a weekend retreat from his law practice in Edinburgh, and when the Glasgow to Edinburgh highway was completed Armadale became perfectly situated and turned into one of the new towns of the Industrial Revolution. Armadale contains a wealth of stories and characters from the past, and its development over the last century is one of the most fascinating we have come across.

Being halfway between the two cities, a regular stage coach route was established, and passengers would break for a rest and perhaps have a meal while the horses were changed in the middle of this twelve hour journey. There was also a toll house here, and it was once described as a "small one-roomed hut with a window lookout in each wall". We presume this was to keep an eye open for those who might try to slip by without paying.

At the beginning of the 19th century Armadale was the scene of a daring highway robbery, involving a stagecoach named the 'Prince George'. On a cold winter morning the stagecoach set out on its usual run from Glasgow to Edinburgh. It had one passenger apart from the driver. This passenger had only paid for a ticket to travel on the outside, yet he asked for a large tin box he was carrying to be stored in the boot below the driver's seat and secured to the floor with padlock and chains.

Outside Glasgow the stage was stopped by two men who looked like labourers. They also paid to travel outside and climbed up on top. Further on the coach was stopped yet again, this time for a well dressed couple who had already bought their tickets and they climbed inside without further delay.

As the weather was cold and the sleet had turned to snow, the driver noticed that the two workmen had produced a length of chain and were continually 'cleaning' this rather heavy piece, whilst making a noisy racket in the process of doing so. He thought no more of it and did not think to complain as the wind was blowing hard and he knew that they had already paid their passage and would soon be getting off.

The stage was nearly at Armadale when indeed, first the young couple dismounted followed not long afterwards by the two labourers on the top. The stagecoach continued its journey until it reached Uphall, which is midway between Armadale and Edinburgh. Here, as the horses were changed the driver was asked to check the box concealed beneath his seat for the first passenger. To their horror they discovered that the box had been broken open and all that remained of its contents was a torn one pound note. The passenger immediately revealed that he was in fact a plain clothes agent for the Commercial Bank and that the trunk had in fact contained £6,000 in notes, gold and silver.

Stage Coach

It was decided that the young couple had in fact been breaking open the box from inside the coach whilst their accomplices had been making as much noise as possible on the top with their chain.

The owner of the Prince George was eventually arrested and hung for organising the robbery, which he had done to save himself from debt. His accomplice and the young woman of the couple was in fact a young man by the name of Davidson who had been disguised. The two workmen were also caught but later released due to lack of evidence. Davidson meanwhile escaped the gallows and eventually escaped from jail to live in America where he ended his days as a recluse afraid to venture out in case his part in the robbery should become known. He finally died in 1904.

The toll at Armadale was the main point for the distribution of gossip in the town. Apart from the stories which were spread from here, other news would come into Armadale via the letter carrier, who would arrive from Bathgate at 10.00am blowing a horn to annonce his arrival to those not living directly on the main route. The first post office was opened in 1855, and resulted in Armadale producing another of its renowned characters in John Easton, known as 'John the Post'. He walked the same post round for twenty five years and it was said that he knew exactly how many steps it took to complete his double trip, as the residents of Armadale demanded two deliveries a day.

The Goth, Armadale

There was only one day when 'John the Post' failed to deliver his round. The villagers set out to search for John, as they were worried and it was snowing at the time. They eventually found him buried in a drift, frozen by cold though still alive. They dug him out, and took him to a nearby house whereupon he was thawed out and insisted on continuing his round.

Armadale's first licensed premises was located at the toll by the cross. The toll at Armadale however also doubled as a dairy, so that anyone who was seen wandering home slightly under the influence was said to have been for the milk again. It is here in Armadale, in South Street, that we found **La Nuit** the ideal place in West Lothian for an impromptu meal, or indeed for a function or special occasion.

From outside you will see that La Nuit is not at first glance the most aesthetically pleasing of buildings, and because of this we have instead included an illustration of the restaurant's plush interior. The warm welcome you will receive from Jeff Oyman and his staff more than makes up for any lack of exterior charm, as does the quality of food on offer, made only from the best and freshest ingredients.

Specialising in French cuisine, La Nuit offers such mouth watering dishes as lobster, served hot or cold, Chicken a La Nuit, and Scotch steaks, all served with a bouquettiere of fresh vegetables. Jeff's own speciality is Steak a La Nuit, and he admits, "It took me eighteen months to get it right"!

At lunchtime, diners can choose from La Nuit's business lunch menu, or eat a la carte. Those who enjoy high teas are also well catered for in the evenings.

To complement your meal you can choose from a superb range of wines, one hundred and seventy two in all. Jeff offers one of the biggest and best ranges of champagne in Scotland, with over thirty seven to choose from for that special occasion. Those wishing to take advantage of the facilities offered in the recently refurbished function room can be sure of a good night out for up to one hundred and twenty people.

A family outing at La Nuit is never a problem, for the restaurant caters well for children, and provides facilities for the disabled.

La Nuit

The atmosphere created by Jeff and his team can only be described as intimate and friendly. Their aim, to make you feel well and truly pampered, is fully achieved, and Jeff's boast of being the best value for money in the area is ably borne out by his succulent sixteen ounce T-bone steak, with all the trimmings, for just £8.00. Beat that for value!

From Armadale you may like to take a look around nearby **Westfield**, situated on the river Avon. Westfield, like other towns on Avon, has its base in the paper industry. Westfield Mills has been going for over one hundred years, and is now the last remaining paper mill in West Lothian. On the edge of the village you may see **Bridge Castle**, which was a fortified mansion and the home of the Earls of Linlithgow.

We were pleased to be near Muiravonside Country Park, situated in the southeast corner of Falkirk District, an area rich in historic, industrial and wildlife interests. Formed around an original, virtually self-sufficient estate, itself part of a much larger family estate, its history can easily be traced back for eight hundred years.

Reginald de Tinsdale gifted the estate at his daughter's marriage to Richard de Melville in 1189. At this time it is believed that the remains of the Anglo-Norman 'Maiden Castle', just outside the country park, may have been the hub of the estate.

The estate was married on to the Ross family in 1471, although in 1513 Sir John Ross fell at the Battle of Flodden. His heir died shortly after, although the estate stayed in the Ross family. The original Muiravonside House was built in 1609 while under the ownership of the Rosses, and was later extended in the eighteenth and nineteenth centuries.

By 1724 the estate was in MacLeod hands. Leading up to the '45 rebellion, these Jacobite sympathisers were amongst those plotting the return of the Stuarts. Also involved was a leading Scottish advocate and MacLeod's friend, Lord Grange, whose wife, Lady Grange, threatened to expose his Jacobite sympathies and his plots to the Crown. For her troubles she was abducted and taken to the Hebrides, via Muiravonside, by Alexander (Sandy) MacLeod, son and heir of the estate.

Come 1835, the estate had changed hands again, this time to the Stirling family. It was now that Sir Charles Stirling decided he ought to make his estate as self-sufficient as possible. He built limekilns, which you can still see on the estate, and then carried on to set up his own clay draining works. Sir Charles also turned his attention to turning an old grain mill into a productive sawmill, as well as finding the time to oversee the Muiravonside coalfield which had been in operation since the eighteenth century.

The family had therefore transformed Muiravonside into a profitable working estate which extended well beyond the present country park. Since the beginning of the twentieth century the house itself was partially let out for various uses, particularly during the Second World War when eleven British soldiers were billeted here.

All good things come to an end however, and by the 1960s the estate was virtually abandoned. The once grand old house was badly vandalised and frankly unsafe come the mid-seventies. It was then, in 1977 to be precise, that Falkirk District Council adopted Muiravonside to be its first country park, and the estate once again underwent the developing process of change and revitalisation.

It now comprises one hundred and seventy acres of woodlands, parklands and gardens, with many features designed to meet the informal recreational needs of the district's population, as well as the area's many visitors.

The old Home Farm has become the Visitor Centre, with reception, toilets, auditorium and exhibition areas. There is also a seventeenth century dovecote and the old Newparks Farm which has been transformed into a children's farm with many rare breeds of domestic animal and fowl.

The park offers panoramic views, a spectacular river gorge and relics of industrial archaeology, linked by a network of paths through a diverse ground flora. Over eighty species of bird have been recorded here; a true bird watcher's paradise.

Muiravonside Coiuntry Park

Wherever you wish to go in the park, and whatever you wish to do, a helpful ranger service will try and steer you to experience Muiravonside at its best.

This area of Scotland proves to be an excellent centre for not only taking advantage of looking around Falkirk but is not far from the splendid city of **Stirling,** which is easily reached by the superb systems of motorways linking them to the major centres of Glasgow and Edinburgh. Before we rushed off again however we were careful not to miss the town of **Denny,** in which we wanted to spend some time visiting an old friend. The Stirling-shire town of Denny is surrounded by a motorway system, so we recommend that you keep a sharp look out for the Denny exit points, for you will then be fortunate enough to find **The Horsemill Inn.**

The Horse Mill Inn

As the name suggests, The Horsemill Inn has been created from the skilful conversion of genuine farm buildings. Once filled with cattle, horses and grain, The Horsemill has been run by the same family for over a century and is now in the capable hands of Fraser Taylor.

What you will find most appealing about The Horsemill Inn, which specialises in 'Taste of Scotland' dishes, is the wide range of food on offer. You can choose from bar lunches and suppers served in the lounge bar, high teas on Sundays, a fixed price four course table d'hote menu, or savour the full a la carte menu in the Harness Room Restaurant.

Whatever your choice, you will find that all meals are prepared to the highest of standards. Vegetarians eating at here will also be pleased to find themselves well catered for.

This is a favourite watering hole for travellers on the way to and from Stirling, and the historically famous battleground at Bannockburn. The cities of Glasgow and Edinburgh too are only a forty five minute drive away from Denny.

The restaurant is open seven days a week between mid-day and 10.00pm, and all major credit cards are accepted. Recommended by the Loch Lomond, Stirling and Trossachs Tourist Board, you can always expect a warm welcome at The Horsemill by Fraser and his team. We're sure you'll consider it well worth your while to break your journey at Denny.

We have come as far north as we are going to in this chapter, and it is to some of the most beautiful border country that we are now going to turn our attention, taking us to the south-west of Scotland and towards some of the most spectacular coast in Europe.

Dumfriesshire

Caerlavbrock Castle

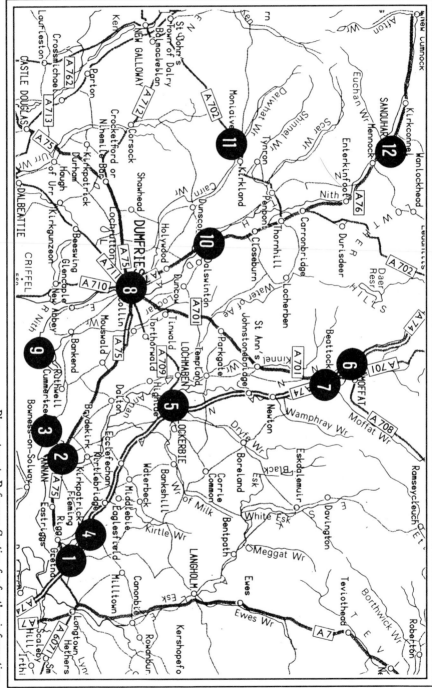

Please turn to Reference Section for further information.

CHAPTER SIX

Dumfriesshire

We begin our journey in this chapter just across the Scottish border in that place renowned for its runaway couples and hasty marriages, **Gretna Green**. We were interested to find out that marriages by declaration could in fact take place at any house or shop, provided there were two witnesses available.

In 1856, after much indignation from the church and even local people, who were not too happy with what they saw as 'immoral practices', the law was changed. The new legislation demanded a residential qualification of three weeks for one of the runaway couple, which we would imagine was not quite so helpful to those in a hurry.

Even when the couples had been married their problems were not always over, and there have been several cases of bridegrooms being arrested on their return to England. In one particular case, where a music master was wed to his twelve year old pupil, he was sentenced to nine months in jail for abduction.

In 1940 marriage by declaration became illegal, although the age of consent was still lower than that in England, and therefore the attraction of Gretna Green continued to lure young couples. This attraction only really declined when the age of marriage without parental consent was lowered in England from twenty one to eighteen years, in 1970.

We spent some time looking around this most famous and interesting place. The blacksmith's shop today has a range of curiosities and souvenirs from the marriage trade and, if you are lucky enough, you may even be involved in a mock ceremony.

Gretna itself is situated on the River Sark, which flows into the Solway Firth, and we decided to stay with the coastline and follow the A75 westwards to the town of Annan. It is sad that so many visitors to Scotland these days rush through the border spurred on by the thought of reaching their next destination. They are the unlucky ones who will miss out on some of the most delightful towns and scenery to be found in this country. It is of course a pleasure for us to try and bring you a small sample of these hidden places, which are so often neglected in the hectic pace of modern life.

The small red stone town of Annan sits overlooking the Solway Firth and the mountains of the Lake District. This ancient burgh was in fact founded by the family of Robert the Bruce, and displays the Bruce coat of arms, a red saltire on gold, as its own.

Standing close to the border as it does, Annan has many times been subject to the unwelcome attentions of the English, and was destroyed repeatedly between 1298 and 1660. It was, however, the waters of the river Annan which brought about the first of many tragedies for this burgh. A curse was put on the town by the renowned mystic Saint Malachy, who was angered by the decision of one of the lords of Annan to execute a robber on whose behalf he had interceded.

The site of the castle, which was formerly in the churchyard, still bears the scars of river erosion. The town today, however, bears little sign of those turbulent years and we found it pleasant and peaceful in this lovely riverside setting.

If you wish to take advantage of a stay in this restful place, then why not look for the **Northfield Guest House**. Dating back to around 1750, the building is grade II listed for its architectural interest, and sits on a delightful spot overlooking the river Annan.

This is a top quality guest house, offering a high standard of care and attention in these tranquil border surroundings.

There are three bedrooms, all on one level, with en-suite shower, toilet and washhand basins. Proprietors James and Mary Airey have earned a reputation for delicious cuisine with the emphasis on fresh produce. They do point out, however, that although they are not licensed, guests are quite at liberty to bring their own wine, and no corkage is charged.

Small things like electric blankets, colour television, hairdryers and tea making facilities in the rooms are not overlooked and make all the difference.

Northfield Guest House

Northfield House is undoubtedly a place for relaxing. There are twelve acres of beautiful grounds here, with private fishing and mature gardens. Nearby you will find **Powfoot**, with its long, sandy beach and close by is Gretna Green where we started our journey.

Overall, Northfield House is the ideal place for a 'get away from it all' break. Once you arrive, you will see that James and Mary's aim is simply to make you feel as warm and comfortable here as you do in your own home.

Annan was once an important shipbuilding and trading centre, and we enjoyed a stroll around the attractive riverside park. There are many walks nearby around **Hoddom Castle**, and there is a golf course with lovely views over the Solway. Why not stay for a while by this scenic coastline?

Hoddam Castle

Not far from Annan, near to the small hamlets of Powfoot and Cummertrees, we found the **Queensberry Bay Caravan Park**. The thing about caravan parks today is that they frequently vie with each other in a continuing competition to provide all varieties of entertainment on site. Certainly there are many tourists who actively seek such an entertainment based holiday, but many more prefer to escape to a quiet site where the sort of leisure activities available are more natural than man-made.

If you are looking for a caravan holiday where peace and quiet are the order of the day, then Queensberry Bay Caravan Park could be exactly what you're looking for.

The park is owned and run by James Graham, and sits next to the beach near the village of Powfoot, some twelve miles from the Scottish border along the A75, turning off at the B724 Annan bypass.

The site itself covers twelve acres of level grounds and offers facilities for touring vans, campers and tents. There are showers, a laundry, a public telephone and a well-stocked shop.

Queensberry Bay's surroundings enjoy some of the best in seaside and countryside beauty. The beach next to the caravan park is rarely crowded, and nearby there are many miles of country walks. Golfers can enjoy a round at Powfoot's eighteen hole golf course and shoppers are just four miles away from Annan town centre. Only a short distance away is the beautiful **Ruthwell village**, where you will find the **Duncan Savings Bank Museum**, site of the first savings bank in Britain. Also worth a visit is

Ruthwell Church, where you can see the famous Runic Cross.

Queensberry Bay Caravan Park

Queensberry Bay is a well tended, easy going sort of place, and as such is ideally situated for those looking to make the most of this peaceful corner of Dumfriesshire.

We crossed back over the picturesque River Annan once more, and took the B6357 towards the village of **Kirkpatrick-Fleming**. We were very hungry, and keen to sample the delights of a place that had been recommended to us called **The Station Inn**, a perfect example of the sort of charming country inn you can find in Scotland, if you take the trouble to get away from the main roads.

Proprietors Maureen and Willie Hunter offer a warm welcome and a delicious bill of fare at some extraordinarily reasonable prices. Where else can you enjoy a ten ounce sirloin steak for just over #5.00? Indeed, much of the menu contains meals for under two or three pounds, including some tasty vegetarian dishes.

The Station Inn is over two hundred years old, and is now a family run business. Maureen and Willie, we discovered, have always lived locally and are ably assisted by Maureen's father, now retired. Needless to say, the inn enjoys a strong local trade and everyone is made welcome. Families with children are easily accommodated, both in the beer garden and inside. Quiz nights are popular in the pub, as well as darts, dominoes and regular summertime barbecues.

Inside, the theme is, not surprisingly, railway based, and there is plenty of fascinating memorabilia. Some of this is related to Quintinshill Signal Box, scene of Britain's worst rail disaster in 1915, when two hundred and twenty six people died in a collision between a coal train and a train carrying British troops to Gallipoli. Most of them didn't make it, and many died inside the carriages which were locked from the outside to deter deserters.

On a lighter note, the Hunters will tell you of a more recent mishap when, in 1985, the artist painting the new sign outside fell from his ladder. Locals claim that this is the only time a sober man has been seen hanging from the sign.

The Station Inn

With the whole of Dumfries before us it was not easy to decide where to head next, so we decided, in keeping with our main intention to avoid the main routes, to take the B6357 to **Canonbie**, which proved to be a welcome discovery. Standing on the left bank of the river Esk, it is set in a particularly picturesque valley. The parish church here dates from 1822 and is situated on the opposite side of the river, which emerges dramatically from between the red sandstone cliffs. We were interested to note that it had been designed by William Atkinson, the architect of Sir Walter Scott's Abbotsford.

The A7 follows the river from Canonbie back towards its source, and we followed this road upwards to **Langholm**, a typical border town in appearance, situated on the river with its narrow streets. Like Edinburgh, Langholm is divided into a new and old town. It is hard to believe that three rivers join here, and not surprisingly there are three bridges. As the famous engineer Thomas Telford was born nearby, we wondered if he had a hand in the building of any of these bridges.

Being a true Border town, Langholm has an annual Common Riding which takes place on the last Friday in June. A feature of this day which we found fascinating is that the colours worn by the Cornet for his ride are the same colours of the winner of the Epsom Derby each year. Try as we might however, we were unable to find out the reason for this custom which has been going for some one hundred years. Perhaps you can do better than us.

If you are lucky enough to be here for this special event you will be treated to a day full of the most exciting spectacles, including horse racing, foot races, wrestling and Highland dancing.

In the evening, if you have any energy left, you can take part in an open air dance. Be warned though; the celebrations of the day start at five o'clock in the morning.

We thought Langholm to be an excellent centre for exploring the quiet valleys and hill country on foot, but, if you prefer, there are marvellous opportunities for cycling, or even driving. There is also excellent fishing nearby.

To the north of Langholm, and in the heart of some of most magical forests and scenery, we came across the strangely named village of **Eskdalemuir**. In 1905 an observatory was built on the moors, and there is also a weather station here. Some of the lowest temperatures in the winter are recorded at this station.

As we looked around, we were pleasantly surprised to come across the **Kagyu Samye Ling Tibetan Centre**, which, you may not be surprised to learn, is a Buddhist centre. This is a thriving international community, and holds pottery, woodcarving and carpet-weaving workshops. There is also an art studio and a printing press. If you are of a mind, then you can take the chance to learn some relaxation here. Meditation, healing and Buddhism are also taught. The centre is a highly unusual place, and one which we are sure you will enjoy visiting as much as we did.

When we eventually and reluctantly left Langholm, we took the B7068 which passes through some spectacular scenery, as it winds its way towards **Lockerbie**. This pretty town was of course the scene for that dreadful tragedy which killed so many people when, in December 1988, a Pan American jet was blown up by terrorists on its flight to America from Germany, via Heathrow. There are few words to describe the horror of the world which watched the result of the carnage unfolding, via the media, in this small town which may forever be linked with this unfortunate disaster.

The origins of Lockerbie however go back to the 16th century, when it grew as a market town in this largely agricultural area. The character of the town has been retained, and there are many interesting shops and fine buildings dating from the 17th and 18th centuries.

If you wish to sample some of these period delights and relax in style, then just off the B723 and half a mile from the bustling town centre of Lockerbie you will find the **Lockerbie House Country Hotel**.

The hotel is housed in an imposing, magnificent building dating back to the 18th century, and was originally built by Dame Grace Johnstone and Sir William Douglas, Marquisses of Queensberry. It was in this very building that the Queensberry rules of boxing are said to have been formulated; a direct result of the 8th Marquis' passion for boxing, among other things.

Today, the Lockerbie House Country Hotel still retains most of its period charm, enhanced by original wall panelling and a superb collection of artwork. There are twenty six rooms, all prettily furnished in antique style, with en-suite facilities and all the modern conveniences you would expect in a top class hotel. These include a courtesy tray, tea and coffee making facilities, central heating, colour television, trouser press, hairdryer, direct dial telephones and room service. All VIP rooms contain traditional four poster beds.

The restaurant enjoys wonderful views over the surrounding lawns and woodlands and, with its subtle lighting and magnificent wood panelling, provides the perfect atmosphere in which to relax and enjoy the superb cuisine. There is a delicious selection of new classical dishes, as well as traditional English and Scottish food. An extensive wine list ensures that there is something here to suit all tastes and complement every dish.

Lockerbie House is ideally placed for touring the Borders and Solway Firth. The hotel offers free golf at Lockerbie and Moffat, salmon and trout fishing and clay pigeon shooting by prior arrangement. Tuition in all of these pursuits is available.

A special service offered by the hotel is a two day break offering full a la carte dinner, bed and full Scottish breakfast. These breaks are available any two weekdays throughout the year.

However long your visit, whether for a couple of days or a couple of weeks, proprietors Mr and Mrs Byerley are always on hand to ensure your stay is a pleasant one.

Lockerbie House Country Hotel

Near to Lockerbie is **Lochmaben**, and here we found the ruined castle of Robert the Bruce. We were able to spend a delightful time on the shores of the castle loch watching the sailing boats and the fishermen trying their luck. The loch is also an ideal place for bird watching. We departed the peaceful surroundings and made our way the short distance to our next stop, **Moffat**.

We had heard that Moffat was a picturesque town, and were not disappointed. Its wide main streets, with attractive shops and hotels, make for pleasant strolling. Do spend some time in the fabulous gardens and parks which have helped earn Moffat the title of the 'Best Kept Village in Scotland' award twice in recent years.

In the centre of the town is a handsome square with the Colvin Fountain, surmounted by the famous ram. This statue proclaims the importance of sheep in this area and the role played by Moffat as a sheep and wool trading centre. Those of you with a taste for traditional home cooking will find that Moffat has a rich heritage of food. Why not search out some traditional Moffat toffee, or even try the famous Scottish haggis?

You can still find a traditional bakehouse in the old part of the town, in which the **Moffat Museum** is situated. The Scotch oven, an old furnace used for baking bread, is an interesting feature on the ground floor. The museum also has an exhibition, tracing local history which follows Moffat's rise as a health resort in the mid-eighteenth century due to the discovery here of mineral springs. As a result of this, Moffat became famous as one of the few spa towns in Scotland. The Old Well and Hartfell Spa have both been restored, and make fascinating visits.

How often have you thought about trying your hand at the magical art of fly-fishing? This sport has always held a fascination for us, and we were overjoyed to find a place near Moffat where we could try the sport for ourselves. Just three hundred yards out of Moffat on the A708 Selkirk road is **Moffat Fishery and Fish Farm**. Set in the beautiful surroundings of the Upper Annandale Valley, Moffat Fishery offers you the opportunity to see, feed and catch the fish.

Moffat Fishery and Fish Farm

Proprietor Peter Hesketh has established a working fish farm here, as well as two spring fed lochans stocked with rainbow trout and quality brown and American brook trout.

There is a family fishing loch and a separate secluded fly only fishery. Full day, half day and evening permits are available and rods, bait and tuition can be provided.

The fly fishery is run on a catch and release basis using barbless hooks, where anglers can catch and return fish all day, or indeed take them home if they wish to. On the family loch you will find that rods and bait are all included in the charge. Any fish taken away is of course charged for, and it is best to check the price with Mr Hesketh.

For those who enjoy the taste of fish but are not so keen on catching them, the farm shop sells fresh trout. Frozen and smoked trout and salmon produce is always available too. There are hot drinks, ice cream and snacks on sale as well, in case you need a little extra sustenance.

Open all day, every day, and catering for coach parties too, Moffat Fishery and Fish Farm is simply a great day out for all the family, as well as being within easy walking distance of Moffat town centre.

Apart from fishing, Moffat can offer a wide variety of activities for the visitor. There are many beautiful walks around the surrounding country-side, and if you take the time to go a little out of your way you will be able to take in the wonders of the Grey Mare's Tail, for which we followed the Selkirk road, with its spectacular waterfall.

Horse riding, pony-trekking, cycle-hire, sailing and swimming are all available locally. Did you know that the annual South of Scotland Tennis Tournament held here actually pre-dates Wimbledon?

If you have a young family with you, we could not think of a better idea than to spend some time at the **Holm Park Holiday Centre**. It is here in Moffat that two enterprising women have created the ideal family holiday at Holm Park Holiday Centre, in the town's Ballplay Road.

Mrs Sage and Mrs Druce describe their listed Victorian mansion as a "small, licensed hotel set in three acres of grounds." It is the three acres that makes Holm Park so different.

Holm Park Holiday Centre

The house has an open air swimming and paddling pool, riding stables, animal pens and a recreational hall. Pony trekking is popular here, and tuition is available for novices, as well as donkey rides for the very young. An archery range inside will provide a challenge for those with a strong arm

103

and a steady eye, supervised of course, by a qualified instructor. There is also a shooting gallery if you fancy a little target practice with air rifles.

For animal lovers there is a little 'Garden of Eden' where the children and adults can go into the small enclosures with the pets to feed and stroke them. There are peacocks, geese, rabbits, goats and many other small breeds.

These facilities are available whether you choose to stay in the main building, take a residential caravan or, by prior arrangment, bring your own touring caravan.

All rooms in the house are spacious and comfortably furnished. Each has its own television, so in the evening your room is converted to a cosy sitting room, should you simply wish to relax with the children.

The Tack Bar Restaurant is used for breakfast and lunches, as well as meals and snacks. In the evening you will see it converted to a romantic, candlelit restaurant with an affordable menu offering a wide range of dishes.

We thoroughly enjoyed our time here. Moffat is an ideal centre for touring not only the borders but also the south and west. It is also handy, being close to the main A74, for forays into the exciting cities of Edinburgh and Glasgow. Whether you intend to take in the whole of Southern Scotland or explore more local phenomena, such as the intriguingly named Devil's Beeftub and the Grey Mare's Tail, you probably won't find a better hotel than the Auchen Castle as a base.

The Auchen Castle Hotel and Restaurant can be found just north of **Beattock** village on the A74. Centrally situated between east and west coasts, and just over an hour's drive to Edinburgh and Glasgow, the hotel is set in fifty acres of beautiful grounds.

There are magnificent views and, as well as fishing on a trout stocked loch, you can enjoy the sight of some superb specimen trees and shrubs which provide a blaze of colour in season.

Here you will find that the warmth of welcome you receive from Mr Beckh and his team makes every visitor feel rather special. All bedrooms have en-suite facilities, and fifteen of these are in the main building which dates back to 1849. There are ten further bedrooms in the Cedar Lodge, a fairly recent addition to the hotel. Parents will be glad to see that children are well catered for, and a baby listening service is provided.

The restaurant, which is very popular among non-residents, serves a wide variety of delicious food. 'Taste of Scotland' dishes are a regular feature of the menu here, with no trace whatsoever of convenience foods. Fresh local produce is used extensively, including game in season.

The Auchen Castle is four crowns commended by the Scottish Tourist Board, and is also Egon Ronay recommended. Prices, however, remain extremely competitive, and represent what is probably the best value for money in the area.

We know that you, like us, will be very impressed by what is offered here. All we do say though is that you should remember that old proverb about 'all work and no play', and be prepared for the hotel to be closed for three weeks over the festive season, when Mr Beckh takes the opportunity to enjoy a well- earned rest.

Auchen Castle Hotel

After our relaxing stay at Auchen Castle, we decided to take the A701 southwards past the **Forest of Ae**. We took our time and made the most of the wonderful scenery in this beautiful area, which truly is the heart of Dumfriesshire. There are many stopping places along the road, and seasoned walkers may well find that the challenge here is irresistible.

Crossing the Ae Water we found that we were only a small distance from the royal burgh of **Dumfries**, which lies in the heart of the district of Nithsdale. This area takes its name from the river Nith, which winds its way southwards from the Lowther Hills to the Solway. It is truly a picturesque river, running through such a variety of countryside that the area is sometimes referred to as "Scotland in miniature".

The river reaches the Solway at Dumfries, and here we planned to spend some time exploring the locality of one of Scotland's most celebrated sons, Robert Burns.

If the Borders are associated with the tales and legends of Walter Scott, then Dumfries and Galloway are forever associated with the poet Robert Burns. He lived in Dumfries and worked as an exciseman here until his death in 1796. There is a statue in the High Street commemorating this town's most famous citizen.

There is surely no one who has not heard of Robert Burns, but what was his connection with Dumfries and the area? Many people come to Dumfries each year to visit the monuments and places associated with the poet, and this period in his life is widely considered to be one of his most productive. Whilst the French Revolution and the Napoleonic Wars were going on, and the country was alive with rumours and alarms, there were food shortages and riots in Dumfries. It was during this time that Burns produced some of his best work, despite being heavily in debt and suffering from a serious illness.

He first came to Dumfries in 1787, though did not eventually settle here until some four years later, after finding his farm Ellisand to be uneconomical. He first lived in Bank Street, and the building can still be seen. In 1793 Burns moved to a larger house in what is now called Burns Street. Here he worked until his death three years later. We visited this two storey house where he spent his last years, which is now a museum, and saw many items associated with the poet. Burns is buried in the graveyard of nearby St Michael's church.

While Burns was in Dumfries he was no stranger to the taverns of the town, and one with special Burns links is the **Globe Inn** just off the High Street. In the small panelled rooms it is fascinating to think of the poet sharing a glass of port or a tankard of ale with his friends.

His favourite armchair is still there, but before you try it out for size be warned, as anyone who sits in the chair can be called upon to buy a round of drinks for everyone present.

In 1790 Burns had an affair with a young barmaid and she bore him a child, which his wife later took in and cared for as one of her own.

For a full explanation of the poet's links with this town, why not take a look at the **Robbie Burns Centre** situated on the banks of the Nith. This building houses a permanent exhibition and an audio-visual presentation on the poet. You may also enjoy the bookshop here, where we relaxed with a cup of tea in the lovely cafe with its spectacular views over the river.

The most familiar landmark in Dumfries is the Midsteeple, and this has been witness to some famous characters from the past. Bonnie Prince Charlie would have passed it on his way through Dumfries with the bedraggled remains of his army.

Dumfries Mid Steeple

Do you remember how we told

you of the shoes that were made for his army in Selkirk before their march to England? Well it seems that they needed some more shoes on their return journey, only this time the folk of Dumfries were not as forthcoming. A request for one thousand pairs of shoes only resulted in two hundred and twenty five being offered, whereupon, according to legend, the soldiers began to stop people in the street and take their shoes from them.

If you look at the Midsteeple you might notice something odd about it. Well you'd be right, as it now leans over, although we were told that it is in no danger of toppling.

We walked around the streets and were able to look at many interesting buildings, from the elegant Trades Hall to the quaint Queensberry Square with its old-fashioned closes.

Did you know that Dumfries was the inspiration for the story of Peter Pan? We were surprised when we were told that the young James M Barrie was a pupil at the predecessor of Dumfries Academy.

In 1860 Barrie came to Dumfries, and was at one time in the school's amateur dramatic club. He even wrote one of its earliest productions. When he returned to Dumfries, some years later as Sir James Barrie, he revealed that it was while playing in the gardens on the banks of the river Nith that he conceived the original basis for Peter Pan. The house in which he stayed whilst at the Academy is in Victoria Place, and is marked with a plaque.

Another excellent outing took us down towards the Solway by the B725, to find **Caerlaverock Castle**. This castle is one of the finest and most imaginative we have come across in our journey so far, and we will certainly not forget its unusual design and magical setting within its moat.

Caerlaverlock Castle

No one is really sure who is reponsible for the design of the castle, although it is believed to have been built in the last quarter of the 13th century. Its dazzling red sandstone gives the impression of a fortress of tremendous strength, and yet the Renaissance style buildings within are refined and intricate. These were built later, and include wonderfully carved scenes from classical mythology covering the walls.

Nearby is the **Caerlaverock Nature Reserve**, covering some 13,594 acres of saltmarsh and sand along the coastline of the Solway Firth. The marshes and mudflats stretch for six miles along the coastline, and in winter the reserve is home to great flocks of barnacle geese and other wildfowl. It also provides a breeding ground for the rare Natterjack toad. The wildfowl reserve is open from mid-summer until the end of April.

If you have time, it is well worth paying a visit to nearby **Ruthwell**. In the parish church you will find the Ruthwell Cross. This seventeen foot high cross is a testament to the faith of the early Christians, and has survived many attempts to destroy it. Dating from the early 8th century, we were captivated by the intricate and beautiful carvings, illustrating episodes from the Gospels.

Sadly we had to leave the Solway for a while, but we wanted to follow the river Nith towards its source as we had heard that the Nithsdale valley would be full of pleasant surprises.

Following the A76 northwards we passed **Ellisland**, where Burns had his farm. This is now open to the public, and we found the Burns relics, including the old farmhouse kitchen, fascinating.

We made a small detour and branched left at the B729, which led us to **Glenkiln Reservoir**, and to an unexpected surprise, for we found here on the hillsides surrounding the loch a wonderful collection of sculptures by Henry Moore and other artists. It was a strange experience watching these figures, though we were not allowed to approach them since they are on private land.

From the loch it is an easy drive back towards **Dunscore**, and then the A76. We took the left turning off at **Auldgirth** and drove towards **Penpont**. This is a very relaxing and scenic route, and enabled us to see a particularly interesting example of a fortified house now being run as a hotel.

The south west of Scotland is particularly richly endowed with historic castles, peel towers and fortified houses. Many of these date from the late 16th and early 17th centuries when a side effect of the reformation was to release a great deal of land from the hands of the church. At this time the area was wild, and torn by feuding and violence.

In a none too successful effort to subdue this problem, King James VI gave parcels of the released land to his supporters, making it a condition of each grant that the new owner build a fortified house on the land. His idea was that these houses would provide a safe refuge for the population in times of strife, but in practice their owners seem to have found them more useful as a base from which to attack their enemies.

Be that as it may, future generations inherited a wealth of architectural diversity as the buildings developed from the original square towers to L-shaped and, subsequently, to Z-shaped towers decorated with gables, balustrades, corbels and other features. There is a strong French influence in many of the designs, as the Auld Alliance brought to Scotland courtiers and architectural advisors who adapted the pepper-pot turrets of their own chateaux to the rigours of the local climate.

A handsome and uncompromising example of the L-shaped version is **Barjarg Tower**, which forms the north east corner of a mansion house lying on the west side of the River Nith some four miles south of Penpont and twelve miles north of Dumfries.

Approaching from the south, we turned left off the A76 at **Auldgrith** and then, threequarters of a mile up the hill, turned right on the road signposted to Penpont. 'Barjarg' means 'the red hill top'. The original tower dates from the late 16th century when it was built by one of the Earls of Morton and gifted by him to Thomas Grierson. A later owner, a Mr Erskine, planted the magnificent Wellingtonia trees that have stood guard behind the house since the beginning of the 18th century.

In 1740, the property passed to a Reverend Hunter, a Doctor of Divinity from Edinburgh, who was related to the Hunters of Hunterston in Ayrshire, the remains of whose castle is now a near neighbour of a nuclear power station. Dr Hunter was the founder of the Hunter Arundell family who have owned the property and its surrounding estate for some two hundred and fifty years.

Early in the 18th century the main part of the house was built with a symmetrical frontage and a matching tower at the west end. However the old tower is well preserved and visitors can see the original iron yett gate and many other features.

Barjarg Tower

Inside, a number of the well-proportioned rooms have Georgian fireplaces;

there is beautiful plasterwork and much fine oak panelling. All of this was carefully preserved by Mary and Archie Donaldson when they bought the house in 1985 and converted it into a small, but lavishly appointed hotel. The panelling now glows beside rich fabrics and beautiful flower arrangements.

To this splendid enviroment the Donaldson family, and their pet dachshund Ruari, welcome their guests, offering personal service in a tranquil atmosphere. Several comfortable lounges provide ample room for those who seek a degree of privacy. The ambience is that of a country house where guests can regard the dedicated owners as their hosts and relax in the comfort and attention lavished upon them. The oak-panelled dining room contains a magnificent fireplace reputed to be a copy of one in the ancient Scottish palace of Holyrood House. Set within the carving over the mantel is the coat-of-arms granted to the Hunter Arundell family in 1825. In this setting, the emphasis is on fine freshly cooked food, good wine and personal friendly service.

The hotel, which is open throughout the year with the exception of Christmas, has eight double bedrooms all with private bathrooms. Each has its individual character but all are beautifully appointed, offering such facilities as direct-dial telephones, colour televisions and trouser presses. Most of the rooms offer a panoramic view of lovely Nithsdale and the surrounding Lowther Hills.

Guests can fish on the river Nith or play golf on one of the many fine local courses. However, it is as an excellent base from which to explore this relatively little known, and correspondingly quiet, area of Scotland that Barjarg Tower excels. Within easy reach are **Maxwelton House**, which was the home of Annie Laurie, and the beautiful gardens at **Threave**. **Drumlanrig Castle**, the home of the Dukes of Buccleuch, is about five miles distant and is open to the public during the summer months.

The area was host to Robert Burns in the closing years of his life, and there are many places of interest associated with him. Above all, however, it is the peace and beauty of this vast and diverse countryside that makes those who know it return again and again.

We took the A702 at Penpont and made our way to the small village of **Moniaive**. Set between **Craigdarroch** and **Dalwhat Waters**, the streets are small and narrow and we particularly liked the brightly painted houses. Moniaive is a village renowned for its peaceful atmosphere and beautiful surroundings and it is here that you will find **The George Hotel**.

The George has long been an intrinsic part of this small Dumfriesshire village which sits some six miles from **Thornhill** on the A74. The loss of parish records obscures its earlier days, although it was long established by 1740 when it reappears in local records. Its architecture and roof construction indicate its origins as being nearer the mid 1600s. Inside, the old bar still exists and is barely altered from its original design. The flag floor and fireplace are both originals, and perhaps the most intriguing feature of the fireplace is the 'Tramps Hole'. This was a small hole where money was left by the people of Moniaive for any passing tramps. The custom still continues today although the money is donated to charity as the last tramp known to roam the area disappeared a few years ago.

There are three bars, and the restaurant adjoining the lounge bar serves excellent food in attractive surroundings. The restaurant is open all day in the summer months and there is also a games room as well as the old public bar.

The hotel's two bedrooms sit upstairs past the old covenanter's hiding hole. You will find them tastefully decorated, and more than cosy. Proprietors Richard, Marjory and Alan Price will do all they can to ensure you have an enjoyable stay. An adjoining chalet is ideal for families and is close to the hotel. it has three bedrooms, a bathroom, kitchen and lounge and sleeps up to eight.

The George Hotel

The George is one of the oldest hotels in Scotland. The welcome may be old fashioned here, but the facilities and service are thoroughly modern.

Moniaive is special to us because it was here that both our grandchildren were christened. Our daughter married into the Gourlay family who farm much of the land around the village.

We have heard many references to the Covenanters in these parts, and were curious to learn more about them. We discovered that they were Presbyterians who were persecuted for refusing to renounce their faith during the reigns of Charles II and James II. They were often cruelly put to death without trial, and due to this the 1680s later became known as the 'Killing Time'.

We rejoined the A76 at **Thorburn**, which has lovely wide streets lined with the lime trees planted by the Duke of Buccleuch in 1861. The monument at the end of the street was erected by the Duke of Queensbury in 1714, the Pegasus being his winged emblem. The town is dominated by the magnificent Queensbury mountain which stands at 2,285 feet.

Our next stop was to the romantic **Drumlanrig Castle**, which is a beautiful stately mansion and is open to the public. The mansion was built by the first Duke of Queensbury between 1679 and 1690. It was indeed a departure from the style of most Scottish castles, and reminded us somewhat of a fairy tale castle with its superb, pink sandstone walls and enchanting roof. You may like to spend some time within its walls, as there is the finest collection of furniture, paintings, silver and china in Scotland. Bonnie Prince Charlie slept here on his retreat northwards from Dumfries in 1745. His bedroom can still be seen as can a few of his mementoes and personal relics.

The castle has a magnificent setting and there are lovely views of the surrounding countryside. There are forty acres of garden, and you may be interested to have a look at the craft shops while the children take advantage of the adventure playground. Drumlanrig is a stop worth making, and we are sure you will enjoy a day spent here.

We followed one of the back roads that lead from Drumlanrig northwards, and found ourselves before long in that town with the beautiful name of **Sanquhar**. This name, which conjured up for us any number of exotic images, apparently means simply, 'old fort'.

The post office here is the oldest in Britain, and still retains some of its old world charm. We were amazed to find out from some of the local folk that at one time workers in the mines here were subject to laws of bondage, which meant that miners and their whole families could be bought and sold as slaves. They could only avoid this iniquitous system by escaping and staying free for a whole year and a day. Capture, however, would result in brutal punishment. It was not until the end of the 18th century that the final traces of this custom were removed by an Act of Parliament.

There is an interesting local museum in the old tolbooth of 1735, which is now a visitor and information centre.

We have come as far as we intend to in this area of Dumfries, and it is to neighbouring Galloway that our attentions will turn in the next chapter.

The Queensberry Monument

Kircudbrightshire and Wigtonshire

Lochnaw Castle

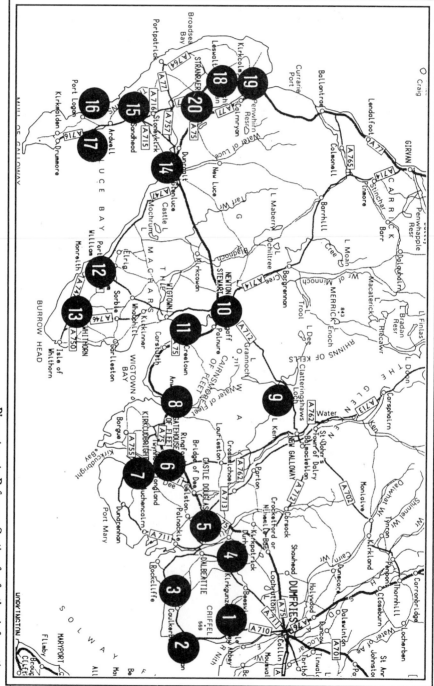

Please turn to Reference Section for further information.

CHAPTER SEVEN

Kircudbrightshire and Wigtonshire

We wanted to travel west from **Dumfries**, and found ourselves with a choice of three roads leading into Galloway. We think this area of Scotland is one of the most beautiful, with its mild climate warmed by the Gulf Stream, enabling even palm trees to grow in some of the gardens.

As a result, this part of the country is particularly attractive and mild in both spring and autumn, making an out of season visit well worthwhile. We found the roads a pleasure to drive along, as here there are no busy motorways or huge traffic jams, only lovely country roads that crisscross the open countryside. This enabled us to drive from loch to glen to forest with the minimum of fuss.

For our venture into Galloway we started by leaving Dumfries on the A710 which took us down once again towards the Solway Firth. This road follows the Solway Coast Heritage Trail, a recommended route of particular interest, which led us past the small hamlet of Mabie.

Seven miles south of Dumfries, we came across the picturesque village of **New Abbey**. This unspoilt haven thoroughly charmed us and we made a point of visiting the ruin of **Sweetheart Abbey**, which is right at the bottom of Criffel Hill. The Abbey was built in the thirteenth and fourteenth centuries by Lady Devorgilla in memory of her husband John de Balliol. You may remember that their son was the King of Scotland for a short while, chosen by Edward I.

Sweetheart Abbey

There is a popular story that after her husband's death Lady Devorgilla carried his embalmed heart in an ivory casket wherever she went. When she eventually died, some twenty-one years later, the casket was buried with her in front of the high altar. The name of the Abbey comes from the Cistercians who, as a tribute to this lady, called it 'Dulce Cor' or Sweetheart.

If you are feeling energetic, then why not attempt a climb up nearby **Criffel Hill**? This hill is one thousand eight hundred and sixty eight feet high, so it is not really for the faint-hearted. The granite can be quite steep and rough in parts, making the wearing of a good pair of stout walking shoes advisable. We took it on good authority that the views at the summit are spectacular.

After a morning spent looking around the Abbey we were keen to pay a visit to the delightful **Shambellie House Museum of Costume** which is just a quarter of a mile to the north of the village. The building itself is notable for having been designed by the architect David Bryce in 1854 and the house reflects the rich characteristics of Bryce's style, referred to as "Scottish Baronial,". We were particularly fascinated by the crow-stepped gables, towers and turrets. The Scottish heritage was uniquely reflected in the appearance of the building with the suggestion of battlements which reminded us of the many castles we have seen in this part of the country.

Inside, the building houses the most fascinating exhibition of clothes, mainly from the eighteenth and nineteenth centuries, which were collected by Charles Stuart of Shambellie, an illustrator who developed this collection over a period of years starting before the Second World War.

There is so much to see in this lovely town; we took our time to absorb it all and make the most of our stay. Something we often do when visiting a town is to base ourselves in the nearby countryside, so as to be able to have the best of both worlds, and it was in a village near New Abbey that we came across a remarkable couple. It is always refreshing to read a story of a dream come true and that's exactly what happened to Mr and Mrs MacKail at the Mabie House Hotel.

Mabie sits just two miles outside the village of New Abbey, and only four miles from the county's largest town, Dumfries. When the MacKails first acquired Mabie House the building was in a very poor condition. They were told by many that the conversion they were about to embark on was an impossible task.

The critics have been proved wrong however. With not a little help from their friends and relatives, the MacKails have skillfully converted Mabie House until today it is Grade B listed. They talk of much that they would still like to do, but this is a lifelong project for them. It is something they want to share with visitors of all nations who come to enjoy the peaceful and relaxed atmosphere here. Children are of course welcome, and there is a special play area for them, as well as a games room.

What was originally the house's morning room is now an elegant dining room, where home cooking and 'Taste of Scotland' dishes are the order of the day, and only the freshest of local produce is used.

Mabie House Hotel is the home of the Dumfries jazz club, 'Jazz Pzazz', and the Riverside Jazz Band. There is live music every Sunday night and the hotel hosts regular concerts featuring some of the top names in international jazz. The highlight of the year is the jazz festival. This is held on the lawns and those performing in the marquees attract audiences from all over the country.

At present there are nine rooms available, all of which are beautifully furnished, and some have en-suite facilities. A phone call to reserve a room before you arrive may be a wise move, especially during peak holiday periods and festival time.

Mabie House Hotel

The amount of effort the MacKails have put into the transformation of Mabie House is certainly beginning to pay dividends, although we are sure you'll agree that it is richly deserved.

After such a pleasant stay in New Abbey we continued on the A710 past **Overton** on the coast and down towards the little village of **Kirkbean**. At **Arbigland** nearby there is a fascinating house and gardens which are open in the summer. John Paul Jones was born in 1747, in one of the cottages. He was to become one of the area's most famous sons and later became known as the "father of the American Navy".

The story of John Paul Jones is very interesting and definitely worth a mention here, as he was not solely regarded as a hero. Indeed some people, including the British, branded him a pirate.

When he was only thirteen he boarded a boat at nearby **Carsethorn** and began an apprenticeship that was to last for seven years in the Merchant Navy. His travels took him around the world visiting such beautiful places as Barbados and Virginia, and eventually he assumed command of his own ship.

In Tobago however, he killed a man in self defence whom he claimed had been a mutineer, and as a result was forced to leave the navy, spending a year in America. When he discovered that officers were needed for the Congress' new navy he signed on as a first lieutenant. His most notable involvement in the colonial conflicts came when he staged raids against the port of Whitehaven and across the Solway at Kirkcudbright Bay.

Legend has it that he planned to seize the Earl of Selkirk as a hostage, but upon finding that the Laird was away from home he gave his men permission to loot the family plate. After the conflicts were over, however, Jones apparently purchased the plate and returned it to the family.

John Paul Jones continued his exploits throughout America and Europe where his feats brought him recognition as a war hero. He was awarded a gold medal in recognition of his services by the US Congress, and in France a dance was named in his honour.

He was even invited to Russia where he helped the navy of the Empress Catherine defeat the Turks. In 1953, the US Naval Historical Foundation and the Daughters of the American Revolution presented a plaque to be erected at his birthplace.

We made a worthwhile visit to Carsethorn where the **Steam Packet Inn** still stands, and saw the remains of the old wooden jetty where John Paul Jones left to start his adventures. An interesting fact we discovered was that once upon a time, a regular steam ship service left from here to go to Whitehaven and Liverpool.

We were intrigued to find out that, although these old ports on the Solway seem to be relatively sheltered, they suffer from unusually high tides and strong currents, making them extremely difficult to navigate.

The Lighthouse at Southerness

We paid a visit to the lighthouse at **Southerness** which was built in 1748 and has the distinction of being the second oldest purpose built lighthouse in the country. The lighthouse is no longer in use, though many people come to Southerness today for it is a delightful holiday village with many attractions, including a famous golf course with nineteen holes.

With its many creeks and tidal rivers, we were not surprised to learn that the Solway was at one time notorious for smugglers. This was especially true since, until 1876, the Isle of Man lay outside British Customs regulations, encouraging regular dealings in contraband goods. Sir Walter Scott wrote a vivid account of smuggling in this area in his book 'Guy Mannering'.

We followed the A710 which moves slightly inland through **Caulkerbush** and then rejoins the coast at the village of **Sandyhills**. Here we came cross the perfect combination for a holiday. **Barend Holiday Village** is a high quality development of luxury log chalets close to the village of Sandyhills and within half a mile of beautiful **Sandyhills Bay.**

Barend Holiday Village .

The chalets are all built in the Scandinavian style and are specially designed for families who enjoy a self-catering holiday. All enjoy a south facing setting and overlook a well stocked man-made trout loch.

This is a fantastic place for golfing enthusiasts, walkers and sailing buffs. The centre offers trout fishing on the loch and riding at all standards, with either instruction from one of the BHS qualified instructors, or pony trekking through the lovely surrounding countryside. The new swimming pool, sauna and a games room complex are an added bonus to the site and certainly add to the luxurious facilities on offer.

There is a public telephone and a small launderette on site, and video recorders can be hired for evenings and perhaps the occasional wet day.

If a break from domesticity is what is required, then the high quality home cooking of the Granary Restaurant, along with a drink from one of the two bars, should do the trick. Both are to be found in attractively converted farm steadings.

A telephone call before your departure is all that is required to ensure that a supply of groceries is in your chalet on your arrival.

Galloway is beautiful all year round, not only in summer, and Barend Holiday Village is perfect for an off season holiday or a weekend break, as well as making an ideal summer retreat.

For those who do not want a self catering holiday but would like to stay in Sandyhills, we can think of no better place than **Cairngill House Hotel,** a charming country house hotel set in three acres of beautiful gardens.

Cairngill House commands panoramic views over the coast, the Solway Firth and beyond to the Cumbrian Hills. The hotel has eight bedrooms, six of which have en-suite facilities and all beautifully furnished with elegant antique furniture.

Proprietors Brian and Anne Downes always ensure that the atmosphere is relaxed and friendly, especially in the intimate Dining room. Here you will enjoy home cooking of a deliciously high standard from a menu which changes daily and makes full use of fresh local produce including game in season.

Cairngill House Hotel is lucky enough to enjoy a tranquil setting while at the same time being ideally situated to make the most of everything this area has to offer. Play a game of tennis on the hotel's own court or venture further afield where you can enjoy coarse game fishing, golf, horse riding and pony trekking. Shooting can also be arranged throughout the winter months. All year round there is an abundance of bird life and relaxing country walks to gladden your heart in this peaceful corner of the Solway Firth.

Cairngill House Hotel

There is much to do in this area and we paid a visit to **Rockcliffe** and nearby **Kippford**, which are on the estuary of the River Urr. Kippford, or as it used to be known "Scaur", is a fascinating place and at one time ships would set sail from here for the industrial areas of Northern England and Central Scotland with cargoes of barley, meal and potatoes. Kippford has a delightful setting and, with its old inn and jetty, is today one of the foremost yachting and sailing centres in the south-west.

Close to the Urr and a couple of miles inland is the town of **Dalbeattie**. You may notice that this distinctive town has mostly been built in the same colour granite. This is the grey granite that was quarried in the area and was a very useful source of income for the town, making it famous throughout the world. This striking material was shipped to many places and was used to construct London's Embankment. We enjoyed walking in the forest nearby and in the pleasant riverside which proved to be a most interesting excursion.

Four miles to the south-west is **Orchardston Tower** which is a unique circular tower house built in the 15th century.

If you feel in need of refreshment, then we can recommend that you travel to the pretty little village of **Kirkgunzeon** which sits on the A711 between Dalbeattie and Dumfries. Here you will find **The Anvil Inn**, owned and run by Jim and Christine Smith

Jim and Christine bought their inn in 1977, when it was the village shop, and converted it into the charming village inn you see today.

Enjoy a drink or snack in the friendly public bar, or challenge the locals to a game of pool, darts or a hand of dominoes. The lounge bar is comfortable and quiet and the whole inn enjoys pleasant surroundings in a cosy village atmosphere. The beer garden is popular on sunny days and is especially convenient if you have children with you.

Jim is certainly a bit of an entrepreneur and has recently been involved in the local resurgence of cockle fishing. Being a blacksmith, he designed and built his own boat, took it down to the sea in four parts and welded it together. With no previous experience of fishing Jim says, "I'd always fancied fishing and enjoyed the challenge." So if you see cockles on the bar, Jim may have caught them himself!

The Anvil Inn

Well, you don't have to be a fisherman or an entrepreneur to enjoy a visit to The Anvil Inn, but you will find it the ideal place to catch your breath. There is plenty to do locally from a visit to nearby **Drumcoltran Castle** to fishing, walking and gliding at the local **Gliding Club**.

Travelling north out of Dalbeattie on the B794 we came to the **Motte of Urr**. This is an impressive site and is the most extensive motte-and-bailey castle in Scotland. It's siting here is something of a mystery as there does not seem much to commend the position. It is possible however, that the river once surrounded it, making it an island. The circular mound here is eighty feet high.

In the nearby village of **Haugh Of Urr** there is a bridge over the River Urr, built in 1760, and we were of a mind to take advantage of some of the pleasures available to us on this small salmon river, which also has a good run of sea trout in high summer. The village is ideally placed for plethora of country pursuits such as fishing and shooting and of course walking. There is an abundance of forest, coastal and cliff walks to enjoy, with many fascinating Heritage Trails amidst the Galloway Hills and the Colvend Coast.

Standing at the cross in the village of Haugh of Urr, **Woodburn House** was established in the early years of the last century when it was a coaching inn by the name of The Dog and Duck.

Woodburn House

The inn was built as a staging post, conveniently sited on the old military road connecting **Portpatrick**, via **Castle Douglas**, to **Dumfries**. Its main line of business was servicing the mail coaches that plied their route at that time.

Woodburn House is now run as a small guest house specialising in home cooking and baking, and a warm family welcome. There are also a handful of fully equipped and serviced caravans available for holiday hire, in the house's pleasant garden.

Mr. and Mrs. Wormald intend in the near future to make supervised painting and sketching holidays available in the house and outdoors; we thought this an ideal opportunity for the artistic among you to realise your ambitions.

Feeling much refreshed after our stop we joined the A75 on the other side of Haugh of Urr and drove steadily towards **Castle Douglas**. This is a popular destination for travellers along this area of the Solway coast, and those looking for a charming family run hotel in elegant and exclusive surroundings need look no further than the **Longacre Manor Hotel**.

Just one hundred metres from the A75, on the northern outskirts of Castle Douglas, Longacre Manor stands in one and a half acres of grounds which provide a blaze of colour in springtime.

Run by the resident proprietors Elizabeth and Walter Meldrum, the house itself was built in 1927 and faces southwards with magnificent views to Screel and the Galloway Hills.

All four bedrooms have ensuite bath/shower rooms, colour television, radio alarm, tea/coffee making facilities and are centrally heated throughout. In addition, each is equipped with trouser press, hairdryer and direct dial telephone.

The proprietors are members of the Taste of Scotland Scheme, which means good wholesome food using the best of local ingredients and the highest standards of preparation. A table licence allows you to enjoy fine wines with your meal. The hotel is also Scottish Tourist Board Four Crowns and Commended.

The market town of Castle Douglas is only ten miles from the Solway Coast and its sandy beaches. The surrounding area excels in natural beauty and fishing; sailing and riding are all available either locally or within easy motoring distance.

Longacre Manor Hotel

The streets of Castle Douglas have a certain planned elegance about them as a result of the town being developed by an enterprising landowner named William Douglas, who had made his fortune in America. He encouraged the development of the town as a cattle market and today it is still a focal point for the local farming community.

We spent an hour or two wandering around the many shops and then we went in search of a suitable reward. Do you find that you tend to watch what you eat these days? We would like to say that we do, though we admit to 'forgetting' every now and again. However, health conscious travellers to Castle Douglas need look no further for refreshment than the **Rendezvous Restaurant**, owned and run by Lesley O'Rourke.

This is a small, friendly restaurant where a warm welcome is always guaranteed and where the most is made of the fresh, locally produced goods. All food is home-cooked and prepared, based mainly on traditional English and Scottish recipes.

Lesley is a trained dietician and with a little notice can always prepare a meal to suit any special dietary requirements.

The Rendezvous is not open on Mondays and is closed at Sunday lunchtimes, although Lesley otherwise caters for both luncheon and evening patrons.

Lesley's prices are certainly very competitive and the warmth of welcome on offer here means that The Rendezvous offers unquestionable value for money.

Rendezvous Restaurant

Not far away is the lovely **Carlingwark Loch**, where we rowed out in a small boat to look at the swans and were rewarded with the bonus of a wonderful view of nearby Screel Mill. There was once an ancient causeway that led to a dwelling on an artificial island at the centre of this loch.

A stones throw away, are the delightful **Threave Gardens**, which you will find approximately a mile from the Loch. These gardens and the visitor centre stand majestically in sixty acres surrounding a Victorian mansion.

The house is used by the National Trust of Scotland for their School of Gardening. There is much to see here including rock gardens, heathers, herbaceous and rose beds and in the spring time nearly two hundred varieties of daffodil provide a dazzling display. On the River Dee we were delighted by the many species of wild geese and duck.

Threave Castle makes a lovely sight here and is accessible by a short boat trip. This castle was once the stronghold of the Douglas' and is built on an island in the River Dee. From here, the family oppressed the local population, defying even the authority of the king himself. On one infamous occasion, a Douglas captured the sheriff of Galloway. On being ordered to return him, he had the sherrif beheaded in Threave, afterwards sending the body to the awaiting king's messengers, with the insolent remark that he was "somewhat wanting in the heid!"

We left Castle Douglas by the A75 travelling southwards towards **Kirkcudbright**. We sometimes feel the need to get away from it all and to indulge ourselves with nothing more than peaceful surroundings and perhaps a good book. We found the perfect place for providing this relaxing atmosphere at **Barncrosh Farm**, nestling in the rolling Galloway countryside on the banks of the River Dee, halfway between Castle Douglas and Kircudbright.

The farm covers approximately five hundred acres, of which twenty five acres are managed woodland and the home and place of work of Ronnie and Liz Ball.

Self-catering accommodation has been developed on the farm by the conversion of three disused cottages and the old stable block. This varies in size from a spacious three bedroomed farmhouse to compact flats for two people. Each building has been carefully modernised to provide the highest standards of comfort as well as preserving a relaxed and homely atmosphere.

Barncrosh, a corruption of Bal-na-Cross or The Place of the Cross was, in the 10th century, one of the satellite abbeys of Tongland. It was famous for being the home of Father Damien who, to prove that Man could fly, tied feathers to his arms and jumped off the ramparts of Stirling Castle. Unfortunately, he was proved wrong and broke his leg into the bargain.

Barncrosh was at one time the site of a Norman motte and at one time a parish in its own right. It was sold by the Earl of Selkirk in an Edinburgh coffee house in 1805 for the sum of eighteen thousand pounds to the Boone family. They, in turn sold it in 1945 to the family of the present owners.

Amongst its claims to fame is the fact that it was tenanted in the 1780's by one Dalziel, who entertained Robbie Burns and who is thought to have conducted the first modernisation of the Old Farmhouse, later renovated by Ronnie and Liz in 1975. At the time of the railway boom in the 1850's John Carrick-Moore, a relation of Sir John Moore of Corunna fame, was the tenant.

Nowadays, no-one famous lives at the farm but the properties, which are to let, have been renovated and equipped to a high standard. No entertainment is available on the site except for the simple joys of bird watching, relaxing and admiring the view.

We can certainly recommend Barncrosh farm to anyone who has a desire to 'escape away from it all' for a while.

Barncrosh Farm

We crossed the River Dee at **Tongland Bridge** taking time to look closely at this structure. Although it is shrouded by trees and not immediately obvious to the traveller, this handsome bridge is a fine piece of engineering. It was designed by Thomas Telford in collaboration with the famous Edinburgh architect and painter, Alexander Nasmyth. It is interesting to note that the single span bridge had to be built to cope with the tide which would rise six metres or more. The difficulty of this was brought home to the builders when the original foundations were washed away on the first attempt. We learnt that the three small arches to either side are designed to help cope with the flow of water at high tides.

From here it did not take us long to get to the county town of **Kirkcudbright**. This beautiful town and harbour proved to be a welcome discovery with much to recommend it. Take a look around the streets here and you will find many examples of seventeenth and eighteenth century buildings. What struck us as particularly pleasing was the fabulous colour used thorughout the town with reds, blues and blacks producing an effect that is almost continental.

Kirkcudbright is an ancient place with quite a history. As far back as the 8th century the Vikings established the church of St Cuthbert near the town. The town seal today still reflects the rather bloody times of old with a picture of St Cuthbert with the head of the martyred St Oswald, king of Northumbria, in his lap.

Facing England across the Solway meant that the conflicts between the two countries were reflected in the fortifications and defences around the town. These included a water filled ditch and wall enclosing the town. The ruins of **Maclellans Castle** date from a period when building reflected a combination of the need for safety and a certain amount of comfort. It was built in the sixteenth century by Sir Thomas Maclellan who benefitted from the dissolution of the monasteries by acquiring the lands and buildings of the Greyfriar's convent on this site. He even built his castle with the stone from the dismantled buildings.

We recommend that you take a look around this ruin, there is much of interest to see. We were intrigued by the fireplace which is some ten feet wide and would have had a fire burning continuously throughout the winter months. A closer inspection will reveal a small hole in the back of the fireplace, which puzzled us. Apparently, this was a spy hole located in a small room reached from the stair. Here, Maclellan could watch and listen to what was being said, without fear of discovery.

Besides Maclellans Castle, **the Tolbooth** is another interesting building dating from the same period. Overlooking the market square, the Tolbooth was the point where taxes were paid and prisoners incarcerated. Pronouncements would have been made from its steps and it is fascinating to see the original manacles that were used to hold the prisoners during their punishment.

The area was caught up in the persecution of both witches, and later, Covenanters. The case against witches usually began with a series of events or disasters occurring within the community, until eventually someone came to be suspected of causing them. The case of Elspeth McEwen is a typical local example. She was accused of making her neighbours' hens stop laying and of having a movable wooden pin at her command that was capable of drawing milk from their cows. The unfortunate woman was imprisoned and tortured in Kirkcudbright Tolbooth until she confessed and was subsequently found guilty "of a compact and correspondence with the devil and of charms and accession to malefices". She was executed in 1698.

Later in the 17th and 18th centuries the town developed along more civilized lines with smart new dwellings arising for the merchants and lawyers. A walk along Castle Street or Old High Street gave us a clear indication of the elegance of Georgian Kirkcubright. It was an important town for shipping, trade went as far as the West Indies and the North American Colonies. As a result it became a centre for Customs and Excise Officers engaged in the capture of the smugglers who were operating from France, Ireland and the Isle of Man, running contraband along the shores of the Solway.

In the late 19th century there was an artists colony established here and the town has become associated with many fine painters and craftsmen. One famous resident was E.A. Hornel (1864-1930) and his house in the High Street contains a display of his paintings and furniture. Do try and visit if you can and have a look at the garden which in summer is particularly attractive. Close by, is the house of the artist Jessie M. King (1875-1949) and examples of her work can be seen at the **Stewartry Museum** in St Mary Street. We were also very interested to see here a host of articles and information on this pleasant town. Visitors during the mid July to August period will be in luck as there is an annual Summer Festival, which provides an extensive programme of entertainment.

We decided to leave Kirkcudbright by the A755, though we soon rejoined the A75 and headed north-east towards the village of **Twynholm.**

It is not unusual for us to come across enterprising couples on our travels, we are always glad to report on their ventures and especially so when they have achieved a measure of success in their field. John and Pat Middlemas' search for a business to purchase started some five years ago when they sold the family business in Kelso. With twenty five years experience in the wholesale licensed trade, the idea of buying a pub seemed to make most sense.

The Star Hotel

Having travelled up and down the country without seeing what they wanted, the Middlemasses were finally rewarded when a property agent told them of **The Star Hotel** at **Twynholm.** A preliminary visit quickly confirmed that The Star was exactly what they were looking for and it became their home in September 1985.

John and Pat were immediately impressed by the warmth and friendliness of the local people. Indeed, The Star itself is an extremely friendly place to visit, either for a drink or something to eat. Bar snacks, sandwiches and bar lunches are speedily provided and made freshly on the premises. In the evening you can wine and dine at your leisure, choosing from the a la carte menu. The Star is a popular local venue, however, and John recommended that we call and make a reservation in order to avoid any disappointment. Whatever you do, you will find a pleasing welcome awaits you at The Star. John and Pat are always happy to tell some fascinating anecdotes about some of The Star's previous owners and patrons, and of course there is nothing like a smile of greeting to cheer you at the end of a hard day's fishing, walking, driving or sightseeing.

From Twynholm it is only a few miles to the town of **Gatehouse of Fleet**. We thought that this place was fascinating with its brightly coloured buildings and scenic setting. It did not immediately spring to mind that this town was once at the forefront of Scotland's Industrial Revolution. However, a closer look reveals that many of these bright buildings were at one time working mills in a town that was built to rival the centres of industry in the North of England.

The town was planned and built in the late 18th century as a centre for cotton manufacturing and other industries. It once boasted six cotton mills employing a workforce of more than five hundred people. The industries did eventually decline in response to better transport related businesses elsewhere. There is a visitors centre in one of the former mills.

Had we realised before we came here that the late 18th century had brought about the expansion of this town, we would have understood that it needed Banks and that is why there is a nice hotel at 47 High Street, named **The Bank Of Fleet Hotel**. Originally it was built as a bank but as the town declined so it was acquired as a suitable site for a hotel.

The Bank of Fleet Hotel

The conversion has been well done lending it a friendly and informal feeling. It is a listed building so care has been taken to preserve the past. It is run by the Wright family who originally came from Yorkshire. They have been at The Bank of Fleet for 2 ^{1}/2 years, during which time they have improved the bedrooms considerably. There are 5 in all, simply furnished, with comfortable beds and prettily colour co-ordinated curtains and bed-covers.

Obviously food plays a great part in the success of any hotel. The Wrights talented son Alastair, a trained chef, has produced a well chosen Continental menu. He is insistent always on fresh produce being used.

There are two bars and a separate TV lounge where you can sit yourself down at the end of a day touring around or perhaps after a hard day's business.

We found the Wright family welcoming and fun to talk to. They have definitely made their mark here and on the community.

Today Gatehouse provides us with a quiet and unspoiled place from which you may take advantage of the wealth of nearby hill and woodland walks.

Those of you with an interest in the haunts of the poet Burns, will be interested to find that the **Murray Arms Hotel** is reputedly the place where he wrote 'Scots Wha Hae'.

We decided to leave the main routes behind once again and headed north on a small road that led us deep into the countryside by the **Forest of Glengap** and deep into the **Laurieston Forest**. Here we had a chance to walk and stretch our legs in some of the most refreshing scenery. The road finally emerges at the village of **Laurieston** and opens up to one of the most renowned beauty spots and activity centres in this part of the country, **Loch Ken**.

We decided to start our journey at the south end of the Loch and took the B795 to the **Townhead of Greenlaw** where we were able to join the A713 which follows the shore of the loch up to **New Galloway**.

Whether you are a birdwatcher, water skier, rambler, sailor or fisherman you will find that there is something to cater for you on Loch Ken. We were able to hire a suitable dinghy at **Glenlaggan Marina, Crossmichael**, and enjoyed an afternoon's sailing.

There are a large number of tracks and footpaths for either more experienced walkers or novices. Fishermen amongst you might like to know that apart from salmon and sea trout, Loch Ken has become famous for the size of pike that have been caught. If you have enjoyed pony trekking in some of the other places we have visited, then you will enjoy the facilities on offer here as the surrounds are ideal for this activity.

The A713 took us right to the top of the loch where it reaches **New Galloway**. The road is notable for its lovely scenic views of the waters and more than once we were tempted to stop and take a deep breath.

New Galloway is itself a very attractive little town which is actually the smallest Royal Burgh in Scotland and, standing on the River Ken, it is a popular base for anglers. Those of you who like to spend time browsing in craft shops will find much to look at in the surrounding area, especially in nearby Balmaclellan and **St John's Town of Dalry**. The latter town derives its name from a stone on which St John the Baptist is reputed to have rested.

We crossed the River Ken at New Galloway and travelled on the A712 towards **Clatteringshaws Loch** and the **Galloway Forest**. Clatteringshaws Loch is surely one of the most scenic spots in Galloway and we were transfixed by the marvellous views over the waters to the hills beyond. This road takes us through the **Galloway Forest Park** and the route was offically opened as 'The Queens Way' in commemoration of the Silver Jubilee of Queen Elizabeth II in 1977.

The park takes in a massive area of Scotland and the road gave us splendid views of mountains, lochs, and waterfalls. If you are lucky you may well spot red deer or even wild goats.

To get thoroughly clued up on the park and its wildlife we stopped at the **Galloway Deer Museum** at Clatteringshaws. Here there is a display on the history of the area and the wildlife in the park. Opposite Clatteringshaws Loch is the famous 'Raiders Road' which is a trail following an old cattle rustler's route alongside the Black water at Dee. We were amazed by the beauty of the park and would recommend that you spend some time making the most of the spectacular attractions of its natural scenery.

All the fresh air however, gave us large appetites and we decided to travel to **Newton Stewart**. After a pub lunch in a local inn, we walked around this busy little market town which has a fine selection of shops, hotels and restaurants. It is here that you will find **Creebridge Caravan Park**, owned by Robin and Ray Wither.

Creebridge Caravan Park

Over the years, holiday makers and tourists coming to stay here have been intrigued by the fact that the site was at one time a Prisoner of War Camp housing Italian and German prisoners. Robin and Ray have produced a small but informative brochure on the site and its history; be sure to ask for one, it is well worth reading.

The caravan park itself nestles in a sun trap half a mile from the Minigaff junction on the A75 and is only five minutes walk from Newton Stewart which sits just across the River Cree.

Creebridge is open for touring caravans and tents from 1st March to 31st October, as well as providing luxury holiday caravans for hire, all with colour television. Hard standings as well as grass areas make the park ideal in mixed weather conditions.

On site you will find a well stocked general store, launderette, indoor and outdoor games facilities and a playpark. Caravan accessories and calor gas are available from a shop in the park's reception area. Hot water is provided free of charge for essentials such as showers, basins and dishwashing. Electric hook ups are available too and site lighting adds to the safety and comfort provided by Robin and Ray here at Creebridge.

Leisure facilities close by include golf, tennis courts and bowling greens. The park is only five miles away from the nearest sandy beaches and the countryside around Newton Stewart is a haven for hill walkers, nature lovers, archaeological and history buffs, fishing enthusiasts and climbers.

Although the new owners are undoubtedly making continual improvements, Robin and Ray intend to maintain the quiet and peaceful atmosphere so inherent in this serene Galloway countryside.

The River Cree flows down towards the sea and we followed its path on the A75 southeast towards **Creetown**, six miles from Newton Stewart at the head of Wigtown Bay. We were thoroughly charmed by this warm and friendly village which features as 'Port-an-Ferry' in Scott's 'Guy Mannering' and has a history steeped in smuggling legend. The village is built in the local 'silver' granite, which we thought to be most attractive.

We were looking for somewhere to stay in Creetown that would reflect the character of this area and we found exactly what we were looking for in the **Hill Of Burns Hotel** where visitors are greeted by old fashioned hospitality, elegant public rooms and spacious surroundings. Standing in three acres of fine gardens, the hotel commands magnificent views across the Cree estuary and offers a pleasantly high standard of comfort.

The Hill of Burns Hotel is an early 19th century grade B listed small mansion house, carefully converted to a delightful country house hotel and boasting a magnificent central staircase. The furniture here is mostly antique and reproduction, blending in   well with the overall charm and elegance of the interior.

There are eight charmingly furnished bedrooms, three of which have en-suite bathrooms. All the rooms are equipped with colour TV, tea and coffee making facilities and direct dial telephones.

The candlelit dining room has a curved bay window overlooking the estuary. Mr and Mrs Stephen Moore, proprietors here, offer stylish home cooking from an imaginative menu where fresh local produce is used extensively. All dishes can be easily complemented by the fine selection of wines available.

The dining room is open to non residents and is, not surprisingly, very popular, so we recommend that you call to book a table ahead.

For after dinner relaxation you can linger over a drink in the drawing room or retire to the hotel's traditional billiards room, which houses a full sized table.

The Hill of Burns Hotel enjoys a particularly attractive setting, sitting as it does on the edge of the Galloway Forest Park. This area is good for climbing and walking and there are many Forestry Commission marked walks and trails. Excellent salmon and trout fishing is available locally and golf is free for residents on local courses.

Hill of Burns Hotel

A break at the Hotel is ideal at any time of the year, either in the summer when the surrounding trees and gardens are in full bloom, or in autumn when it is surrounded by a blaze of golden colour. Whatever the season, the welcome is always warm and you can be sure of a peaceful stay and the best of personal attention.

There is much to do in this lovely village and we were surprised by the amount of facilities on offer to the visitor. For ourselves, we wandered over to the King George VI playing fields where we thoroughly enjoyed a game of tennis. There are also facilities for children here in a well equipped play area. There are many walks, from along the **Minnipool Burn** with its pleasant surroundings, to the slightly more ambitious **Cairnsmore of Fleet** which, at 2,329 feet, is one of the highest hills in Galloway. The views are stunning and take in the Isle of Man, England and the Mountains of Mourne in Ireland.

It was said to Queen Victoria that the road from Creetown to Gatehouse of Fleet is 'the finest in the kingdom', the next finest being the road from Gatehouse of Fleet to Creetown! Whatever you decide, you will agree I'm sure that Galloway is a truly beautiful place.

Crossing the river Cree at Newton Stewart we entered one of the most fascinating corners of Scotland and Galloway. We turned south on the A714 coming out of Newton Stewart and followed the road to the little town of **Wigtown** that overlooks Wigtown Bay and the mouth of the River Cree. The feeling of calmness in the town today belies its previously fierce competitive spirit as the former county town of Wigtownshire, fighting for the royal burgh's trading 'freedoms' (which mean monopolies) over Whithorn and Stranraer.

We were interested to note that the site of the ancient town reputedly lay more than a mile to the east which, if you look at a map, would have placed it firmly within the grasp of the sea!

There is a small church on the east side of the town that was erected next to a ruined church dedicated to St Machitis. There are some solemn reminders of the fate of the Covenanters here. For example you will find a headstone, located in the burial ground. This was erected in memory of the sad fate of eighteen year old Margaret Wilson, who with Margaret Lachlan, aged sixty three, was drowned for her religious beliefs tied to a stake in the sea. A stone post now within dry land marks the site of the drowning.

Taking the B733 from Wigtown, we came across the **Torhouse Stone Circle**, which is a captivating sight of nineteen boulders on the edge of a low mound dating from the Bronze Age.

Set in the heart of the picturesque moors of Wigtownshire and six miles from Wigtown itself, **The Corsemalzie House Hotel** is a fine example of a 19th century Scottish country mansion. The house has been skilfully and tastefully renovated throughout. The end result being a delightful and well-appointed hotel providing the sort of friendly atmosphere that is essential for a good holiday.

Corsemalzie House Hotel
Under the personal supervision of resident proprietors, Mr and Mrs Peter

McDougall, the Corsemalzie offers all the facilities you come to expect from such a hotel. All rooms are furnished with ensuite bath or shower rooms, radio, direct dial telephones, colour TV and tea/coffee making facilities.

The hotel is four crowns commended by the Scottish Tourist Board and specialises in Taste of Scotland dishes. Only the freshest of local produce is used in their variety of mouth watering meals. This is very important to Mr McDougall, who has a Swiss background and a very special interest in cuisine.

Corsemalzie is superbly situated so that residents can enjoy a wide variety of relaxing pursuits. The golfer can choose from a marvellous array of nearby courses where free golf is provided by the hotel. Full arrangements can be made for individual or party shooting, and for the fishing enthusiast the hotel has exclusive salmon and trout fishing rights on four and a half miles of the River Bladnoch, plus eight miles on the River Tarff. The surrounding countryside itself is ideal for horse riding, hiking and walking.

In short, if what you seek is a 'something-for-everyone' holiday, or simply a chance to relax in the atmosphere of a family run, friendly hotel, then Corsemalzie House Hotel is the place for you.

We rejoined the A714 just south of Wigtown taking time to visit the distillery at **Bladnoch**, which is a fascinating place, especially if you have a taste for the delights of malt whisky. There are tours available at the distillery, which is open all year round.

After we had left here, we took the B7004 which led us down to the village of **Garlieston** overlooking the bay. The small port was founded in the 18th century by Lord Garlies. His father, the 6th Earl, built nearby **Galloway House**. The house is not open to the public, although we did enjoy a quiet afternoon in the gardens which cover nearly thirty acres with superb displays of daffodils, rhododendrons and azaleas. There are lovely old trees here and the position of the garden, which leads down to a sandy beach by the sea, is delightful.

Whithorn is a few miles further south on the B7063 and the fact that this ancient town is on the very tail end of Scotland did not diminish its importance, for we know it existed as far back as the second century.

It was here, in AD 397, that St Ninian established the first Christian centre in Scotland. The site of the chapel which he founded is thought to have been a few miles further south, close to the Isle of Whithorn and the area has long since been the focus of pilgrimages.

Robert the Bruce came here in the last months of his life, severely weakened by years of hard campaigning and suffering from leprosy. He had, apparently, to be carried in a horse-litter as he was too weak to support himself. Another noted visitor had no such problem. He was James IV who came here many times reputedly walking on foot from Edinburgh. Mary Queen of Scots also made this journey in 1563. Indeed, such was the influence of this place that, after the Reformation, an Act of Parliament was passed to make the practice illegal.

The Isle of Whithorn was, as the name implies, originally an island, although this charming seaside village is now joined to the mainland and is a popular spot for yachting.

The area is rich in religious interest with a wealth of crosses and the **Priory**, itself the focus of attention for pilgrims. There are also a number of notable sites for the budding archaeologist, with a team digging here throughout the summer. We found the excavations to be fascinating. We cannot help but admire the patience of these dedicated people, who are painstakingly revealing the history of this ancient area, and the folk who have lived here throughout the centuries.

In the midst of these peaceful and historic surroundings you will find **The Castlewigg Hotel**. Over two hundred years old and with a character all its own, the Castlewigg enjoys some wonderfully scenic views over the Galloway countryside, as well as being conveniently close to Whithorn's beautifully sandy beaches. The hotel is superbly situated for enjoying the enviable fishing, shooting and stalking facilities available in this area and Irene Bushrod, owner of the Castlewigg, can arrange residents' participation in all of these activities.

The Castlewigg Hotel

The Castlewigg has seven guest rooms, four of which have en-suite facilities and one of which has a four poster bed. All rooms are equipped with tea and coffee making facilities and the ground floor room with en-suite bathroom is ideal for disabled visitors.

The intimate restaurant is open to non residents and offers a varied selection of dishes. Fish and game are the chef's specialities here during the Winter season. The menu is well complemented with wide choice of wines and champagnes.

This is a hotel with a homely ambience which permeates throughout the building. Log fires crackle in the TV lounge as you enjoy your favourite programmes, as they do in the cocktail lounge where you can enjoy an aperitif or an after dinner liquer.

In summertime, the hotel's beautiful rose garden is a joy to behold, and at any time of the year the surrounding countryside is a haven for walkers. Golfers have two good nine and eighteen holes to play close by, and of course the nearby Whithorn excavations are not to be missed.

The Castlewigg Hotel is an ideal destination for those seeking a relaxing holiday. You can rest assured that Irene will do her very best to ensure you have an enjoyable stay in this historic part of Wigtonshire.

Do spend some time looking around as there is much of interest here. There is a "Dig" shop that will provide you with a wide range of souvenirs and local crafts. There is also a visitor centre and museum providing much detailed information, with a guided tour of the site available.

Make your way to **Port William** on the eastern side of **Luce Bay**. Here is a small and attractive fishing port and **Monrieth Bay** nearby has fine sands. You may notice in the bay a small statue of an otter overlooking the water. We discovered that this is a tribute to the author Gavin Maxwell who wrote lovingly about the area in his book, "The House at Elrig". If you would like to bide here a while, and we recommend that you do, you will find at Port William, backing on to the sea the charming **Eagle Hotel**, owned and run by Colin Hawes and his wife, Sally.

The Eagle Hotel

The traditional inn is over a hundred years old although its history is somewhat obscure. However, the welcome certainly is not. You will find that the Eagle has five rooms available for those who wish to stay a little longer in this beautiful fishing village.

The restaurant here is light, spacious and comfortable with some pleasant background music, which induces a wonderfully relaxed atmosphere. There is a good selection of traditional dishes complemented by a wine list offering eighteen varieties of good quality wine.

All the rooms have tea and coffee making facilities and there is a residents' television lounge. The public bar holds a full sized pool table, or visitors can join the locals in a game of darts.

The hotel can easily arrange fishing facilities nearby on either sea, loch or river. If you're more of a history enthusiast, the local **Whithorn Dig** is fascinating and of course Wigtownshire is the home of Christianity in Scotland. There are some beautiful sandy beaches within yards of the hotel, as well as a golf course nearby, and some ideal terrain for walkers who can take advantage of Wigtown Council's Walkaboutabit Scheme.

Colin and Sally will be glad to provide you with the necessary details you need for whatever pursuits you wish to follow. They, and the Eagle Hotel, offer a true Wigtownshire welcome to all who enjoy this beautiful part of the world.

Close to this sleepy and attractive harbour village we found **Monrieth House**. Built in 1799, it has charming gardens and a park. The White Loch is here also and we were told that even in the coldest of winters it never entirely freezes over.

The area boasts an abundance of prehistoric sites and we took a look at the **Drumtrodden Standing Stones** which were three upright stones (though one has now fallen), and also nearby the fascinating "cup and ring" markings, which were probably carved during the Bronze Age. Theories abound as to the meaning of the cup and ring markings which can be found in many places in Scotland. One source lists a remarkable one hundred and four theories that have been put forward to explain their meaning and usage. The most likely explanations are either that they had some connection with metal prospecting and smelting activities, or that they had some religious meaning perhaps related to sun worship or astronomical observation.

The coast road is the A747 from Port William. We followed it northwards and were rewarded with a refreshing view of Luce Bay as we made our way to **Glenluce**. This village sits on the edge of the Water of Luce and close to Luce Bay. It is fascinating to think that there has been a settlement in this area from as early as 6,000BC.

A mile to the north is **Glenluce Abbey** which was founded in 1190 and was visited by King Robert I, King James IV and Mary Queen of Scots on their pilgrimages to Whithorn. The abbey is said to have associations with a 13th century wizard named Michael Scott. Legend has it that he managed to persuade some witches, who were paying him too much close attention, to spend their time spinning ropes from the sands of Luce bay. The results of their task can supposedly be seen at very low tides.

Another interesting story that we came across was that of poor Gilbert Cambell, who was apparently haunted by the devil of Glenluce for four years from 1654 to 1658. Fortunately the local Presbytery was able to eventually rid him of his unfortunate possession.

We were very impressed by the amount of facilities on offer in this small village where the sea is never far from view. Apart from the many lovely walks, the more adventurous among you will be able to try your hand at wind surfing or even water ski-ing. For those of you who prefer a more leisurely pastime, why not play a round of golf or simply walk along the beach? We spent some of our time looking around **Glenluce Motor Museum**, which houses a splendid display of vintage cars and motorbikes.

Glenluce Abbey

We were keen to explore the southern peninsular of Galloway and journeyed down on the A715 from Glenluce and came to the charming little town of **Sandhead**. Here, in the town's Main Street, overlooking nine square miles of sandy beach, voted the cleanest, safest and warmest in the area, is the **Tigh Na Mara Hotel**, owned and run by Norman and Ellis McIntyre.

Tigh Na Mara Hotel

Behind the spotless but deceptively small facade of this historic building lies a busy hotel packed with ambience, offering attractive eating places, a public bar with a real log fire, and seating for one hundred and thirty in the large function room to the rear.

Discerning diners come from far and near to enjoy food from the hotels imaginative a la carte and bar meal menus. There is no such thing as frozen foods here and Norman and Ellis can justifiably boast that local crabs and salmon caught that morning are on the tables by lunchtime. A large but carefully selected stock of fine wines is another source of pride for the restaurant.

All guest rooms are spotless and comfortable each having colour TV, tea and coffee making facilities and washhand basin. Three rooms have en-suite bathroom facilities too.

There is a large floodlit car park with attractive shrubs and outside tables. Golfing, fishing and shooting are all available and the hotel will gladly make the necessary arrangements.

After a visit to Sandhead and a stay at the Tigh na Mara, we think you'll agree with the sentiment of one of the hotel's many satisfied customers: "You always hear of these places but can never usually find them".

We had heard much praise of the **Logan Botanical Gardens** and we found them just off the B7065. Here, practically surrounded by the sea, we found the most amazing collection of exotic plants. Although usually associated with the southern hemisphere, they are thriving due to the mildness of the climate warmed by the Gulf stream. We thought that the famous cabbage palms and tree ferns were especially interesting, though you will also enjoy the walled gardens and many varieties of flora on show.

From the gardens, we travelled down to **Drummore** which is the most southerly village in Scotland. The people of this village are said to have visited the well of the "Co'" which is near St Medan's Cove on the Mull of Galloway. We were told that on the first Sunday in May, they would come down to bathe in the waters which were widely accredited with having healing properties. Coins have been found in the well which date as far back as the reign of Charles I.

There is a lighthouse situated beyond the "Double Dykes" which was built in 1828, and from here on a clear day you will be able to see both the Isle of Man and Ireland, some twenty six miles away.

Rumour has it that the Picts brewed a drink from heather that was sweeter than honey and stronger than wine, and when the Scots invaded from Ireland, they were most keen to learn the secret of this renowned brew. It was here at The Double Dykes that the secret is said to have died with the final defence of the Picts against the invaders. The story goes that a treacherous Druid betrayed the chief and his two sons, to whom only the secret of the drink was known. One son promised to reveal the secret, if his father and brother were first thrown off the cliffs, to prevent them witnessing his treachery. This request was duly obliged and then the remaining son flung himself off, shouting that the secret would die with him.

At **Port Logan** on the western side of the peninsula, sits a small fishing village where we were interested to see a tidal pool on the bay. This was built in 1800 by a McDougall laird as an artificial sea-water larder to keep himself supplied with cod. The pool is thirty feet deep and fifty three feet in circumference. The cod today however, have no worse fate than being fed by hand and are so tame that they rise to the surface whenever a bell is rung.

On the road back up towards Sandhead we passed **Ardwell House**. Here there are more lovely gardens and we were able to enjoy walking around the two attractive ponds which look out to sea.

From Sandhead, we took the B7042 which brought us to the popular holiday village of **Portpatrick**. This is the largest village on the west coast and is dominated by the impressive Victorian hotel on the cliff top. The village has the feeling of an amphitheatre about it and is in fact quite exposed to the winds and sea. There was an artificial harbour built here due to its proximity to Donaghadee, which is a mere twenty one miles over the Irish Sea. Unfortunately the harbour was constantly damaged by the elements, so trade was eventually moved to the safer haven of Stranraer.

We left Portpatrick on the B738 which took us up to Lochnaw Castle, a place we particularly wanted to visit. **Lochnaw Castle** dates back to 1426 and is one of the few 15th century castles still in existence.

Lochnaw Castle Guest House

This charming and historic country residence was for centuries the ancestral home of the Agnew family, hereditary Sheriffs of Galloway. Built along simple Norman lines, the castle stands at the very edge of the loch, unspoilt and undisturbed.

This is not just another historic building to look over. Lochnaw Castle also offers top class accommodation in its rich historical setting.

Lochnaw Castle Guest House is situated at **Leswalt**, near **Stranraer**. Throughout the whole of the year this area is one of the warmest in Britain. Its climate is conditioned by the Gulf Stream and because of this, the area is rich in subtropical foliage which mingles with acres of rhododendrons surrounding the loch, and providing a blaze of colour in springtime.

The castle is heated throughout, is exceptionally comfortable and delightfully furnished. The restaurant is open all year and is also open to non-residents. Morning and afternoon teas and coffees are available, right through to luncheon and full table d'hote dinner. Lochnaw has helped lead the trend towards organically grown, home produced food for twenty years and is noted for its simple and delicious menus. Many people therefore come here purely to enjoy good food in beautiful surroundings.

But Lochnaw is not only a unique place in which to eat, drink and sleep. There is a wide range of activities available with something to suit everyone. Fishing enthusiasts can enjoy the thrill of catching a Loch Leven trout on the castle's own forty six acre loch. There is rough shooting over one hundred and fifty acres of fields, moss beach forest and reafforestation lands. At the end of the day a good bag might include pheasant, woodcock and hare. The castle has a first class equestrian centre where riding is on novice or quality mounts with hacking available through forest or hill country. The cost is determined either by an hourly or daily rate. There is a first class squash court in the castle, and a choice of two golf courses nearby.

The castle's craft shop and boutique offers an attractive range of goods including Scottish handicrafts, with the emphasis on natural fibres like wool, silk and cotton. All facilities are available to non-residents except on Sundays.

For those who prefer to go self-catering there are three fully furnished and heated cottages available on the estate.

Situated, less than two miles away, from some wonderfully secluded sandy beaches and within an hour's drive from the beautiful Galloway mountains, Lochnaw Castle is the ideal setting for a totally self indulgent holiday, any time of the year.

Do not miss the small charming village of **Leswalt** which is close by, and why not follow the coast road up towards **Kircolm**, on the banks of Loch Ryan. We were told the legend of a ghost that at one time was said to haunt **Caldenoch Castle** on the west shore. This ghost had the rather nasty habit of seizing old women and flinging them into the water, and also would drown the voices of ministers who tried to stop its anti-social behaviour. Eventually one particularly long-winded minister proved to be too much for the ghost, causing it to utter, "Roar awa, McGregor. I can roar nae mair!"

On the north west tip of Wigtownshire, near Kircolm, you will find **The Knocknassie House Hotel**, owned and run by Stuart and Lucy Nabb. Stuart and Lucy maintain that the Knocknassie is ideal for those looking for a 'get away from it all' holiday, where relaxation and conversation with local characters is preferred to discos and nightclubing.

There are seven rooms here, all elegantly furnished in antique style. All have colour TV, tea and coffee making facilities,and three have en-suite bathrooms.

The cosy restaurant seats eighteen and here you can enjoy local Galloway beef and game, as well as some delicious seafood: plaice, trout, salmon, lobster, king prawn and scampi all come from local bays, river and fisheries. A choice selection of wines mean you can easily complement your meal with your favourite grape and vintage.

Dogs are welcome here and have their own kennels where a minder will ensure they are well looked after. The Knocknassie is the perfect place to take advantage of the great outdoors. There is sea angling, golf, pony trekking and shooting. There are several beaches nearby and you can even enjoy a boat trip around the coast.

The Knocknassie House Hotel

The house itself was once owned and lived in by Ross, of North West Passage fame, and enjoys magnificent views of rolling hills and the Irish Sea. Ireland is in fact only a ferry trip away, twenty miles across the sea.

Whether you take advantage of the facilities in nearby Stranraer, or simply relax in the hotel snooker room or cocktail lounge, each day you spend will leave you relaxed and refreshed in the capable hands of Stuart and Lucy, and the Knocknassie House Hotel.

At the head of Loch Ryan, **Stranraer** is a busy seaport which attracts many visitors each year. It is of course, as we have mentioned, the port which operates a regular ferry service to Ireland having taken over from Portpatrick. Adjacent to the ferry port in Stranraer you will find **The Downshire Arms**, an excellent place to wait for your ferry or to relax after your arrival.

The pub is popular with locals, ferry workers and passengers alike, and

145

proprietor Graeme Miller explained to us that The Downshire takes its name from the Downs of Ireland and the Shires of Scotland.

The tastefully decorated lounge bar is ideal for families and is a comfortable place to enjoy some delicious home cooking or perhaps a baked potato; Graeme has a good selection of fillings to choose from. Children are welcome in the pub until 7 pm which will be a relief for the parents among you.

The Downshire enjoys excellent sea views over the port and surrounding hills, so relax and enjoy the views in the lounge or join the locals in the bar. Here you will find the ferrymen an intriguing source of fascinating anecdotes about their life and work on the ferries. Fishing trips can be arranged in the Downshire Arms' own boat, the 'Sea Lion'.

The Downshire Arms

While the destroyed harbour in Portpatrick is a fitting testament to the power of the sea, there is a more solemn tribute in Stranraer's, **Agnew Park**, which commemorates the loss of one hundred and thirty three lives in the sinking of the ferry in 1953. Before the ferry came to Stranraer, the local people, in the 18th century, made a living from the seasonal shoals of herring in Loch Ryan, until the fish began to die out in the early 19th century.

There is a castle here and parts of it remained in use as prison cells until 1907. It was also used by John Graham of Calverhouse during his persecution of the Covenanters in the 17th century.

The earliest surviving municipal building is the former town hall of 1776. There was a guide book published in 1877 which referred to the town hall as "like some ladies - not Stranraer ladies, however - very much indebted to paint for its good looks". **The Old Town Hall** is now an interesting museum with plenty of information on local history as well as changing exhibitions. If you are looking for something to eat then why not pop along, as we did, to see John and Irene White who have plenty to offer at the **Alexandra Restaurant** in Stranraer's George Street.

The restaurant is on two levels. On the ground floor is the cafe and coffee room, open from nine in the morning for the early starters amongst you. Both are ideal for a quick snack and a welcome break during a shopping trip or the like.

On the first floor is the Alexandra's tastefully decorated restaurant, equally popular with locals and visiting television personalities. The restaurant, open until 9pm, is licensed and serves full a la carte cuisine based on traditional home cooking and baking, with some delicious fresh cream cakes and gateaux too. There is also a comprehensive wine list if you're looking for a tipple to accompany your meal. Vegetarians can easily be catered for on request and children are well looked after with high chairs and half portions.

John and Irene offer excellent value for money at the Alexandra. If you are in the vicinity for more than a few days, your first visit is sure to tempt you to return.

Alexandra Restaurant

To the east of Stranraer you will be able to visit **the gardens of Castle Kennedy** which are open to the public and are famous for their displays of rhododendrons, azaleas, magnolias and embothriums.

We travelled to the north east and passed the 16th century **Craigcaffie Castle** on our way to the small coastal village of **Cairnryan**, which, we were interested to learn, was a base in the Second World War for handling transatlantic traffic. Here too were made the parts for the Mulberry Harbour which was vital to the success of the Normandy landings in 1944. It is fascinating to think that those massive Sunderland flying-boats also used Wig Bay as a base, the remains of which can still be seen.

Ayrshire

Dean Castle Country Park

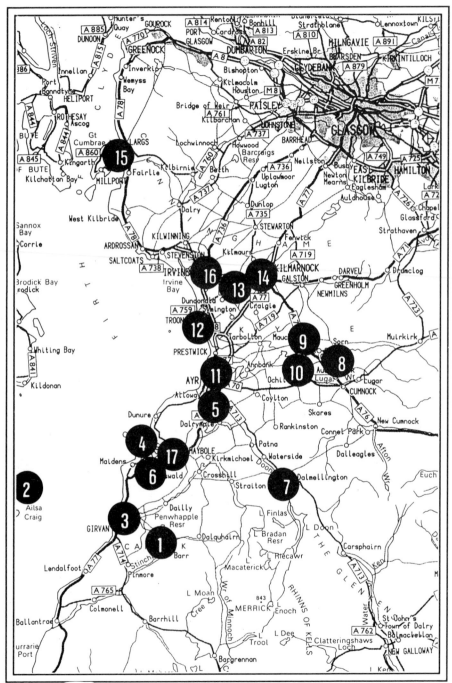

CHAPTER EIGHT

Ayrshire

Those of you familiar with Robert Louis Stevenson might recall the novel 'The Master of Ballantrae'. Although **Ballantrae** was not the setting that he used for the plot, it is, however, a pretty seaside town popular with visitors. It is also, the starting point for our visit into Ayrshire, where the river Stinchar, well known for its trout and salmon fishing, runs into the sea. At the delightful harbour, we enjoyed the sight of both fishing and pleasure boats, whilst, above the river and the old bridge, stands the ruins of **Ardstinchar Castle**. Between the coast and the rising hills is **Lendalfoot** which was once the haunt of smugglers and is dominated by the ruins of **Carleton Castle**.

Just to the north of Ballantrae lies **Bennane Head** and it was here, we are told, lived a rather nasty piece of work by the name of Sawney Bean. Apparently he and his family were cannibals and preyed on travellers passing their cave. The cave can still be visited by more intrepid visitors without, we might add, the fear of being eaten.

The small churchyard at Ballantrae bears witness to a vicious local feud that once took place between members of the Kennedy family. The Bargany Aisle in the kirkyard is a memorial to Gilbert Kennedy of Bargany who was killed in a fight with his near relative, the Earl of Cassillis, in 1601. Theirs was a family torn by conflict for over forty years, beginning when the fourth Earl of Cassillis kidnapped and roasted one Allen Stuart until the unfortunate man signed over his lands. On a later occasion, the wicked earl was only just persuaded not to blow up the castle at Ardstinchar, which was the home of the Bargany branch of the family, on the grounds that it might displease the king, not to mention cause the deaths of many innocent people. The eventual outcome was reached when the feud was ended in the High Court in Edinburgh in 1611, leaving the Earl a little chastised although still the supreme ruler in the family.

The hill on which the village of **Colmonell** sits is known as 'Knockdolian' which derives from the Gaelic words for hill, 'cnoc', and 'dall', meaning 'to mislead'. It seems that in times past the hill was mistaken by mariners, in bad weather, for Ailsa Craig which lies off the coast.

This pretty village takes its name from Saint Colmonella who died in AD 611 and the village has many old castles of interest. Nearby, there is the one time hiding place of Robert the Bruce, **Craignell**. We stopped to take a look at the marvellous view of the surrounding countryside and the river

Stinchar laid out below. The road follows roughly the passage of these waters, and we took the A714 northwards for a mile and then turned off at the B734 which, still following the course of the river, would take us to the village of **Barr**.

Barr is a charming little conservation village nestling on the banks of the River Stinchar, seven miles south of the fishing port of Girvan.

This parish is the largest in the Scottish lowlands and around sixty years ago was said to have been populated by the most sheep and fewest people! These days the hub of the village is **The Kings Arms Hotel**, a two hundred year old coaching inn where hosts, Mr and Mrs Norton, can always be relied on to provide a warm and friendly greeting, and where children are made particularly welcome.

The Kings Arms Hotel

The cosy lounge bar, complete with wood burning stove, provides comfortable surroundings in which to enjoy the excellent home cooking. A satisfying three course meal certainly won't break the bank here and the menu contains some delicious old favourites including Barnsley chops, not often seen in these days of nouvelle cuisine.

The first class wine list, with a choice of over thirty bins, should ensure you find something to provide the perfect accompaniment to your meal.

Snacks are available all day too, as well as morning coffee and afternoon teas.

Barr is an attractive village in a beautiful and peaceful setting. There is, however, a lot more to it than meets the eye. You may therefore decide to enjoy the Norton's hospitality a little longer and stay in one of their three guest rooms, all comfortably furnished and with TV, tea and coffee making facilities. You can then explore Barr and its surrounds to the full. For nature lovers the countryside abounds with bird and plant wildlife as well as being well provided with forestry walks. This part of Ayrshire is steeped in history and its days are well chronicled in Barr's village hall and parish church. The Kings Arms can certainly offer value for money, and the Nortons will ensure that your stay in Barr is as comfortable and interesting as possible.

Looking around the churchyard, we again noticed two headstones in memory of Covenanters who had died. There is also, a richly sculptured stone showing one Reverend John Campbell, whose unfortunate demise occurred in his pulpit.

At Barr, the road winds northwards and we followed it up toward the strangely named villages of **Old Dailly** and **Dailly**. The latter village grew up with the mining industry though there seems to be little evidence of this in the surrounding landscape. We have often found that a good place to look, to get some idea of the history of a place, is in the churchyard. Indeed, we were not disappointed on this occasion; evidence of this industry lies here. We came across a headstone to the memory of one John Brown, who was a sixty six year old collier who became trapped underground by a roof fall in the pit in 1835. He was eventually brought out alive after 'having been twenty three days in utter seclusion from the world and without a particle of food'. Ultimately however, John Brown only managed to survive for three days after being set free. What a constitution the man must have had!

You may not help noticing the large mausoleum of the Bargany family in the churchyard as it is as high as the church.

At Old Dailly, you will notice two large stones inside the churchyard. These were known as the Charter Stones and were used in local contests of strength to see who could lift them.

Not far away is Girvan, and it is here that we were heading to take full advantage of this renowned seaside resort. The town can boast one and a half miles of safe sandy beach, which stretches southwards from the harbour, a hive of activity and a bustling centre for the fishing fleet. We stood for a while watching the catches being landed.

There is plenty going on here, although the summer months boast a larger range of activities for visitors to enjoy, especially those located by the promenade which range from a boating lake to children's fun fair. We were able to relax here and had great pleasure from the putting greens, while the youngsters made full use of the trampolines.

At the Beach Pavilion, you might like to catch one of the many family shows, whilst children are extremely well catered for with an array of entertainments and games. If the sea is too cold for you, why not take the opportunity to make use of the excellent heated swimming pool; it is, after all, supposed to be the best form of all round exercise.

No-one looking out to sea will fail to notice the large island that is some ten miles offshore. This is **Ailsa Craig** which is the plug of an extinct volcano. A number of boatmen operate trips out to the island from the harbour and it makes for an interesting excursion. If you go, you will have a chance to see where the fine grained granite was mined to make some of the highest quality curling stones. There was even a castle perched high on the island, this was once the subject of an invasion by Hew Barclay of Ladyland, who attempted to seize the island for Philip of Spain.

Today however, the Ailsa is home to one of the largest colonies of gannets in the British Isles. If your visit coincides with low tide, you will be able to walk around the island and look up at the breeding colonies. The isle was once known as 'Paddy's Milestone' as it is thought to be located halfway between Glasgow and Belfast.

Other activities available include golf, and of course, bowling and tennis. If you take a stroll into the town, as we did, you will discover a good selection of shops and cafes, possibly not as healthy a temptation, and usually more expensive, but part of the joys of travelling are the little self indulgences, are they not?

Although the necessary town charter was granted by Charles I in 1668, Girvan is known to have been occupied since at least 5,000 BC. As late as 1961, archaeologists have been discovering more and more about Girvan's past, including a site of Bronze Age urnfields located off Coalpots Lane, east of the town.

Nowadays, as well as being a busy fishing port, Girvan plays host to many visitors who come from all over the world to explore Burns Country, and take advantage of the varied facilities available in and around this thriving Ayrshire town.

The Southfield Hotel

Whatever your interests, Christine and Peter Jones will offer a refreshing welcome at **The Southfield Hotel.** Situated in The Avenue, this imposing building is over 150 years old and was originally the first bank in Girvan. The hotel has eight comfortably furnished guest rooms, all with colour television, tea and coffee making facilities, two of which have en-suite facilities.

Christine and Peter are justifiably proud of their reputation for serving delicious home cooked dishes and vegetarian meals. We always try to find those who only use the fresh local ingredients, and here they are certainly the order of the day, to be enjoyed in the tastefully furnished dining room where you can partake of a la carte dinners and high teas. Sunday's speciality is a traditional four course roast lunch, and every day there is a satisfying selection of bar lunches and suppers from which to choose.

Your forte may be swimming, fishing, golf, bowls, tennis, shooting or simply walking. Whichever it is, participation in any of these pursuits can be arranged by the hotel for you.

Whether it's business or pleasure that brings you to Girvan, it's unlikely you'll find a more friendly or relaxed atmosphere than that offered at the Southfield Hotel.

In getting to know this lovely town, the many parks and gardens were a source of delight. You will be able to relax on a Sunday afternoon listening to the sound of the brass band, and on Thursday evenings, treat yourself to a display of Highland dancing.

We took the A719 north from Girvan which follows a delightful coast route up towards **Turnberry** where there are a few remains of a castle that was the main seat of the ancient earldom of Carrick. This was inherited by Robert the Bruce and indeed, it is believed to have been the place of this great man's birth. It is also where Bruce landed to begin his return to Scotland in 1307. The lighthouse now commands the most prominent position. We however, are familiar with Turnberry for another reason, as it is here that the famous golf course lies, which held its first Open Championship in 1977.

It is not far from the castle to one of the most famous and best examples of Scottish 'strongholds', situated in a magnificent country setting. **Culzean Castle and Country Park** is the most visited National Trust property in the world, and with the range of interests and activities it offers, it is easy to see why. In 1988 over two hundred and seventy six thousand sightseers enjoyed sampling this, one of Scotland's major tourist attractions. 1989 saw an even greater number of visitors, in what is the country park's twentieth anniversary.

The castle itself was built by Robert Adam between 1772 and 1792, and is noted for its magnificent oval staircase and round drawing room, which are now considered to be among Adam's most outstanding achievements. Of particular interest is the Eisenhower Room, the contents of which record the progress of the general's career and his close association with Culzean. The National Guest Flat, formerly General Eisenhower's holiday base in Scotland, is available for residential guest lettings of up to twelve people. Frequently used for smaller board meetings, conferences and seminars, the flat is also popular as a venue for dinner parties and wedding receptions.

Hardly a weekend passes at Culzean without there being a special attraction or entertainment, and the mix of different ocassions means that this is the ideal place for a family day out. The Classic Vehicle Show was the main event when we visited, along with numerous supporting attractions.

Of course, there are many other permanent visitor attractions at Culzean, including the exhibition, shops and Visitor Centre. A visit to the fully licensed restaurant is a must, especially if you've made your way round the deer park, swan pond, adventure playground and walled garden!

For those who wish to make the most of Scotland's first country park there is a Ranger service based at the Visitor Centre. The Rangers are invaluable in helping visitors take as much enjoyment as possible from the various guided walks available.

Culzean Castle and Country Park totals five hundred and sixty three acres in all, and almost every acre offers something for everybody, young and old alike, whether it be seashore, cliffs, ponds, deerpark, gardens or woodland areas.

It simply is not possible to come to this part of Scotland without hearing the name of Robbie Burns, and it is, of course, fitting for us to mention here Scotland's most cherished poet.

Culzean Castle & Country Park

In this area of his birth and upbringing there are many places that associate themselves with the man and the country, which has become known as Burn's Country. So let us talk a little of this renowned figure who is so much a part of the landscape.

It was in the small village of **Alloway** that William and Agnes Burnes (the name was later adapted to Burns by the poet) were married and settled down to make a home. On the 25th of January 1759, Agnes gave birth to their first son, whom they named Robert. The cottage at Alloway is now preserved in much the way it was during their time and is a shrine for those interested in the poet, as it houses a fine collection of furniture, books and personal possessions associated with him. As the family grew, they leased a farm called Mount Oliphant that lay some two miles above Ayr.

Although quite poor they were well educated for the time and Robert was sent to school at Alloway Mill each day. Eventually the family brought in a tutor, shared with the neighbours, to educate the children further, and it was under the influence of this tutor that Robert received his first introduction to literature and grammar. It is generally accepted that Burns had a reasonable education and this, combined with the influence of his mother's love of traditional song and the tales and stories of those who visited the house, helped to form the basis of the stories and poems that he was to make so famous.

Most of the family's time was spent working on the small farm and indeed the work was quite hard on them all, with his father being over fifty and showing the signs of a hard life's work. There was a girl, called Nelly Kilpatrick, with whom Burns worked when he was fifteen during the harvest. He seems to have become enthralled by her and for the first time he committed to verse his feelings of love.

Burns continued his education where he could and spent some time with his teacher, then a period in Kirkoswald receiving not only education in books but also in life, learning about smuggling tales in the local public houses. Many of Burn's relatives lived in the locality and it is thought that some of them were probably involved in smuggling. Again he fell in love, this time with a lass by the name of Peggy Thomson who, according to the young man himself, thoroughly distracted him from his work.

Life at home had become no easier, and the family were forced to move to yet another farm where the living was not much better. Robert gathered about him a new set of friends and acquaintances, not always to his father's approval.

He became a Freemason and played a large part in forming the Tarbolton Bachelors Club, which was a debating and literature society run by the poet and his friends. It is around this time that Robert's friends began to notice the poet's charm and ease when he was with the fairer sex, an ability that he was to make the most of throughout his life.

His father died after a lengthy law suit had taken its toll on his health and Robert became the head of the family, moving with them to a another farm a few miles away at Mauchline. His attempts at being a farmer were not however a success, although the poetry that he wrote during this period was considered to be some of his best work.

Subjects chosen by Burns for his work would range greatly, from romance, to comments on the people and the world around him, to hard satire on life in the eighteenth century. His own life was further complicated when a girl by the name of Elizabeth Paton, brought in to help in the house, fell under his spell and bore his child.

Soon after this event, another local lass called Jean Armour was expecting Burns' child and, although he pledged to marry, her father broke the couple up, sending her away to live with relatives. Burns thought it prudent to leave Scotland for a while and planned to go to Jamaica. In order to raise funds for his journey, he decided to publish his poems to pay for his passage. The publication of his work, however, changed everything for him as, when 'Poems Chiefly in the Scottish Dialect' appeared in 1786, it was an immediate success, receiving praise from layman and intellectual alike.

Burns became the toast of Edinburgh, and by all accounts enjoyed his reputation, as there were a string of affairs. With two more volumes in print and successful tours behind him, Burns married Jean Armour, who was again expecting a child by him, and they moved to the farm at Ellisand near Dumfries. This we have mentioned in a previous part of this book.

Robert Burns died at the age of thirty seven and his life story is one of both tragedy and romance, and yet full of colourful character. It is his honesty and ability to express himself that people find endearing the world over. He has come to represent the vitality and spirit of this corner of Scotland,and is an important part of its living history.

Burns characters at Souter Johnnie's Cottage

Our journey has reached the village of **Kirkoswald**. We have already talked about Burns' links with this place as he was here studying Surveying for a short period. You may still visit Souter Johnnie's Cottage which was built in 1785, and occupied by John Davidson the shoemaker. Robert Burns took the real man and turned him into an immortal character of fiction in his celebrated poem 'Tam O'Shanter'. Douglas Graham, the actual model for Tam O'Shanter lies buried, as does John Davidson, in the old parish churchyard.

We were fascinated to find that the ancient font, discovered at Chapel

Donan and now in the kirkyard at Kirkoswald, is rumoured to have been used for the baptism of Robert the Bruce.

Almost two hundred years ago Burns himself wrote about the Kirkoswald hostelry, **Kirkton Jean's**, in his poem Tam O'Shanter. Since then Kirkoswald has been put firmly on the Burns heritage trail, and Kirkton Jean's today is a popular watering hole for those exploring and living in Burns country.

Proprietors, Derek and Maureen Braid, took over this historic inn in June 1988 and have since completely refurbished the dining room, lounge bar and all nine of the guest rooms. All the bed rooms have en-suite shower, toilet and washhand basin plus colour television, tea and coffee making facilities.

Kirkton Jeans Hotel

The cosy dining room is traditionally furnished and here you can eat from an excellent a la carte menu offering a selection of imaginative and mouth watering dishes, including the chef's speciality, Beef Wellington. The table d'hote menu is ideal for those looking for some traditional Scottish fayre, or try a bar lunch or supper; everything on the menu represents excellent value for money.

The Braids have created a charming beer garden which proves extremely popular in the summer.

With so many local courses in the area, Kirkton Jean's makes a super base for a golfing holiday. Call Derek before you arrive and he may be able to provide you with details of any golfing packages available.

There can be no doubt about this hotel's popularity with Burns and his cronies in the 18th century, but it is also evident that, thanks to the commitment of Derek and Maureen, Kirkton Jean's remains the place to eat and stay whilst here.

The A77 took us out of Kirkoswald and towards the town of **Maybole**. We passed the fine ruins of **Crossraguel Abbey** on the way and we were impressed by the state of preservation which gives an interesting insight into life in this 13th century settlement. The abbots who lived here apparently made the most of the plentiful seabirds who nested on Ailsa Craig, as they were often served here on the dinner table. It was the unfortunate owner of the lands of Crossraguel after the Reformation, Alan Stewart, who was himself basted and roasted by Gilbert Kennedy.

An interesting note about the monks who lived here was that they actually minted their own pennies and farthings. Not surprisingly, these coins are much sought after by collectors.

Maybole Castle, at the town itself, was the stronghold of the Kennedys and their descendants now occupy **Cassillis House** which is situated four miles north east of Maybole, high above the river Doon. The position of Maybole is somewhat lofty, set two hundred to three hundred feet above sea level. The town is the fifth largest in Ayrshire and commands a wonderful view of the area. Apart from visiting the castle, the town offers splendid opportunities for walks as well as a golf course and an indoor heated swimming pool.

We were now not far from Ayr; however we wanted to take in a little more of this wonderful countryside and decided to follow the B7023 from Maybole, which would take us down towards **Dalmellington**. We travelled slowly, taking our time to look at the pretty villages of **Crosshill** and then **Straiton**.

Dalmellington makes an excellent base for exploring the river Doon, immortalised by Burns in verse. Its source is at Loch Doon and we spent an enjoyable day with a picnic on its shores. The road actually follows the shoreline of the loch and provides ample opportunity to just stretch your legs, or perhaps take up the challenge of a more invigorating walk.

The castle here dates from the early fourteenth century, though you may be surprised to learn that it has actually been removed from its original site on an island in the middle of the loch. This ambitious scheme was undertaken as the waters of the loch were raised in the 1930's, and the castle was removed to the west bank to prevent it being lost forever. This must have been quite a task, since the walls are seven to nine feet thick. The island can still be seen from time to time as the water level tends to fluctuate.

The loch has been the base for a number of madcap schemes, one of which was the siting of a gunnery school during the First World War. You can still see the remains of the concrete blocks which carried the monorail target for the school. More recently, in 1978, the area was targeted by the nuclear industry for the deposition of nuclear waste. It is thanks to the vigilance of the locals, who fought tooth and nail, that the scheme was abandoned to let us enjoy the peace and calm of this beautiful place today.

Cathcartson Interpretation Centre in the centre contains an interesting display of weaving, mining and other aspects of the area's industry and the town is full of fascinating buildings from the eighteenth and nineteenth centuries.

The B741 continues through the area of **Kyle Forest** and gave us some lovely views as we made our way towards the A76 and the village of **New Cumnock**. Only recently, thanks to a prolonged dry weather spell, was it realised that the Romans used this road on their way to the Clyde from Hadrian's Wall, nearly two thousand years ago. Ariel photographs revealed a hitherto unknown batch of forts along the road. Underneath this area ran rich coal seams that provided much of these towns with their industry for many years.

Turning left at New Cumnock, we travelled for six miles on the A76 to the village of **Cumnock**. We were fascinated to learn that this town was once famous for the manufacture of snuff boxes. James Kier Hardy, regarded as the founder of the Labour Party, lived here and built himself a house nearby.

We were intending to travel north towards the town of Mauchline, but our curiosity for exploring out of the way places made us turn off on the B743 and head for the little village of **Sorn**. We can well advise you to pay a visit to this picturesque village. This really is a most attractive place, nestling as it does on the banks of the River Ayr and with a peaceful atmosphere all of its own.

In 1976, Sorn was voted Best Kept Village in Britain and you will understand why when you see how charming and beautifully cared for the village and its houses are. **The Sorn Hotel** is no exception, with its whitewashed elevations and traditional country inn appearance.

The Sorn Hotel

The Sorn is over two hundred years old and today is personally owned and run by Tony and Toni Smith. They offer guests the choice of eight comfortably furnished bedrooms, all with tea and coffee making facilities. The dining room exudes an intimate atmosphere, for here you eat in snug booths containing beautifully polished mahogany tables. Home cooking and traditional fare is graciously provided, and there are some excellent Scotch steaks.

This is a popular little restaurant with the locals though, so if it is simply a meal you're coming for, we strongly advise you to book a table beforehand.

If you're looking for a quick nip or perhaps something to relax with after your meal, enjoy a drink in one of the Sorn's four bars, or try your hand at a game of pool or darts with the locals.

The Smiths are happy to provide assistance with children, who are always welcome here, and you can even bring the dog if you discuss the arangements before your arrival. They can also arrange permits for shooting in the area and for fishing in the River Ayr, which flows directly past The Sorn.

The B743 takes us firmly back into Burns country as the town of **Mauchline** was immortalised by the poet. It was near here that the family moved after his father's death and to which Burns returned to live with his new wife, Jean Armour, who came from the town.

We paid a visit to the room where the couple first abided, as the house on Castle Street is now the **Burns House Museum**. There is a wonderful collection of memorabilia here. We were saddened by the sight of the graves of four of Burns' daughters in Mauchline churchyard. Across the road is **Poosie Nansie's ale house**, which inspired 'The Jolly Beggars' and is still in use today.

Did you know that at one time Mauchline was a centre for the manufacture of curling stones? Well, evidence of this and other local industries may also be seen in exhibits at the museum.

Burns House Museum

While you are here, take some time out for a walk to a spectacular local site, and one of Scotland's most magnificent river scenes. Follow the A76 south to where the road crosses the river Ayr. Use the old, two arched bridge to make a descent which will take you on a path to the river along the rim of the **Ballochmyle Gorge** and under the railway viaduct. We're sure you will agree that the view of sweeping woodlands and the river far below is breathtaking. The viaduct itself is of interest as a great feat of engineering, being the highest railway bridge in Britain, at 51 metres, and the main span also having the longest masonry arch railway bridge in Britain, being 55 metres in length.

Following the road back to Mauchline, we turned west onto the A758 passing through the hamlet of **Failford** where there is a monument commemorating the last meeting between Burns and his lover, 'Highland Mary', who died the following autumn. There is a path from Failford that leads you to Stair through some charming countryside in the **Ayr Gorge Woodlands Wildlife Reserve**.

Whether you make the trip on foot or drive via the B730, we recommend that you find time to discover this pretty little village. Here, standing on the banks of the river Ayr, is **The Stair Inn**. A listed building of considerable character and dating back to around 1670, this is a traditional country hostelry situated in a beautiful conservation area. We were greeted by a inviting atmosphere, a cosy log fire, and the sort of warm welcome that makes visitors feel at home as soon as they step into the bar. Pictures of Robert Burns adorn the walls reminding you that this inn was frequented by the poet in his lifetime.

Hosts, Mr and Mrs Cameron, offer comfortable accommodation in two guest rooms which can be let as single, double, twin or family. Reduced rates are available for children and also for those enjoying week long holidays.

The Stair Inn

Residents and customers of The Stair Inn regularly enjoy a weekly ceilidh where an accordionist plays traditional Scottish and Irish music, as well as some good old golden oldies to dance or sing along to.

Neighbouring the inn are the farmlands and woodlands of the Earl of Stair, and just across the river is the only hone stone mine works remaining in Britain. This still produces the celebrated Tam O'Shanter and Water of Ayr hone stones.

In the past the inn was used for church services when the local church roof leaked. After the service, every member of the congregation received a jar of ale and it's been said that these were the best attended services ever!

The Stair Inn is well situated for visiting the many local attractions of historical interest as well as being only a short distance from the famous Troon and Turnberry golf courses. International travellers will find it easy to reach the hospitality of Mr and Mrs Cameron since it is only a short drive from Prestwick airport. Hidden in the heart of the Poet's land, this is truly a gem and one that all visitors to this beautiful part of Ayrshire should make a point of seeking out.

We rejoined the A758 and made our way slowly to the principle town in Burns country, **Ayr**. We had heard that there would be much to see and do here and indeed we were not disappointed.

This busy resort is one of the most popular and beautiful on the west coast of Scotland. The town has developed from settlements in Roman times, but always retained an attraction due to its extensive sandy beaches, golf courses and many recreational activities. You may choose to enjoy some of the traditional seaside entertainments or perhaps walk around the many excellent, colourful parks in the town. Here, of course, is the famous racecourse which hosts meetings throughout the year. We used the opportunity to catch up on some shopping as here we found a good range of shops. The evening can be entertainingly spent with a visit to one of the two theatres.

Ayr has a history of trading and markets, and there is a busy fish market at the South Harbour which makes an interesting visit. Today the Ayrshire Agricultural Show takes place every year in April. Around 1900, the cattle market in Ayr was relocated to its present site in the town's Castlehill Road. Here you will find the aptly named**Market Inn**, a well known watering hole for Ayrshire landowners and farmers seeking refreshment after a hard morning's bargaining.

The Market Inn

Farmers, as you know, are famed for having an eye for value, and it's worth following their example by trying out the Market Inn rather than the town centre with its parking problems.

The inn, owned and run by the Morris brothers, still boasts its original mahogany horseshoe bar and on the gantry you will see a fine selection of malt whiskies, you will spy many a rare and fascinating bottle.

There are two dining rooms serving traditional Scottish food and the Burns decor surrounding the rooms adds to the brightness and gaiety of a family atmosphere. The family room is a bonus for parents, and of course there is a special children's menu for the younger members of the family.

Bar meals are available too and, with the average meal costing under £3, it's easy to see why the Market Inn is so popular with the farming community.

There are two bridges that cross the river. The Auld Brig and New Bridge were written about by Burns in 'The Brigs of Ayr' where he correctly forecasted that the old bridge would outlast the new. In the poem, the Old Brig says to the New; "I'll be a brig when ye're a shapeless cairn". Indeed, the New bridge fell down in a storm in 1870. The connections between Ayr and Burns are very strong, especially as Alloway, where the poet was born, is now a suburb of the town, though it was once separated by two miles of countryside. Visitors to Alloway are able to go to another **Burns Interpretation Centre**, this permanent exhibition, like the other mentioned before, displays events, characters and memories of the life of the poet. Nearby you will be able to see the cottage where he was born and spent the first five years of his life.

We were interested to visit the **Auld Brig O'Doon** where the chase in the epic poem 'Tam O'Shanter' took place. The story in the poem is an interesting one, for those who have read it, indulge us whilst we try in brief to capture its content, for those who have not.

A farmer who had been to Ayr on market day was delayed by business until, by the time he left to cross the river Doon and reached Alloway, it was the hour of wizards, between night and morning. As he came to the gate of the kirkyard, he was surprised to see, through an old gothic window, a dance of witches. The farmer recognised many of their faces as those of local women, and was taken by surprise to see one particular female of his acquaintance dancing around in a smock that was somewhat too short. Unable to stop himself, his humour got the better of his senses and he burst out in a loud laugh.

The farmer recovering from his impetuous laughter, took saner council with himself judging a hasty retreat across the bridge would be prudent, sharing in the common belief that no power could pursue him once across a running stream. Fortunately for the farmer, the Doon was not far away and he reached the middle of the bridge as one of the pursuing witches caught up with him, and sprang to seize him. She was, however, too late and the only thing caught in her grasp, as she stood on her side of the bank was the tail of Tam O'Shanter's horse, which had given way as he escaped across the water. The farmer, now safe, was able to warn all others not to stay too late in the Ayr Markets!

As we left the fair city of Ayr, we were lucky enough to discover **Crofthead Caravan Park**. This is conveniently but peacefully situated just off the Ayr bypass, and can be found by following the caravan site signs about a mile along the A70 out of Ayr.

Crofthead makes an unbeatable base for touring as you can easily head north to Troon and further to the Ardrossan ferry terminal for Arran or south to trace the Burns Heritage trail. Ayr itself is only two miles away so you are also within easy distance of its beautiful beach and lively shopping centres.

Proprietors, Margaret and Vic Borland, originally come from Edinburgh but have settled in Ayrshire after moving up here from the south of England, where Vic held down a high powered job involving a great deal of international travel. Now they have decided to take life at a slower pace opting for the tranquillity of this particular Ayrshire spot.

Crofthead Caravan Park

Crofthead Caravan Park sits in ten acres of green countryside with facilities for static vans, touring vans and campers. On site you will find the facilities are comprehensive and include a shop with an off licence, showers, laundry and a public telephone. There is a large grass play area for children and if you do get a wet day at some point during your stay, never fear, for there is an excellent recreation building.

Ayr itself is of course well served with facilities. There are beautiful gardens at Belleisle, theatres and cinemas and popular activities include wind surfing, horse riding, sailing, swimming, ice skating, fishing and of course golf.

The Caravan Park is beautifully situated and enjoys a handsome view of the Ayrshire hills and beyond, offering the delights of scenic rivers and countryside. With the option of Ayr, being so close by, and the picturesque tranquility of Crofthead, here you can enjoy the best of both worlds.

As far back as the beginning of the 18th century the attractions of coastal towns like **Troon** were becoming clear to those who lived in the cities and industrial areas. Indeed, Troon was considered at the time to possess "an excellent situation for sea bathing". We are happy to report that on this count Troon is unchanged, and this small fishing town is still a popular holiday resort that can boast two miles of soft, sandy beaches stretching from either side of the harbour.

The harbour itself is a fascinating place with much going on. We strolled down by the marina to watch the yachts arriving and berthing. Anglers were trying their luck but we were far more interested in exploring all the nooks and crannies of the many rock pools.

The Anchorage Hotel

We enjoyed a walk into town to find momentoes of our visit and for a general browse around the shops. These, together with cafes and restaurants are ideally situated, with a wide range suitable for most tastes. The Anchorage Hotel in Templehill is the oldest licensed premises in Troon, dating back as it does to 1812. It was originally built by the Duke of Portland as a coaching inn to service the harbour traffic, and was then known as the Portland Arms Inn.

It was here in 1878 that Royal Troon Golf Club and its constitution was established. Troon is of course a Mecca for golfers and boasts some of the finest golf links in the world. Royal Troon Golf Club has hosted the Open championship on numerous occassions, most recently in 1989, and the course itself is only a short distance from the Anchorage.

You will certainly appreciate the comfort and personal attention provided in this family run hotel. The welcoming Fo'c's'le Bar offers a fine selection of traditional ales, wines and malt whiskies; apparently the largest selection of real ales and single malts in Ayrshire.

Food is traditionally Scottish, prepared to a very high standard and of course includes some excellent fish dishes. Bar lunches are served during the day and certainly represent excellent value for money. If you have something special to celebrate or are perhaps looking for a suitable conference venue, then you may well find the Anchorage's recently refurbished function suite, which can cater for up to ninety, an ideal choice.

Accommodation at the Anchorage comprises fourteen comfortably furnished guest rooms, all with private bathroom, colour television and telephone.

There is no shortage of things to do in Troon and its surrounds. The hotel staff here will gladly arrange visits to nearby places of historical interest such as Culzean Castle. Riding stables and a beautiful sandy beach are located nearby, and fresh water and sea fishing trips can easily be arranged: another example of the efficient and personal attention you will find here at the Anchorage Hotel.

The delights and attractions of Troon and other towns on the west coast began to draw the trippers from towns such as **Kilmarnock**. They would arrive here on the steam railway that ran between the two towns. We found out that it was the development of the harbour in Troon that led to the arrival of one of the earliest steam passenger railways in the world.

It was the Duke of Portland who pioneered its development as a way of transporting coal mined on his lands at Kilmarnock. Before the engines came however, wagonloads of coal were pulled by a team of horses, and on summer Saturdays the wagons were scrubbed out to bring passengers from Kilmarnock to Troon and the coastal resorts. A silver model of the locomotive 'The Duke' was made for the silver wedding of the 6th Duke and Duchess and can be seen in Troon Town Hall.

We also noticed 'The Duke' on the coat of arms on the lamps outside. On the edge of the town is the Fullerton Estate which was once owned by the Duke, and makes a delightful spot for walking and is an ideal place for enjoying a picnic.

The main route out of Troon to the east is the A759, and we left the town on this road which runs through Loans and then crosses the Dundonald Hills. We stopped and marvelled at the lovely views and imagined that they would be spectacular at sunset.

We passed through the village of **Dundonald** which developed beside the site of the castle, dating from 1390. The street of houses near this castle are quite picturesque and we stopped to have a look at the beautiful 19th century church.

At Gatehead, the road crosses the railway line and we turned in towards Kilmarnock. At Gatehead we found **Laigh Milton Mill**.

As its name suggests, this listed building is an old mill which sits on the River Irvine and has now been partly converted into a first class restaurant.

The Mill has fishing rights on the river itself and opposite is an excellent example of an old railway viaduct, and in fact one of the first railway bridges to be built in Scotland. We recommend you take the opportunity to see this splendid example of railway architecture, since bridges like these are certainly disappearing rapidly in Britain today.

The Yildirim brothers are owners here and, although they have a Turkish background, they specialise in continental cuisine. The emphasis here is on French and Italian dishes, with flambe meals which are prepared for you at the table. There is also a comprehensive selection of wines to choose from ensuring that you find something to accompany the adventurous recipes on offer. Vegetarians are well catered for too and for those who are looking for a light snack, bar meals may be partaken of at lunch and dinner times.

Laigh Milton Mill Restaurant

Laigh Milton Mill is open lunchtimes as well as evenings although, according to plans in hand, the Yildirim brothers will soon be catering for visitors on an even grander scale than now. They intend to turn the rest of their building into a sixteen bedroom hotel with banqueting hall, sauna and jacuzzi.

If the owners' skills as hoteliers are as well developed as those they so obviously have as restauranteurs, then clients can certainly be assured of an enjoyable stay.

It is not far from here into **Kilmarnock** and we were keen to take a look around this interesting town. You may remember that the first edition of Burns' poetry was printed here and became known as the 'Kilmarnock' edition. In Burns' day the town was full of handloom weavers who lived and worked in their cottages. The industrial heritage has continued throughout the years, and today Kilmarnock is a busy producer of many goods. Not the least of these was the target of our first visit: the **Johnie Walker Bottling Plant**. We were taken on a very enjoyable tour of the plant, which gave us a fascinating insight into the production of this world famous whisky. After the tour we were also pleased to enjoy the free dram.

Just off the Kilmarnock bypass, north of the town centre, we discovered

Dean Castle Country Park. This is the sort of place where the whole family can spend a super day out for there's a variety of activities to while away the hours. Apart from an adventure playground woodland walks, children's corner and riding school, there is Dean Castle itself with its dungeons and museum.

Dean Castle Country Park

The stronghold dates back to around 1360 when the main keep was built to defend the lands of the Boyd family, lords of Kilmarnock. The castle then expanded along with the fortunes of the Boyds, until fire destroyed all but the shell of this once powerful family seat.

Now run by Kilmarnock and Loudon District Council, Dean castle was superbly restored to its original grandeur by the 8th Howard de Walden, and houses his collection of European arms, armour and tapestries. There is also the Van Raalte collection of early musical instruments. There is, furthermore, exhibits and displays of medieval life, plus, of course, various artefacts from the life and works of none other than, Robert Burns.

Dean Castle Country Park operates a Countryside Ranger service, should you wish to learn more about the many species of surrounding wildlife. The aim of the Rangers is to create an awareness in visitors as to how they can make the most of their countryside and its wildlife, for example by observance of the Country Code. For guided walks they are indispensable, and for curious children an absolute necessity. Rangers can be found throughout the park between 9.00 am and 9.00 pm during the main visitor season.

The castle's newest venture is its children's corner. This is still being developed but even now houses over seventy animals, including birds, chickens, rabbits, ducks, sheep and goats. More than enough to keep the average youngster amused.

Once you've seen everything Dean Castle has to offer its likely you'll almost have walked your feet off, we certainly had. The sight of the castle's tea rooms was the most welcome of the day!

Regardless of the seasons, there's plenty here to see and do. Dean Castle Country park should certainly not be left out of your arrangements when you're in Ayrshire.

Travelling to London Road we came across the **Dick Institute**. This contains Kilmarnock's main library with a museum and art collection that has many fine paintings, including work by Constable, Corot, Turner and members of the Glasgow School, as well as housing a variety of exhibitions throughout the year.

We took the A71 from Kilmarnock which led us to the town of Irvine, close to the coast this is a wonderful place for a day out. Many of Irvine's activities are based around the attractions of the sea, and one of the most popular is the **Magnum Leisure Complex**. This dominates the harbour area and its features are too many for a complete list but include swimming pools, an ice rink, bowls hall, theatre, cinema, sauna and solarium, plus many other activities inside and outside in the two hundred and fifty acre beach park. We are sure that you will enjoy your time with such a magnificent choice.

A covered shopping mall spans the river connecting the town to the harbour area. In the latter is the **Scottish Maritime Museum**, which includes a shipyard worker's flat, which has been restored to its original 1910 decor. We were delighted to find some fine historic ships moored in the harbour, which we were actually allowed aboard.

Nearby, we paid an enchanting visit to **'Sea World'** which creates an underwater environment for observing marine life, housed in special tanks, ranging from sea anemones and starfish to lobsters and even giant conger eels.

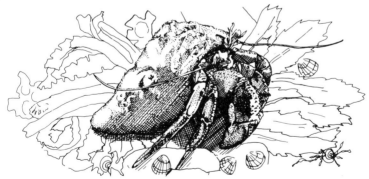

Hermit Crab at Sea World

Back in the town it was fascinating to walk along the narrow cobbled streets of old Irvine, as we looked at some fine examples of 18th and 19th century buildings. Nearby **Glasgow Vennel** was once the main route to Glasgow, though now is traffic free, and was recently the winner of an award for its restoration. Being in the heart of Burns country, you will not be surprised to learn that the Poet came here in 1781, not to pen his verse though but to learn the flax dressing trade. The buildings where he worked, and stayed for two years, are now some two hundred year later, home to the Ayrshire Writers and Artists Society. We took a look at his attic bedroom which is open to visitors and located at number four.

On the opposite side of the house is the **Buchanite meeting house** which was once occupied by an infamous religious sect, led by one Elizabeth Buchan. The agricultural revolution in the late 18th century brought many country folk in to the towns in a desperate search for work. This led to an increase in the general instability and a result of this was the flourishing of religious cults. The most unusual of these were the Buchanites who set up their sect in Irvine.

Elizabeth Buchan talked of the second coming of the Messiah when she and her followers would be taken up to heaven. The townspeople of Irvine were rather taken aback by all this and promptly ran the lady and her followers out of town.

The young novelist, John Galt, later recalled the scene as the psalm singing band of men and women left for Closeburn to await their ascendancy at the appointed hour. Apparently when the time arrived, the Buchanites built three large platforms one of which was higher than the other two, for the special use of Mrs Buchan. The followers had shaved their heads with the exception of a small tuft of hair by which they might be grasped to ease their ascendancy, and mounted the platforms in anticipation. As a breeze sprang up, this was taken to be the sign of the angels coming as their wings were beating in the air. Unfortunately, the ceremonious ascent was marked by nothing more uplifting than the disturbing downfall of the platforms, sending the confused occupants rather violently to the ground.

Coming out of Irvine, the road took us north to nearby **Kilwinning**, where we heard of the strange ancient custom of 'shooting the papingo'. We were intrigued and wanted to learn more. We discovered that a Papingo, or wooden bird on a pole, is set up as a target from the clock tower of the Abbey Church for the Ancient Society of Kilwinning Archers to test their skills. This annual shoot is re-enacted each year, and the table gravestones beside the church have been chipped by the arrows that presumably have missed the papingo! There is a magnificent Silver Arrow Trophy dating back to 1724 that is displayed in the town's library.

From Kilwinning we drove to **Saltcoats** and neighbouring **Ardrossan**, on the coast. Saltcoats, as its name suggests, developed a salt panning industry established here by James V in the 16th century. The harbour was built in the 17th century and coal would come here via a canal for export to Ireland. Since the development of the harbour at Ardrossan however, the use of Saltcoats as a working port declined and only small boats are seen here today, although the place is very popular with holiday makers.

Keep an eye open at low tide in the harbour for you will see the fossilized remains of tree trunks here.

The tower above the school is the **Martello Tower**. We were interested to learn that it was once a gun position to protect the mines from French warships during the Napoleonic Wars. Saltcoats and Ardrossan are divided by the **Stanley Burn** and we crossed to take a look at this 19th century town. There has in fact been a castle here since the 12th century, though, despite its seemingly strong position it was captured by Cromwell, who used its stones to build his castle in Ayr.

There was a very ambitious plan to connect the port and harbour at Ardrossan with Glasgow by linking the two with a canal. Both Telford and Rennie were engaged on the construction. Unfortunately their funding ran out in 1815 and the plan was abandoned. Had it gone ahead the town of Ardrossan might have been a very different place.

Androssan became important for its ferry crossings to the Isle of Arran and to Belfast, and has since developed into a popular resort boasting sandy beaches to rival the best of the west coast.

You will notice **Horse Island** just off the coast and not surprisingly this is a bird sanctuary.

Tempting though it was to take the ferry to Arran, we wanted to save this pleasure until we had explored the region of North Ayrshire a little more. With this pleasurable task in mind we made our way slowly up towards **West Kilbride** on the A78. We doubt if there is a coast road that will take you closer to the sea than this.

We found a local pub in the town and enjoyed some refreshment before journeying inland on the B781 towards the town of Dalry. On the road we came across **Blackshaw Farm Park**, which we found is a working farm where visitors can see real farming techniques at first hand, and enjoy a variety of demonstrations.

Ayrshire Cow at Blackshaw Farm Park

We heard that in North Ayrshire it was common for milk to be turned into 'Dunlop' cheese. The practice, until the early part of this century, was for every dairy farm to make its own cheese from the daily milk, over and above that required by the locality. The increasing sophistication of the storage and transport of milk brought relief of an arduous task for many a farmwife! The Scots eventually tried to export the cheese to England, it unfortunately suffered from more common connotations of the word Dunlop! The cheese was eventually renamed Scottish Cheddar.

The town of **Dalry** is situated on the River Garnock and was developed principally as a weaving town in the 18th century.

We walked around the grounds of nearby **Blair estate** which is to the south east of the town. The house here is quite interesting, it is based around an ancient tower and later developed into a T-shaped plan with three and four storeys. The estate is surrounded by a wall, and there are attractive lodges and an interesting smithy worth looking at.

The Dusk Water flows through the estate and for those of you interested in caves, we suggest a trip to **Cleaves Cove** on the south bank of the water. Excavations here in 1883 show that the caves were inhabited in prehistoric times! These are a series of limestone caves and contain some well known stalactites.

If, like us, you are entranced by the beauty of waterfalls then go to the **Caaf Water** to the south-west of Dalry. Here we followed a path alongside the stream that led us to another fine waterfall and the remains of a mill.

The road up towards **Largs** is extremely picturesque and we drove slowly, absorbing the beauties of both **Camphill** and **Muirhead Reservoirs** which are next to the A760.

Largs faces directly onto the sea, with a stony beach. It was here in 1263 that the Scots defeated an invasion force of Norse invaders, and in 1912 the "Pencil", a distinctive monument on the coast of the Southern end of Largs, was erected to commemorate the victory. In September each year, a Viking festival is held where, strange though it may seem, many Scandinavian entertainers return to celebrate the Vikings only defeat on mainland Scotland.

There are many types of accommodation available in Largs, to suit all pockets. We had decided to spend a few days at the **Elderslie Hotel**, a listed building at Broomfields. The hotel is situated on the sea front, with superb views to the Isle of Cumbrae, and beyond to Arran, which would be our next port of call.

The Elderslie, recommended by all the major guides, has a unique and fascinating feature, which you won't notice at first but which will certainly make you look twice! The chimneys of the hotel are probably some of the most important and interesting in Scotland. They are built as pawns, with the gabled ends carved as knights and bishops, the roof being the chess board.

After a very warm greeting by the staff, the manager explained the history of the Elderslie to us, over a quiet drink in one of the comfortable lounges.

The Elderslie Hotel

Originally, the building was erected as two houses in the 1830's. The main house was built as a holiday home for a Glasgow tobacco baron, whose extravagent, eccentric nature perhaps explains the Chess Set roof. The Elderslie has been a hotel now since the turn of the century, the two houses being joined together in 1912. During the war the house was taken over by Supreme Allied Command.   Lord Mountbatten spent some time here recuperating from injury in what is now Room 2 of the hotel.

The hotel provides 25 bedrooms of which 13 are en-suite. All have central heating, tea-making facilities, T.V. and radio. Ours was extremely comfortable.

We found the food first class. Traditional Scottish fayre is served with "Taste of Scotland" dishes which proved excellent value for money. Local fresh produce is used wherever possible to ensure a varied menu which is changed daily. A facility all patrons can enjoy, at no extra charge, is a walk in the gardens which we found very relaxing.

We can, therefore, recommend the Elderslie to anyone looking for home comforts in elegant surroundings. It ishotel which has retained so many of the traditional values we so rarely see today. You can be sure of the best attention from Mr. Pratt, who gives as much of his energy and experience into the running of his hotel, as he does in his role as Secretary of St Mirren Football Club!"

We travelled south of Largs and spent the day at the historic estate of **Kelburn,** located on the A78 between Largs and Fairlie. **Kelburn Castle** makes an impressive background here and there is much to do in the lovely grounds for all of the family

Whether you want to enjoy the islands or the attractions of the Clyde with its perfect conditions for sailing activities, or merely just to tour around the winding country roads of the region, you will find as we did that North Ayrshire is an ideal place, with Largs being a good centre for all these things.

Kelburn Castle

Visitors can easily travel to Glasgow, for the city is not far from here, alternatively you may decide, as we did, that The Isle of Arran or the Isle of Bute would be exciting places to visit and this is where we shall be heading in the next chapter.

Burns Monument, Alloway

The Isles of Arran, Cumbrae and Bute

Brodick Castle

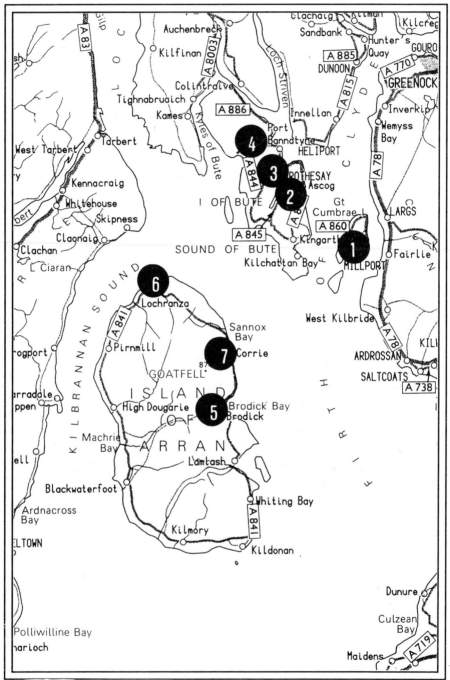

Please turn to Reference Section for further information.

CHAPTER NINE

Arran

Largs is an ideal centre for the touring of North Ayrshire but it is also the place to cross the water to visit **Great Cumbrae Island**, which lies between the Isle of Bute and the mainland. We took the boat over to the island from Largs, and were able to cycle round and explore this fascinating place witnessing some superb views of Scotland from the highest point, the Glaidstane

Millport, on the south side of the island, proved to be a friendly town where we looked around and purchased some mementoes of our visit. There are good pubs here, and we spent a while gazing at the smallest cathedral in Europe, which came as a delightful surprise to discover in Millport.

We found the island to be a very pleasant place and it makes for an excellent outing. Those of you who enjoy a taste for more active pastimes might like to take advantage of the **National Watersports Centre**. You can opt for wide choice of tuition courses in a variety of watersports for beginners and enthusiasts alike. Watching the children down by the sea, it brought back warm memories of our own childhood in Cornwall. Endless hours were spent playing on golden sands, crouching around rock pools and hunting rugged shorelines for sea-life left behind by the tide. Here, on the safe beaches of the Island, we observed the frolics and studied concentration of some youngsters enjoying the same innocent pursuits, and we reflect that the simplest pleasures in life alter little despite the years.

Whilst in Millport we paid a vist to the **Museum of the Cumbraes** which is located at Garrison House, and was originally built by Captain Crauford, of the famous cutter, 'The Royal George', as a barracks for his crew in 1745. The island is a haven for research, and the **Marine Biological Station** and **Museum** is located at **Keppel**, where it has been involved in research since it was opened in 1887. It is open to the public and we were able to enjoy looking at the fine aquarium here.

As we made ready to leave this precious, peaceful island, we were genuinely sad. There is always the comfort and privilege for us that we will certainly return to renew the friendships and memories made. It was for us, and we hope will be for you, a marvellous place.

In order to visit the **Isle of Bute** we had to travel up to **Skelmore**, where we were able to get a ferry to take us across. The crossing however, only took about half an hour and it was not long before we were docking at **Rothesay**. The island of Bute is only about fifteen miles long and just over a mile wide, though we were amazed by the wealth of scenery that it contained. The land at the northern end of the island has a wild feeling about it while the southern end is altogether more soft and gentle. Rothesay itself is a popular holiday resort with an ample choice of activities and entertainments.

The burgh was first granted a royal charter in 1401 and the castle dates from around 1098. In 1398 King Robert III created his eldest son 'Duke of Rothesay', and the title still exists today being held by none other than Prince Charles. Opposite **Mansion House** we came across The Bute Museum, which has a fascinating exhibition covering all aspects of the Isle. If you, like us, are intrigued by the mild climate you will be interested to know that it is, of course, as a result of the effect of the warm Gulf stream. This reaches the west coast, allowing the magnificent palm trees and azaleas to thrive here.

From Rothesay pier, we turned right and travelled north to **Ardbeg**. Turning left immediately after the post office there, we found our destination, **The Ardmory House Hotel**. This cosy informal place had been recommended to us and we were eager to see if it lived up to its praise.

We were delighted to discover that one of its most obvious charms was that of peacefulness. With panoramic views from Loch Striven and the hills of Argyll, to Skelmorlie and Rothesay Bay, this building dates as far back as 1833. The oak beams and huge log fires of the two lounge bars, on the ground floor, create a wonderfully relaxing atmosphere.

Our rooms were well-decorated and clean with full central heating and direct-dial telephones. Efficiently run by Neil and Jayne Haddon, we particulary enjoyed eating Jayne's home cooking in the restaurant, with its breathtaking views across Rothesay Bay and the Clyde Estuary. We learnt that Jayne's fare enjoys a high reputation amongst the locals and after sampling some, we could see why.

The Ardmory House Hotel provided an perfect base for us with its proximity to Rothesay Castle, Ardencraig Gardens and Rothesay Museum. We throughly enjoyed our stay here and were not disappointed in the least. When we heard about the **Kingarth Trekking Centre and Dabbles Workshop**, we felt highly intrigued and could not resist a closer look. They are both based in what used to be Kingarth School. Now converted into craft workshops, visitors can watch demonstrations of the ancient crafts of spinning, weaving and natural dyeing. If you're not content simply to watch, it is possible to stay and learn these crafts of yesteryear as well. Both day workshops and holiday workshops can be arranged at any time for adults or children, and we were assured that you do not have to be experienced to take part. We were advised to ring up before visiting though, especially if we wanted to see the demonstrations.

Kingarth Trekking Centre enabled us to explore the beautiful countryside of the island in a virtually unique way, from the back of a horse. Seated on these amiable animals, we were able to enjoy the pleasures of not only riding but touring a truly lovely place. We were able to cover more distance than we would have on foot, and to reach places which are inaccessible for vehicles.

The trekking centre provides hour rides, half day rides, day rides and even entire riding holidays. The inexperienced rider is welcome here and visitors can stay for an hour or up to a week.

The Kingarth Trekking Centre and Dabbles Workshop really do provide a double helping of enjoyment for the visitor.

Kingarth Trekking Centre

We spent our time here making most of the glorious walks and lovely beaches. You might like to try your hand at fishing or perhaps pay a visit to the colourful gardens and aviary at Ardencraig.

Whilst on Bute, we also visited the **Argyle Private Hotel**. What a super place, the owner, Roderick Campbell, was both welcoming and friendly to us from the moment we arrived.

We discovered that all eleven rooms, one of which is en suite, have comfortable modern furniture and complete tea and coffeemaking facilities. Should you wish to watch television, we noticed there is one in the residents' lounge.

The Argyle's a la carte restaurant opens on Friday and Saturday evenings. We were lucky enough to be there on one of these nights and enjoyed a fine meal from the varied menu. We began with mushrooms stuffed with pate and philly cheese, deep fried and served with salad and garlic dip. After this we suggest you try, as we did, the Tournedos Argyle: a prime fillet steak stuffed with chef's pate, served on a croute and covered with a rich sauce. A meal to satisfy even the most discerning palate, we felt. Roderick told us that they will even cook special meals for children.

The Argyle Private Hotel is open all year around, except Christmas, and is ideally situated on the seafront, near all the amenities, and close to the country and a number of secluded beaches. We had an enjoyable time here, and were pleased by the attention and service provided.

Argyle Private Hotel

Before leaving we spent time at **Woodend**, which is a house built by Edmund Kean, the great English actor of the 19th century.

Back on the mainland, we drove down to **Ardrossan** to enable us to cross to the **Isle of Arran**. This fascinating 10 by 20 mile island is perhaps the most challenging of all the isles we have visited, and with some justification it is referred to as Scotland in miniature. It unfolds dramatically, from mountains in the north capped by Goat Fell at 874m, to the farmlands and rolling moors of the south.

Its history was turbulent, being held not only by the Dalriada Scots from Northern Ireland but also by the Vikings, whose links with the Isle are still celebrated, and finally by the Scottish Crown. Robert the Bruce stayed here in 1307 before leaving for the mainland to continue his struggle for Scottish Independence, which he finally achieved at Bannockburn after some seven years.

The ferry unloaded us at **Brodick**, after a journey time of about an hour. You will find that regular services link the Isle with the Mainland. The name Brodick has Viking associations, as do many of the names of the Isle, it is Norse for 'Broad Bay'. Brodick is the largest village on Arran, and lies to one side of Brodick Bay. From here we were treated to a fine view of the mountains to the north.

A mile and a half from the Brodick Pier we were interested to come across **Brodick Castle**, another fine Trust property. The castle is the former seat of the Dukes of of Hamilton and dates in part from the 13th Century.

Brodick Castle and Country Park

Over the many following decades, additions to the Castle have included a gun battery erected in 1652 by Oliver Cromwell's troops, who occupied the Castle at that time. 1844 was also a busy year for the masons who carried out,at Brodick, work in traditional Scottish Baronial style.

Inside, there are many fine paintings, a large number of which depict sporting scenes and reflect the sporting nature of the Hamiltons. An indicator of the hunting skills of the family are the stag heads which line the walls of the grand staircase.

For those of you, however, who favour less energetic pastimes, there is a fine collection of silver and porcelain to enjoy, as well as the valuable art collection.

The last owner of Brodick Castle was the Duchess of Montrose, daughter of the 12th Duke of Hamilton. It was she who created the magnificent rhododendron collection, now regarded as one of the finest in Europe.

The Castle gardens these daysform part of **Brodick Country Park**, and as well as the Woodland Garden which houses the rhododendrons, there is a Walled Garden which dates back to 1810. Also in the Park is the mountain of **Goatfell,** at 2866ft the highest peak on Arran, and part of **Glen Rosa and Cir Mhor,** 2618ft.

A thoughtful touch is the Nature Trail designed especially for wheelchair users, and for everyone, a Ranger Service is provided to answer the many questions posed by curious trekkers.

Young visitors will love the Adventure Playground, and a visit to the Castle shop and tearoom rounds the day off perfectly.

Visitors to the castle will notice a strong Bruce connection as this stronghold has a room known as 'Bruce's Room'. The story goes that in 1307 Bruce, and his small band of colleagues, waited in hiding for a signal from two companions the King had sent across to the mainland. Their mission was to investigate if a landing would be safe near the King's birth place of Turnberry.

Bruce waited for the signal, which was supposed to be a bonfire lighted on the other shore. However, the tale unfolds that the King and his followers saw an unrelated fire, and in their mistaken assurance that it was the prearranged signal, they set forth, across the waters. Although the misguided depature of the King and his men was somewhat premature, in the end the misunderstanding did not hamper Bruce's arrival. There is another version of the story which claims that the room, from which Bruce watched for the fire, was not in fact in the tower of Brodick Castle but in the now ruined Kildonan Castle which is some nine miles to the south.

The historians who state this theory point out the fact that Brodrick at the time was the headquarters of King Edward's governor, and possibly the last place that Bruce would find refuge, while Kildonan Castle was owned by a branch of the Clan Donald of the Isle, who was a friend and supporter of Bruce.

Whomever is right, we're sure that you will find the Castles and stories linked with them most intriguing. To get an accurate picture of life on Arran up until the 1020's, we recommend that you pay a visit to the Isle of Arran Heritage Museum which is located between the castle and the village. Here we enthralled with the representation of life on Arran, including a Smiddy and an Arran cottage.

Looking around the museum we came across a plaque to the memory of the 112th Scottish Commando. Wanting to find out a little more, we discovered that the Isle was the training ground for the officers and men during the last war. It was this Commando Unit which wasresponsible for a daring raid on General Rommel's headquarters in November 1941.

Going back even further in time, the importance of Arran as an archaelogical centre cannot be forgotten. We were amazed to be told that there have been recently excavated sites, which have been dated back to 2500 BC, and are considered to be some of the most important remaining examples of Bronze and Iron Age finds in Europe. There are many sites to see if you are interested in these ancient monuments, and the Isle can boast a rich choice of tombs from the Neolithic period and circles of standing stones from the Bronze Age.

The same must be said for Arran's importance as a geological centre. Did you know that the local rock is Permian desert sandstone which is 250 million years old? We were also told that James Hutton, who is regarded as the 'Father' of modern geology, discovered an nonconformity at Lochranza, which was the first certain proof of the great age of the Earth.

The Douglas Hotel in the town often plays host to trainee submarine captains who come to Arran, twice a year, for simulated deep sea dives, and attack manoeuvres around the island.

It was while we were in Brodick that we paid an interesting visit to the **Lighthouse and Transport Museum** at Cladach. Housed here is an exhibition of memorabillia of steamers, lighthouse, railways and buses. Brodick is a useful base for a number of walks, one which we tried taking us to **Merkland woods**, quite close to the Castle.

We searched for a restaurant, recommended to us, that was in this vicinity. **The Pirate's Cove Restaurant** can be found after passing Brodick Castle and Merkland Wood. It has beautiful surroundings and gorgeous views across the Firth of Clyde. It is positioned at the sea front below banks of wild rhododendrons.

The Pirate's Cove Restaurant

Michael and Mary, who founded the "Winking Owl" Restaurant in Aviemore, came to Arran sixteen years ago and totally renovated an old croft, retaining much of the original building. What you see today is the result of their continuing effort to provide the sort of warm and friendly greeting, which will make your visit a memorable one.

Amongst many well known personalities who have dined at the Pirate's Cove have been Sir Harry Secombe, Peter Morrison, Lord Goold and Dennis

Norden. Traditional fayre is served in a relaxed but efficient manner, and all dishes are prepared using fresh local produce whenever possible. Michael has chosen a well balanced selection of wines to complement the menu. The letting bedrooms have been found to be ideal for the keen golfer, as they will find that there are seven golf courses within easy reach.

The Restaurant is open from seven o'clock each evening. It is certainly worth the extra effort of booking a table to avoid disappointment. To make your holiday complete, dinner at the Pirate's Cove is a must.

The one main road that circles the Isle is the A841, and we decided to follow this road southwards towards the village of **Lamlash**, which nestles on the shores of **Lamlash Bay**. It is here in 1263 that a naval battle was fought between the Norwegians and the Scots. Prior to the battle, the Viking King Haakon's fleet was anchored off the shore, and every year the village of **Corrie**, which in fact is to the north of Brodick, holds the 'Corrie Capers' to remember this time by burning the replica of a Viking long ship.

We noticed a small island off the shore of Lamlash and we were told that this was called **Holy Isle**, and is a paradise for bird lovers. You can visit the Island, which is only a short boat trip away, and catch sight not only of the birds but also a herd of wild goats which roam around its rocky crags.

Holy Isle also contains **St Molio's cave** to the west of the island, along with **St Molio's Well** and the **Judgement Stone** which is a 7ft sandstone table. The island takes its name from the 7th century St Molaise, who is said to have lived to be 120. Perhaps this is a testament to the healthy life here in the Isles. If you pay a visit to his cave you may notice some 'graffiti' on the walls in 'runic', the old Norse alphabet, which was carved by Norwegian sailors who were here before the battle in 1263. The Vikings lost the battle to Alexander III of Scotland, who effectively ended centuries of Norse control of the Western Isles.

In 1829 the brig, 'Caledonian', stopped here at Lamlash Bay. It's purpose was to pick up 86 emigres who had lost their places on the land as a result of the clearances, when they were forced to leave their homes to make way for the more profitable sheep, whom the landowners were bringing in. There is a monument here to these unfortunate people. Visitors to Lamlash will be able make use of facilities for putting or bowling or even a game of tennis. You will also find a lively marina here, and if you are of a mind, you will be able to hire a boat for a spot of sea fishing. Those of you with a taste for the underwater world may like to hire some diving equipment, and you will be able to get excellent advice on the best places to drive locally.

The cottages along Hamilton Terrace were originally built for estate workers, who would move to the backs of their houses each summer in order to let the main front house to visitors. Another interesting shop in Lamlash is the **Arran Provisions factory** which produces a world famous range of jams, jellies, chutneys and mustards.

The road continues south through **Whiting Bay**, which is a truly lovely spot and close to the **Glenashdale Falls**, a picturesque place of sparkling waters which makes a pleasant excursion on foot from the other side of Whiting Bay.

We noticed th at there is a rich abundance of sea-life around the Isle, and were told that it has been quite common in the earlier part of the summer for sightings to be made of basking sharks in the waters. These huge plankton eating fish can grow up to 40ft in length, and swim around for six to eight weeks before taking their leave.

It is amazing to think that little is known about the habits of these superb creatures, which are fortunately harmless. Another visitor to the Isle is the whale, and both killer and bottlenosed have been sighted around the shores. We can imagine what a stirring sight this would be.

Kildonan is situated at the south of the Holy Island, and is another centre for diving as well as having opportunities for boat hire. We carried on to **Lagg Inn** which is a charming Inn set amongst palm trees, with a lovely tea garden in a wooded ravine just to the west of Kilmory. The creamery at Kilmory manufactures the prize winning Arran cheddar cheese, which, to our surprise, produces over three hundred tons each year!

At **Blackwater Foot** we found a choice of pony trekking and riding centres, this was marvellous as we were able to tour a large area of Arran by horse back. We can thoroughly recommend that, if you have the time, you should see some of the lovely countryside this way.

Not far from here you will be able to visit the legendary cave occupied by Robert the Bruce. Weary and defeated he had taken refuge within its cool shelter, and whilst resting, cloaked in his despair, he watched a spider attempt to make his web. The spider's efforts never ceased despite setbacks and difficulties, and with a relentless determination success was finally achieved. The King was reputedly inspired by this one little spider, and he left refreshed to try again.

As we approached **Machrie Bay** we were able to see some fine examples of the standing stones that we have heard so much about. The bay itself has lovely sands and is an ideal place for a walk or picnic.

If you have been making the most of your opportunity to walk around on Arran, you may have come across the warm-

Kestrel, Isle of Arran

189

ing sight of wild red deer. This is not unusual as the Isle can boast over 2,000 of the species in the wild hill country. They wander around at will and are a most impressive sight. We were fascinated to learn that the Island is also famous for its Golden Eagles, as well as a wealth of other birds of prey including hawks, buzzards, peregrines and kestrels. Bird watchers amongst you will enjoy a rewarding time here.

Travelling to the north of Arran we came to **Lochranza** which is a delightful community situated around the shores of Loch Ranza. Here you will find the ruins of **Lochranza castle**, which was once the hunting seat of Scottish kings, and was built in the 16th century. It stands rather romantically, we think, on a sand spit in the middle of the loch. There are many fine craft industries based here, and we enjoyed looking around the Arran Pottery where we were able to watch the craftsmen at work. We were delighted with the Gold and Silver jewellery produced at the Castle Workshop.

The Lochranza Hotel is located in the middle of this picturesque village, with views on nearly all sides. As we walked up the path to the hotel entrance, we saw the Mull of Kintyre in the distance and the majestic peaks of the surrounding hills.

The hotel was built in the early part of this century and has a 9 hole golf course nearby which is great for golfing fanatics.

Inside, the hotel is warm and very comfortable. The ten guest bedrooms all have tea/coffee making facilities, wash hand basins with plenty of hot water and shaver points. The rooms are spacious and spotlessly clean. Some have wonderful views with so much detail, you could sit and gaze and dream from the window for hours.

The Lochranza Hotel

When we arrived, we were greeted by the hotel owner Mr Stewart. He showed us around the resident's lounge and bar where other guests were chatting and enjoying a pre-dinner drink. The peacefulness of the area seems to permeate the walls, adding to the cosy atmosphere and making us feel very much at home.

After a quick wash and change we went down for dinner. As it was quite chilly outside, we decided to have home made soup followed by a plain sirloin steak served with Garni and chipped potatoes. Both were excellent and very enjoyable. We had chosen from the bar menu which is very comprehensive, although there is an a la carte menu to choose from as well.

After dinner we decided to stroll down to Newton Shore to see if we could spot any of the many grey seals that play here. We were not disappointed as in the distance we glimpsed some cavorting joyfully in and out of the waves, a bit like the Scarlet Pimpernel, now you see them now you don't.

We had not been able to tour this lovely Isle without being tempted to try some of the magnificent walks and climbs that Arran can offer. **Corrie,** previously mentioned for holding the 'Corrie Capers', is a small village of closely packed white cottages. Here we found the ideal base for hill walking and climbing in the area. It is ideal, for instance, for attempting the majestic challenge of **Goat Fell** or **Glen Sannox** which can be seen from the village. The old fishing and mining village of Corrie has seen much in its historical past, although this peaceful part of Arran has now been purely residential since around 1945.

At the northern end of the village, sitting between the mountains and the very shore, is **Blackrock Guest House**. Its name would appear to stem from the layer of black basalt lava found on the shore immediately in front of the house. This, together with other interesting geological features, has resulted in the whole shoreline being designated as a site of special scientific interest.

Blackrock Guest House

Blackrock Guest House is open from March to October, and at other times by special arrangement. Proprietors, Mr and Mrs Wilkinson, have made a great effort to create a warm and homely atmosphere here, and there can be no doubt that they have succeeded,

There are eight spotless guest rooms, all with washhand basin and tea and coffee making facilities. There are special rates available for children, and the Wilkinson's will gladly listen out for them during the evenings.

What you will undoubtedly enjoy about Blackrock Guest house though, is the food. A typical evening menu might include, Yorkshire pudding with onion gravy and Arran roast beef with fresh vegetables as a main course. Afterwards you will be knocked out by their Knuckleduster, the Wilkinson's own sweet of meringue, ice cream, cream and bananas. All followed by cheese and biscuits, tea or coffee, Delicious! The Blackrock is not licensed but you are welcome to bring your own wine which is chilled and decanted at no extra cost.

You will find the Wilkinsons are knowledgeable hosts, well versed in local history and facts. AA listed and two crowns commended by the Scottish Tourist Board, this charming guest house offers first class value for money, and is perfectly situated for taking advantage of all that Arran has to offer.

Our whole stay on Arran was enchanted. The warmth of the people, the sense of the past, the majesty of the terrain and the peace of the place, all were an inspirational joy. Our departure was tinged with regret despite the exciting call of Glasgow, which was where we were headed next.

16th Century Sandstone Portal, The Burrel Collection, Glasgow (see the next chapter)

Strathclyde

Glasgow University

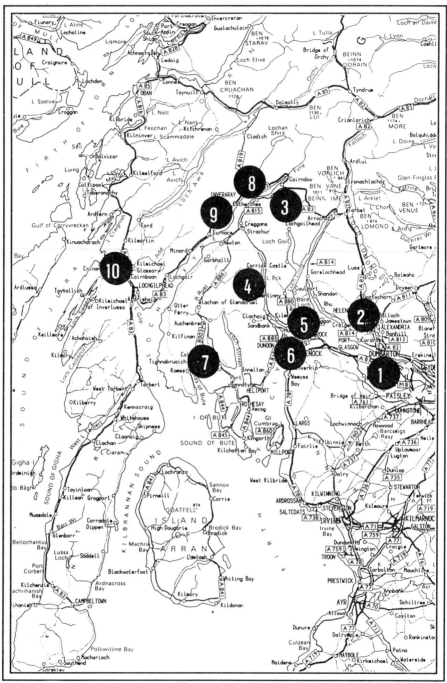

Please turn to Reference Section for further information.

CHAPTER TEN

Strathclyde

There is no possibility in a book of this size to do full justice to **Glasgow**. However, we will just tell you a little about some of the many delights you can find there, and suggest that under no circumstances do you leave it out of your itinerary.

Glasgow has a character and flavour all of its own and unlike anywhere else we have ever visited. It has an abundance of opulent 19th Century architecture, wonderful museums and galleries. Charles Rennie Mackintosh designed the **Glasgow School of Art** in Renfrew Street, and in the famous Sauchiehall Street, much beloved by that famous old variety artist, Harry Lauder, is his **Willow Tea Room**. If you enjoy seeing those buildings then take a look at his **church at Queen's Cross**, which has recently been restored, and the **Hunterian Art Gallery,** Hillhead Street, where you will have the opportunity to see the reconstructions of the interiors of his Glasgow home.

Charles Rennie Mackintosh was the leading spirit of what became known as The Glasgow Style, but he was by no means alone. His wife Margaret Macdonald, their colleagues, Margaret's sister Frances, George Walton, E.A Taylor, Jessie King and many others, many of them from the Glasgow School of Art, all made their mark and together earned for Glasgow a place in the world of Art Noveau comparable with Paris.

It is strange thinking about Paris; we tend to forget that since the days of Mary, Queen of Scots, it has been the French and not the English who have been the dominant influence in Scottish cultural life.

If, towards the end of the last century, you had wanted to buy Impressionist paintings without crossing the Channel, it is to Glasgow that you would have come, not London or Edinburgh. In this fine city, currently the European City of Culture, you would have met several of the leading, distinguished and highly respected dealers of the day. The greatest of whom would have been Alexander Reid, a personal friend of many of the Impressionists.

Today, the most famous collection of art in Glasgow is the **Burrell Collection**. On his death in 1944, a Clyde ship-owner, Sir William Burrell bequeathed to the city his magnificent collection of 8000 items of the ancient world, paintings and oriental art. He was quite specific in his will about how the collection should be housed, and this resulted in a superb gallery being built in Pollok Country Park. There is no question that this is a must for anyone visiting Glasgow.

The Glasgow Art Gallery and Museum in Kelvingrove Park has one of the finest municipal collections in Britain, ranging from Rembrandt to Dali. In various rooms throughout there is a feast in store for you. We were suffering from mental indigestion by the time we left, not only are there these superb paintings but there is a wealth of ceramics, glass and silver, clocks, snuff boxes, pewter, Egyptian antiquities, and a rare arms and armour collection.

If you have a fascination for oddities, as we do, Glasgow can offer a plethora to delight the senses. Perhaps the most memorable is the **Necropolis**, a hill crowned with obelisks, monuments, statues, columns and miniature temples. In Victorian Glasgow, unless you were buried here you were a nobody!

Alongside the Necropolis is **St Mungo's Cathedral**, a building with an exhausting history. A little church was founded here in the 6th century by St Mungo, around which the city of Glasgow grew. Take a look at the Lower Church which is considered to be one of the very best vaulted crypts of Gothic Europe. It is of beautiful proportions and very graceful. In the centre is the simple tomb of St Mungo who was buried on the site beside an ancient well in 603.

So many people just expect Glasgow to be an Industrial city but how wrong they are. Its University for example was founded by Pope Nicholas V in 1451, which makes it the fourth oldest in Britain, after Oxford, Cambridge and St Andrews.

Glasgow University

Glasgow is a place of immense fun as well as culture, there are good theatres and concert halls, good eating houses and hotels. The pubs in Sauchiehall Street are famous, if not infamous, and the Glaswegians are friendly folk even, if at times, you cannot understand what they are saying!

The town of **Dumbarton** lies above **Glasgow** and sits guarding the Clyde approaches. Like Stirling, it has its origins in its fortified rocks, from which it derives its name, and was once the capital of the ancient kingdom of the North Britons, who were a Pictish tribe. The name Dumbarton is derived from 'Dun-Briton' which literally means the fort of the Britons. There was a castle on the rock in medieval days, and William Wallace was reputedly imprisoned here for a short time. It was here also, Mary Queen of Scots set sail for France to marry the Dauphin. The castle was last used as a barracks during the First World War and is now a museum which makes an interesting visit.

Being situated on the river, the town developed an important position, controlling the pass into the Highlands, and was formerly the port for Glasgow until the deepening of the river Clyde in the 19th century. There were famous shipyards in Dumbarton, and one great vessel launched from here, that we had heard much of, was the famous clipper 'Cutty Sark'. The name incidentally was taken from an incident in Robert Burns', 'Tam O'Shanter'.

Today Dumbarton is an interesting blend of old and new, with many lovely shopping streets built around the waterfront area that possess a unique flavour. Here we came across the excellent facilities of the **Meadow Sports Centre**, which is able to offer the visitor a wide range of facilities for sports and leisure.

While we were in the town we paid a visit to the fascinating **Denny Ship Model Experiment Tank**. This was the first purpose-built experimental tank to be used commercially, and was created for the renowned Denny Shipbuilding Company in 1882. For over one hundred years it was used to test designs for hulls and propellors, until it was taken over in 1984 by the Scottish Maritime Museum. We were much impressed by the size of the tank, which is over 100 metres long and has a depth of 2.5 metres. We were also able to have a look at many other interesting exhibits from this fascinating industry, including workshops, model making processes and the drawing office.

If you happen to come across any local cowboys, don't be too alarmed as Dumbarton has become a centre for 'Wild West' shootouts. You will be quite likely to find these enthusiasts at the annual **Dumbarton District Festival,** which takes place in the third week of July. It boasts many parades and activities to keep you enthralled during visits to local distilleries and events, based around the attractions of **Loch Lomond.**

During this particular week, a marquee, complete with chandelier, is erected in Moss O'Balloch Park, and a host of musical entertainment is laid on, including folk music and a fiddlers' rally. Try and get along to another highlight which is the Fun Day in Levengrove Park which has a whole range of side shows, competitions, dancing tournaments and plenty of piping.

The **Anchorage Guest House** dates from 1886 and is set in the historical village of **Balloch**, lying close to the shores of Loch Lomond.

There are eight bedrooms here, four of which are en-suite, and there are toilet and shower facilities for the disabled. Children and families are welcome, and the guest house very thoughtfully provides a range of facilities for children.

Situated directly at the mouth of Loch Lomond, the surroundings are wonderful and visitors are only a short distance away from cruises on the loch. **Balloch Park and Castle** are also within easy reach.

Overbooking is rarely a problem here, as the family residence is immediately across the road. The Bowmans, who run the Anchorage, are only too pleased to welcome extra guests into the hospitality of their own home. This has a further four bedrooms, one of which is en-suite, and a stay here has the added bonus of a large outdoor swimming pool.

The Anchorage Guest House

The Anchorage Guest House is an ideal stopping off place for visitors, standing as it does at the gateway to the Western Isles. It is also a good base for those wishing to spend a few days taking in the wonderful attractions of this most famous Loch.

Loch Lomond is one of the largest expanses of water in Scotland, and we never cease to marvel at its range of beauty. It is big enough to contain its own islands, some of which are inhabited. Many of the isles have legends or stories that surround them. Inch Lonaig or 'Yew Island', we were fascinated to learn, was so named as it was supposed to have been planted with yew trees for the use of King Robert the Bruce's archers.

The A82 takes you up its west coast, whilst you will find, if you are feeling a little more adventurous, the east side of the loch is the sole preserve of the walker. Your trecks will be more than rewarded with the timeless beauty of the scenery, from the southern tip of the loch right up towards the towering form of **Ben Lomond.**

The views around the loch are inspired, and have to be seen with your own eyes to understand why those of us, who have had the heady pleasure, so eulogise on their wonder. Those of you walking on the east side will find yourselves in the **Queen Elizabeth Forest Park;** full of wildlife, you may be lucky enough to come across the marvellous sights of deer or even wild goats.

If you start from **Balloch**, at the south of the loch, you will be able to take advantage of the many boating facilities. Why not just relax and take a tour over the waters in this leisurely fashion, you'll find a good selection of cruises available. If you like, hire a dinghy and take the chance to discover by yourself some of those intriguing islands, or, if you are feeling a little more energetic, how about a spot of water-skiing. Replete with our own exploring, we found equal enjoyment in just sitting back in a small cafe, and watching others expend their energies and humours on the wealth of activities from which to choose.

You may be interested to know that the small village of **Luss**, on the west shore, is used as the film set for that popular television serial 'Take the High Road'. There are many picturesque villages in the area, and we were enchanted by some of the floral decorations and little gardens. This region really is a most magical land.

Loch Lomond is of course well known for that famous song about its 'Bonnie, Bonnie Banks', which has its roots in an old celtic belief that when a man dies in a foreign land, his spirit returns home by the 'Low Road'. The song itself is said to refer to the last moments together of two Scottish soldiers, captured by the English during the '45 Rebellion. One was to be set free, whilst the other was to be taken to England and executed. His spirit would thus go home by the 'low road' while his friend returned by the 'high road'.

Make the most of your time here as you will be in the good company of Wordsworth, Coleridge and Sir Walter Scott, who were also visitors.

The A82 winds its way along the coast of the loch towards **Tarbet**. This town has the fortunate position of being set in between two great waters, Loch Lomond, which is fresh water, and Loch Long, which is salt water. The name, Tarbet, is said to come from the words 'tarrain bata', or portage which stems. They originated from the days when Haakon of Norway allegedly dragged his vessels over the land separating the two waters, and sailed into Loch Lomond to carry on his raids of pillaging and looting.

At Tarbet we took the A83 winding around the top of Loch Long, and leading us westwards into the Dunoon and Cowall Peninsula, which has been referred to as Scotland's best kept secret. Our route wound through the picturesque **Argyll Forest Park,** until we reached the delightfully named spot of 'Rest and Be Thankful'. This is the highest point on the road between Loch Long and Loch Fyne. Here we are 803ft above sea level, and we were able to park the car and just rest our souls before the magnificent view. We would justly suppose that the name of the stop probably derives from the days before transport was so widely available! Even higher than the spot we were looking from, can be seen the glorious peaks of the Northern mountains of the park, which tower to some 3000ft.

The B828 winds down towards the village of **Lochgoilhead**, which is situated towards the head of Loch Goil, strongly reminiscent of a fjord. At Lochgoilhead, and further down at **Carrick Castle,** you might like to take advantage of the renowned watersports facilities which include boating, fishing, sub-aqua, diving and water skiing. Lochgoilhead also possesses a golf course, and at **Drimsyne Leisure Centre,** between November and March, we were assured you will be able to enjoy partaking in the famous sport of 'curling'.

In this same arena during the months of April to October, you may experience Europe's first indoor 'sheep show', which pays testament to the hill farming that has been carried out here for generations. You will be able to see a collection of nineteen different breeds on show. We were impressed by the accompanying talk that explained the difference between the breeds, and their wool and meat. Visitors are also able to see a demonstration of sheep shearing, and that delightful experience of dog and sheep handling which is so essential to life in this area.

Bouquet Garni Restaurant & Herbs Wine Bar

It is in this striking village that we came across the **Bouquet Garni Restaurant and Herbs Wine Bar.** This magical setting is a fine background for this most unusual and intriguing restaurant. We were made welcome by Mike Dimmer who, in keeping with the place, is a real character.

Dining can be a real experience as the food, which is both Scottish and otherwise, is served in a variety of interesting recipes which are a credit to the originality of Mike and his staff. Mike stresses the thought and preparation that is put into the dishes, which cater for everyone's taste, and include some original vegetarian recipes.

Likewise, with the selection of wines and beers, which come from all over the world. You may have the chance to accompany your meal with the best of Texan, Mexican or any number of unusual wines. We thoroughly enjoyed our time at the Bouquet Garni, and were made to feel perfectly at ease with the friendly atmosphere and good music.

Mike is also something of a mine of local knowledge, and will be glad to arrange accommodation for you in the area or point you in the direction of any number of activities, from golf to indoor swimming, bowls and tennis.

Lochgoilhead, we found, made an ideal centre for enjoying the benefits of the Forest Park, and some of the various excusions and leisure pursuits available, such as hill walking, climbing and pony trekking.

After taking a short trip down to see the 14th century remains of Carrick Castle, which lie rather romantically on the waters edge, we turned northwards on the B839. Our route took us to the shores of **Loch Fyne**, from where we made our way leisurely to the village of **Strachur.** We were most impressed by the stream of lovely places that are dotted along this particular stretch of coastline.

If you travel inland from Stachur on the A815 you will approach **Loch Eck,** and come across **The Whistlefield Inn.** We were immediately struck by further beautiful views towards Loch and mountain. Situated close to the edge of Loch Eck, the Inn is surrounded by fields, and visitors have use of a free campsite on the shore with a jetty.

Whistlefield Inn

Formerly a coaching inn, there are many interesting stories surrounding this lovely building. We were amused to hear that the name of the Inn comes from the time when the premises were used to distil whisky. Men would stand in the surrounding fields as lookouts, ready to blow a whistle in the event of the approach of customs and excise men!

The Whistlefield can offer eight comfortably furnished rooms with soft feather mattresses and duvets. The decor in the Inn is a fascinating mix of old and new with many original features, including a Victorian style games room and a log fire. Whether you want to enjoy the cosy, warm family room, the large games room, or the peaceful and informal lounge, you will find the atmosphere to be quaint and friendly.

The restaurant seats up to forty and offers an excellent choice of local, traditional and French cuisine. There are good value bar meals also available, and the inn has gone to a great deal of trouble to ensure that children and vegetarians are well cared for.

Outside the views are wonderful, and the excellent facilities for fishing and boating are readily available. At the loch side there is a small beach which the children will love, and there is plenty of opportunity for walks around the loch, and in to the hills. For sheer charm and character you will find The Whistlefield Inn hard to beat.

The road continues southwards and follows the coastline of **Loch Eck,** despite having so recently come from the splendours of Lock Lomand, Eck we decided, is surely one of the most beautiful of Scottish lochs that we have seen, you can visually drown in its glory. We took advantage of the magnificent scenery to stop awhile and feast on the sights, and a fitting picnic to complement the ocassion. Did you know that the 'Powan' is an extremely rare fish that is common only to this loch and to Loch Lomond? It is a species of fresh water herring that is believed to have been trapped here, and left in the loch at the end of the last ice age.

At the southern tip of the loch we came across the **Younger Botanic Garden**, which has a truly wonderful display of trees and shrubs. There is another beauty spot nearby, which we found by following signs to **Pucks Glen**, where there is a route that follows the river into a gorge, and is well worth a look.

On the Dunoon to Glasgow road there is a turning off at Cot House Garage, which will enable you to find **Strone House,** with its magnificent sea views and garden overlooking Holy Loch and Loch Long. It is only four miles from the junction and we urge you to take this detour, if it be that, nomatter how fleetingly.

A look around these sublime gardens is essential with their delightful shrubs, trees and pond. We found the northernmost cork tree in Europe here.

The mansion itself dates from 1871, and we spent a very contented time browsing amongst the excellent selection of tweeds, tartans, knitwear, pottery and glassware on display. This is an ideal place for gifts and momentos.

Strone House is open daily from 9.00am to 5.30pm, and on Sundays from 1.00pm to 5.30pm. It has a wonderful atmosphere, and there is a bonus in the nearby **Botanic Gardens and Art Gallery.**

Take the road around Holy Loch and you will come to **Dunoon,** a much favoured resort since the 18th century. The peaceful waterfront location with its aura of serene spaciousness, is a far cry from the place in the 17th century, when the old castle witnessed a dreadful massacre. The Campbells of Argyll took advantage of a temporary truce to capture their enemies, the Lamonts. They ruthlessly and bloodily killed two hundred of them, throwing the bodies into a hastily dug pit. The grave was only discovered in the 19th century when a road was being built. A memorial has since been erected to those who died there so dreadfully. The lover of Robert Burns was from Dunoon, and there is a statue to 'Highland' Mary Campbell at the foot of Castle Hill.

Strone House

As a visitor, Dunoon has much to offer, amongst other things a heated indoor swimming pool, bowling, tennis, live entertainment and cinema.

The Enmore Hotel is situated on Marine Parade in **Kirn**, with the most glorious views of the Clyde reaching out from its grand position. The hotel is the perfect place to stay if you wish to enjoy the many attractions of Dunoon, standing at the gateway to the Western Highlands with all its delights. From here you will be able to soak in the atmosphere of this genteel town, with the hotel's modern amenities catering for a wide range of interests and activities.

The fifteen rooms, all with finely tiled bathrooms en-suite, are everything one might expect from this fine hotel with views to the sea, mountains or to the gardens. They are individually furnished, comfortable and welcoming, and the perfect tonic to greet you after a long day's sightseeing.

Our hosts, Angela and David Wilson, were happy to give us guidance on what to see and to do during our stay. This was a great bonus, and helped to make our time here more pleasurable and interesting. It is their personal touch that ensures the hotel is such an inviting place in which to stay, and often guests will find fresh flowers, fruit and chocolates in their rooms upon arrival.

There are three attractive lounges in the hotel, and an inviting cocktail bar, which is just the place to unwind and chat for a while before dinner. The food in the elegant restaurant is superb, and the hotel is justly praised for its five course 'Taste of Scotland' meals and excellent value. To complement our meal there was an extensive wine list which should cater for every palate.

The Enmore Hotel

The hotel even has its own squash court, what better way to work up an appetite.

The Enmore Hotel really is a taste of the best of Scotland and you will enjoy your stay here, whether you come for a short break or make it your base for a longer holiday. The time of the year is unimportant. The warmth of welcome from the Wilsons will more than make up for inclement weather.

Leaving Dunoon we went round the loch and then northwards on the A815, and eventually into Strachur. We were keen to linger awhile in this part of the country and decided to follow the A886 down towards **Tighnabruaich**. On our way, we made sure to stop and have a look at **Kilmodan Church,** which dates back to 1610. A follower of St Columba, known as St Modan, established a monastery in the glen here and if you look on the hill you will find **St Modans Well.**

Here also, we had been recommended by friends to stop at **The Glendar-vel Hotel.** The name Glendaruel is an interesting one which has its origins in a battle fought in 1110 AD between Meckau, who was the son of Magnus Barefoot, the King of Norway, and the Scots. The Scots won and threw the bodies of their slaughtered enemies into the river, which flows through the Glen, turning the water red with their blood. The river became known as the

Ruail, and the glen as Glen-da-ruail or 'glen of red blood'.
Set in the heart of the Clachan of Glendaruel is this small and friendly
hotel. It is both attractive and comfortable, and offers a perfect retreat from
which to enjoy a wealth of country pursuits and pleasures. There are five
well furnished and centrally heated bedrooms, four of which are en-suite.
Every bedroom has Colour TV and tea and coffee making facilities.

You can choose from two bars or take advantage of the relaxing surroundings of the residents' lounge. We discovered to our delight that the dining
room specialises in an excellent range of home cooked Scottish dishes, with
a wide selection to choose from including fresh local fish, meat and game.
The staff will even prepare packed lunches to order for visitors who wish to
treck and explore the surrounding countryside; and there is a wealth of
activity available within easy travelling distance as the hotel is ideally
placed for fishing, stalking, hill-walking, golf and bird-watching.

There is private fishing for salmon and trout in the River Ruel which runs
right behind the hotel. Also, we were told that the hotel will gladly arrange
for the hire of boats for either sea or loch fishing. The plentiful wildlife all
around makes the hotel a natural choice for enthusiasts.

Looking carefully we were rewarded by the sight of deer, foxes, badgers,
wild mink, stoats, weasels and otters. It was tremendously exciting. The
hills are alive too with Owls, kestrels, buzzards and golden eagles.

It is no wonder that visitors and sportsmen alike head for the Glendaruel
to beneft from its warmth and hospitality.

The Glendaruel Hotel

Thoroughly refreshed by our rest, we ventured forth to Tighnabruaich,
where we hired a boat at the Sailing School. As its title suggests, you can
take instruction here and with so much beautiful water around us it would
be an opportunity missed indeed,not to take advantage of the wonderful
facilities on offer.

Down here on the tip of the peninsula there are a multitude of fine walks, views and picnic areas. We marvelled at the peace and tranquility of the area and will surely return here one day. Instead of returning by the main roads, we suggest you find your way onto the B8000. This quiet route will take you on a fine journey back towards Strachur, whilst allowing you the scenic marvel of Loch Fyne. It's a view fit for Gods, and of which we could never tire.

Continuing along the loch shores, and just before the road turns to come down the other side, look out for **Cairndow**, as here there is **Strone Garden,** which is open to the public throughout the summer. If you stop to have a look around you will be rewarded with the sight of the 188ft 'Grand Fir', the tallest tree in Britain.

Following on, around the tip of the loch, you will soon be in **Inverary.** The wonder of Inverary is its magnificent **Castle,** which is the home of the Duke of Argyll. The project of building a new castle was conceived by the third Duke in 1746. The epic result is best known for its decor and interiors. The original building was by Roger Morris, with help from William Adam. Take a look around the interior as the relics, furniture and paintings are superb, including portraits by Gainsborough, Ramsay and Raeburn. Outside the grounds are extensive, with many pretty walks, some by cascading water-falls on the River Aray. There is also a craft shop and tea room in the grounds.

If all this gives you a taste for the good life, then you will be in just the mood for **Dunderave Castle,** one of the most awe-inspiring and romantic castles in Scotland. Standing on the shores of Loch Fyne, Dunderave's stronghold is nearly four hundred years old, and is the principle seat of the MacNachtan clan.

Today this ancient castle offers all the modern comforts, combined with the elegance and attraction of its former glories, to those who stay here. There are seven bedroom suites, all with televisions, telephones, modern bathrooms and central heating. Dunderave Castle has all the hallmarks of the best country house, guests are welcomed and made at home in true Highland style.

The food is widely renowned and of a very high standard, with fine wines available from the castle's own cellars. Guests are even encouraged to help themselves to drinks from the sideboard. The castle seems to be full of fascinating and comfortable rooms, and you may enjoy the peace and quiet of the library or simply relax in one of the snug sitting rooms overlooking the Loch.

What better way to relish this marvellous countryside than to stay here in this splendid style? Outside, and just waiting to be explored, is the beautiful region of Argyll, steeped in history, and, of course, there is the loch with its majestic scenery and changing moods.

You are not far from **Inverary,** and the castle has its own private beaches on the lochside, where often seals and otters can be seen at play on the shore. There are numerous pursuits for the visitor, including swimming, riding, boating, fishing, tennis, skiing at Glencoe and walking.

Built in 1539 by the 12th chief of the clan MacNachtan, the castle itself is a grade A listed building and indeed one of the top five in Scotland. Its success today was ensured when it was restored from a roofless and ruinous state, by Sir Andrew Noble in 1906, who set about making the castle habitable. He retained the original character of the old tower, and added two further wings which enclosed a courtyard.

Today, the wonderful atmosphere surrounding this noble castle is a testament to the skill and sympathy of the restoration, and we feel most lucky to be able to sample this unique experience. Time spent Dunderave will be cherished, and we will not forget our stay here.

We followed the A83 out of Inverary for a mile or two. The road passes close to the **Argyll Wildlife Park**. This 60 acre site has one of Europe's largest collections of wildfowl, with an extensive variety of owls. It is open daily until dusk.

Five miles from Inverary is the **Auchindrain Museum**, which gives a fascinating insight into life on a joint tenancy farm in the late 18th century. There are dwellings and barns of the period, together with traditional farming displays. It really is an informative place for all the family. There is also a useful visitors' centre, shop and lovely picnic area.

Dunderave Castle

We continued down on the same road until we came to **Lochgilphead**. This is a charismatic, quiet resort, and only a small distance from one of the most fascinating and picturesque areas here, **the Crinan Canal**, which links Loch Fyne with the Sound of Jura via a series of fifteen canals. Started in 1776 by James Watt, the canal was designed to facilitate travel for business people and locals who had previosuly had to travel around the Mull of Kintyre. However, the terrain proved to be difficult, skilled labour was scarce, and money ran out several times before the canal was finally opened in 1809, bringing the Western Isles and the west coast of Scotland to within easy reach of Glasgow and the Clyde.

We paid a worthwhile visit to **Crinan** at the head of the canal, which still keeps its delightful character today. Here in Crinan it would not do to miss out on the **Crinan Hotel**, which for over two hundred years has stood within this small fishing community, extending its welcome to fishermen, yachtsmen and visitors to the area alike.

The hotel has twenty two en-suite bedrooms, all with colour TV, radio and direct dial telephone. Some of the rooms have balconies, and the views from each room are breathtakingly beautiful, looking out over the sea and the mountains. The hotel welcomes children, and has facilities for the disabled visitor.

Seven miles from Lochgilphead, this quiet country hotel really is unparalleled in its position, and we found to be the perfect place for a relaxing break.

Crinan Hotel

The hotel has two restaurants, and we were not surprised to find that they have achieved fame in their own right. Situated on the rooftop, "Loch 16", as it is known, is supplied by a steady variety of fresh fish landed only fifty yards away, and the "Telford Room", which is closer to sea level, has won awards for its food and service. Visitors to Loch 16 should remember that jacket and tie is required and dinner is served promptly at eight o'clock in the evening. A coffee shop with all home baking in the converted stables is another attraction.

The surrounding area is extremely interesting and it is fascinating to watch the fishing boats and yachts coming and going. Golf, fishing and shooting can be arranged through the hotel, which all in all makes for a pleasant retreat in a spectacular setting.

From Crinan and Lochgilphead, we are now nearing the end of our journey to this western side of Scotland. Down here on **Kintyre,** it would be worth travelling to **Campbeltown,** complete with its two whisky distilleries, though this seems somewhat tame in comparison with the thirty-four that once existed.

In **Cambeltown Loch** there is a small island called **Davaar.** At low tide you can walk out to it along a single spit. There is a lifesize painting of the crucifixion in a cave here, done in 1887 by one Archibald MacKinnon. He returned at the age of 80 to renovate the picture himself.

We found life down here on the Mull to be undisturbed by tourism in the main and enjoyably peaceful. **The Mull Of Kintyre** (do you remember the song?) is of course unique with its spellbinding views towards Ireland, just 12 miles distant. As you drive back up along the west coast, enjoy the lovely deserted beaches and inlets. This place really is a paradise, and it would not do to rush your journey. Offshore are the **islands of Gigha, Islay and Jura,** what beautiful and fitting names they are. They all have their own characteristics. Jura is where George Orwell wrote '1984', and Islay produces some fine malt whisky.

Now it is time for us to go further into central Scotland and start our journey into the beginnings of the Highlands. We are always sad to leave the west coast, and we are certain that we shall return again, we hope in the not too distant future.

A Piper from the Band of a Thousand Pipers, Playing after the Cowal Gathering in Dunoon

From the Campsie Fells
to the Forest of Atholl

Stirling Castle

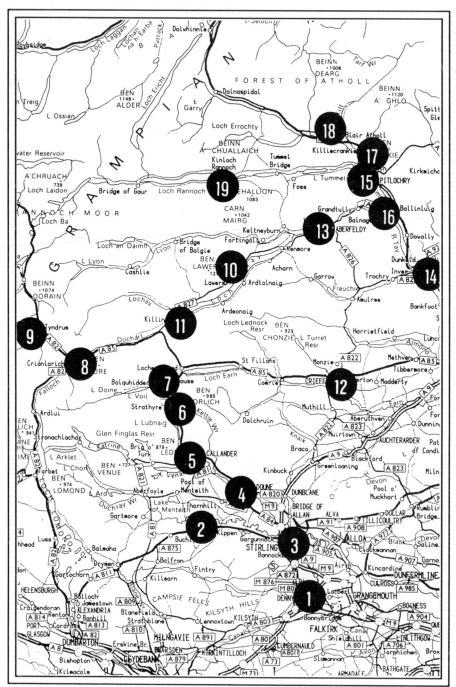

Please turn to Reference Section for further information.

CHAPTER ELEVEN

From the Campsie Fells to the Forest of Atholl

The small town of **Denny** is situated at the bottom of the M80, where it meets the M876, and this is where we started our journey that eventually led us into the Highlands of Scotland. But let us not rush there yet, as there is much to see and do in this central area. From Denny we took the B818 which travels westwards leading up above the Kilsyth Hills, and eventually the Campsie Fells.

A few miles into our journey, we found ourselves deep within the countryside and came across the **Topps Farm Guest House**, an excellent place to stay in order to make the most of the beautiful countryside in the Carron Valley Forest, north of the Kilsyth Hills. It is a friendly, chalet type farmhouse.

Topps Farm Guest House

Your hosts, Jennifer and Alistair Steel, will be glad to welcome you to the warmth and comfort of the 'Woodland' bedrooms, from which you can choose to stay in either family, double or twin-bedded rooms. There are excellent facilities for the disabled in the 'Rowan' room, which has been designed to cater for special needs. Each bedroom is en-suite and has its own special character and decor, based on a particular woodland theme. Tea making facilities are also provided.

A major bonus of a visit here is the excellent food, as Jennifer is a qualified chef and Topps Farm is part of the 'Taste of Scotland' scheme. Both the breakfast and dinner menu reflect the quality and choice that is mouth-watering and irresistible, including some traditional Scottish dishes, as well as some more unusual choices. A small selection of drinks and wines are available to residents, and special diets are happily catered for.

Visitors to Topps Farm will be able to enjoy the surrounding countryside, as well as take advantage of the proximity to Glasgow, Stirling and Edinburgh.

Locally there is golfing, walking, bird watching and fishing in lochs or in the River Carron beside the house. With so much to offer, Topps Farm is surely an ideal base for your stay in Scotland.

From Carron Bridge we continued on the B818, which runs alongside the shoreline of the Carron Valley Reservoir and on towards Fintry where the road divides into the B818 that leads to Loch Lomond and the B822. We followed this up towards **Kippen**, which is a delightfully quiet village.

The parish title 'The Kingdom of Kippen', which seems very grand for such a small village, was constituted in the reign of James 1V when the childless Menzies, proprietor of most of the lands of Kippen, adopted the baby, John Buchanan, as his inheritor, to prevent his estate from being acquired by the comptroller of the King's household. The title 'King of Kippen' was later bestowed upon John Buchanan by James V.

History relates that whilst residing at Stirling Castle, the King sent out his men to catch venison from the nearby hills. On returning with the venison, the men happened to cross the land of John Buchanan who ambushed them and relieved them of their bounty. When the King's men tried to reason that the venison belonged to the King, Buchanan replied that James might be the King of Scotland but he was the King of Kippen. James V was amused and rode out to meet his neighbouring majesty. John Buchanan was cordial to the King, and became so great a favourite that he was often invited as 'King of Kippen' to meet his brother sovereign at Stirling.

Visitors to Kippen would do well to make a point of stopping at **The Cross Keys Hotel,** which is a small family run country hotel in the heart of this secluded and peaceful place.

We were welcomed by Angus and Sandra Watt who run the Cross Keys, and they told us the interesting history of the building, which dates from 1703 and was one of the original hostelries opened to cater for cattle drovers. The hotel was named after its proximity to the cross, and after the one time owner who was a manufacturer of keys.

Retaining much of its old world charm, the Cross Keys today provides a focal point for locals and visitors alike who enjoy the atmosphere and appreciate the wonderful home cooking, which includes pates, home made steak pie, fresh salmon and venison. There are two bars and an attractive restaurant with pictures of Old Kippen.

Angus and Sandra will be delighted to welcome you to their hotel, where you will be tempted to stop for lunch or dinner; try to resist the warming log fire in winter! If you wish to make Kippen your base for a few days, then stay awhile in one of the twin bedded or single rooms.

The Cross Keys Hotel

There are many beautiful walks nearby and around Kippen, and a booklet about the village can be easily obtained in the hotel. With the warm welcome and delicious food, it is not surprising that the Cross Keys is such a hit with the locals.

The Black Bull in Kippen is not a pub, as you might think, but rather a nice building that was restored through the National Trust for Scotland. The building dates back to 1729 and was once the principal hostelry in the village, standing on the back road from Stirling to Dumbarton. It retains its original style of twelve pane glazing and has scrolled skewputs on the gables.

There are a number of excellent walks in which to delight, our favourite was the one that took us up the Main Street and west along the Fintry foothills. The lower road is narrow and tree lined off which lie scattered steadings. We emerged from here onto a road rising from Arnprior up to Kippen Muir. Just past Mill Dam we turned left on the Fintry Road, this took us along the wild landscape of the higher moorland before dipping slowly back to Kippen.

There are still a small number of industries in Kippen which have been going for 200 years or more. The Blacksmiths for example, where the Rennie family have been shoeing horses for all that time. Andrew Rennie, the last of that long line, worked until his death in 1985, at the age of 97, at the Smiddy which is still in operation and is now owned by the National Trust for Scotland.

From Kippen, after saying goodbye to the locals who had been so friendly, we took the A811 outside the village, towards Stirling. We were most interested to see at **Gargunnock** that there was a garden open to the public and so, rarely able to resist such an attractive prospect, we decided to stop and have a look around

We were very impressed by these lovely gardens, situated next to an attractive house that was built between the 16th and 18th centuries, though unfortunately not open to the public without prior written arrangement. However, the gardens are well worth a visit to appreciate the blaze of colours, textures and sheer magic of narcissi, azaleas, rhododendrons and many other flowering shrubs and trees. The combination and sheer beauty of these in the autumn is a rare pleaure, and there is also a small wood here where we discovered a charming walk.

As **Stirling** was now only a few miles away, we decided to drive into this splendid city and take the chance to get to know her a little better.

Stirling Castle

Stirling is surely one of the most atmospheric of Scottish towns, and today retains much of the feeling and charm of the old town. The grand and imposing **Stirling Castle** remains the most striking point on its skyline. You will find the palace's exterior to be one of the most interesting examples of French Renaissance architecture. Historically, the castle played a crucial role in the countrys history, and Stirling is more closely associated with the Stuart kings than any other place.

Situated at the head of the Forth on a strategic rock, it is easy to see why the castle became so valuable. Indeed it was the site of many a Pictish stronghold long before the castle was actually built. It is even said to have been the Round Table upon which King Arthur trained his forces.

If you look at the Stirling coat of arms, you will notice a wolf. We were told that this wolf was supposed to have alerted the Scottish forces to a surprise Danish attack by growling in time to raise the alarm. When James I returned from captivity in England, he held his court at Stirling, and thus began a long association with the castle for the Stuart dynasty.

James II reputedly tried to curb the power of the Douglas' when he persuaded William, the eighth earl, to come to the castle for dinner by offering him safe conduct. However, he then proceeded to kill his guest when he would not agree to break off an alliance that threatened the king.

James IV, a colourful character, made improvements to the castle and laid out the 'Kings Knot', a garden still preserved in outline beneath the castle. He also apparently dabbled in alchemy, which was what passed for science at the time. We were told a story which tells of a time when the king had his court assemble to watch John Damien, Abbot of Tungland, who claimed he had made a pair of wings which would enable him to fly. The assembled crowd watched as the Abbot flung himself off the ramparts of the castle, only to fall to the ground and break his thigh. The Abbot later claimed that his failure was due to the fact that he had used a mixture of eagles' and hens' feathers and that, as anyone knows, hens cannot fly. Unfortunately, history does not record whether the good Abbot made a second attempt, minus the hens' feathers.

James V also spent much of his time at the castle and did much to improve it, including rebuilding the Chapel Royal and, in 1539, building the palace. Incidentally, did you know that he was in the habit of dressing up in disguise and walking around the town incognito?

We have talked much about Mary Queen of Scots in previous chapters, and in fact it was here, at Stirling, that she was crowned in 1543. Her son, James VI, was also crowned here but when he left for England, Stirling's importance as a Royal Seat declined.

Looking around Stirling, we found that much of its original character has been preserved, together with a large collection of buildings from the nineteenth century, when the town rapidly expanded. After an extensive tour around the castle, we walked down into the town past Mar's Wark, the Tolbooth and Mercat Cross until we found ourselves in the location of Stirling's street markets, which were regularly held in medieval times. There is much of interest in the town, and the place abounds with plaques and notices to help you on your tour.

Modern Stirling is best represented in the excellent university, set in its own marvellous grounds outside the town, and the Thistle Centre in town, which has an excellent range of shops. Apart from this, there are many smaller shops selling specialist items, ideal for the visitor or as holiday gifts. For all parents, a marvellous shoppers' creche has been established to entertain your children whilst seeking those bargain buys and holiday momentos, or indulging in one of the many exellent restaurants and cafes.

There are also extremely good sport and leisure facilities in the town which centres on the Rainbow Slides Leisure Centre. Perhaps the best time to taste the lively atmosphere of Stirling is during the town's Tartan Week, held in the second week in July, when there are concerts, open air dancing and a feast of other events.

Leaving Stirling by the A84, we headed towards Doune, where we were eager to have a look at the ruins of one of the best medieval castles in Scotland. **Doune Castle** was built during the late 14th and early 15th centuries by the Regent Albany, who was later executed in 1424. Interestingly, the village bridge across the river was built by one Robert Spital, tailor to James IV, in order to spite a ferryman who had refused him passage.

There is a splendid **motor museum** here about two miles north of Doune, off the A84, which houses a marvellous collection of vintage and post vintage cars. Collected and owned by the Earl of Moray, most of them are in running order. Other interesting local attractions we found include the **Blair Drummond Safari Park** which is a delight for youngsters - of all ages! The park can be found two miles to the south of Doune.

The road winds for seven miles west of Doune, until you reach **Callander**. Tucked midway between east and west coasts at the gateway to the beautiful Trossachs, it is an ideal base from which to explore the Scottish highlands. The town is known world wide as 'Tannochbrae', made famous in the 1960's by the popular television series 'Dr. Finlay's Casebook.' Many readers will no doubt remember Arden House, the home of Drs Finlay and Cameron.

Today **Arden House Guest House** welcomes visitors from all over the world to this beautiful part of Scotland. Situated in one of the finest positions in Callander, the house stands in its own attractive gardens overlooking the town and commanding panoramic views of nearby Ben Ledi.

Arden House

Proprietors, Jim and Dorothy McGregor, provide a warm and friendly welcome to Arden House where they have eight guest rooms, all equipped with tea and coffee making facilities. Six of the bedrooms are en-suite.

Dinner here is a delight and we enjoyed fresh home cooked meals, and also some mouthwatering home baking which accompanied our evening cup of

tea served in the comfortable lounge

The friendly, peaceful atmosphere which abounds will ensure that you have an enjoyable stay. With such a wide variety of activities available in the area, the McGregors are only too pleased to steer you in the right direction, no matter how energetic or lazy you feel. Many visitors return year after year to Arden House and 'Tannochbrae', come see for yourself and understand why.

We continued on the A84, which leads rather romantically up into the **Strathyre Forest**. There are many fine views along here and opportunities for picnics are numerous. This same road took us from Callander on a delightful route along the very beautiful shores of **Loch Lubnaig**. Here, close to Strathyre, we came across an excellent base for caravanning or camping at the **Immervoulin Caravan and Camping Park**.

The site is picturesquely situated alongisde the River Balvaig, and has pitches for sixty caravans, motor homes and tents. The area is ideal for taking advantage of the many walks which vary in length and difficulty in the surrounding forest and hills, as well as the excellent water sport facilities at Lochearnhead some five miles away, and on Loch Lubnaig.

Strathyre itself has much to offer the visitor and has great charm and character. The surrounding countryside is enchanting, and was reputedly the inspiration behind Sir Walter Scott's 'The Lady of the Lake'.

If you are intending to holiday with a caravan or tent, you will find Immervoulin Caravanning and Camping Park is in a unique position and an ideal stopping place.

Immervoulin Caravanning and Camping Park

A little distance from the head of the loch is a small road that leads to **Balquhidder**. Here, buried with his family, is Rob Roy, that most beloved of adventure writers. In the kirk they lie, and their numerous visitors have included no less a personage as Queen Victoria. We wanted to know a little more about this Robin Hood of the North, and discovered that he was born in 1660, was apparently a decently educated man who possessed a strong physique and a masterful ability with the sword. He set out to become a cattle dealer, but he lived in times of constant feuding and rivalry between clans. Faced with the poaching and pilfering rife around him, Rob Roy was forced to put together a band of men to protect his interests from other greedy landowners and landlords.

He was at one time an officer in the Pretender's army at the battle of Sheriffmuir. Eventually the government set a price of one thousand pounds on his head, though he managed to escape capture and the scaffold. He spent ten years on the run and on at least one occasion, was caught and escaped from his captors, until he was eventually pardoned in 1727, and became a convert to Catholicism. He died peacefully in his bed in 1734.

We have rarely come across two self-catering cottages as well kept and delightful to enter as those at **The Steading** at Balquhidder. We were warmly welcomed with shortbread and oatmeal biscuits, and there were fresh flowers in the cottage upon our arrival.

The two cottages form an L-shaped block and have the warm character of the farm buildings they once were, with stone walls and exposed beams. Each cottage sleeps between four and six, and is available the whole year round, complete with everything you might need for your stay apart from the bath towels.

We found the cottages to be spotlessly clean, and were impressed by the high standard of accommodation which is complemented by the wonderful views from the windows. The walls of the cottages are adorned with pictures of Aberdeen Angus cattle, which were the former inhabitants of the buildings, as well as farming scenes from the turn of the century.

The Steading has its own large garden, which is perfect for children to explore, and the windows are particularly large, designed especially so that guests can enjoy the wonderful views. There is much on offer nearby, including water-sports, tennis, golf and walking. We were enchanted to find that the cottages have their own stretch of water on the lovely River Balvais, which provides excellent trout fishing.

The Steading

A break at the cottages is worthwhile at any time of the year, and you will find that you can combine the blissful silence and tranquillity of this place with the many facilities that are within easy reach. Blaquhidder is only a mile away, or journey a bit further to Callander, which is twelve miles away with its marvellous range of shops. There are many other places to discover and explore but we are sure you will agree that the cottages at The Steading will make a fine base for any visit or holiday.

The A84 joins the A85 at Lochearnhead and we followed the road towards **Crianlarich**. Halfway to Crianlarich, you will find the **Glen Dochart** Caravan Park lying midway between Killin and Crianlarich on the A85. It is a quiet and peaceful park situated on 15 acres in an area of charm and character. Open between March and October, the park offers excellent facilities, including a toilet and shower block, a launderette and scullery, a well stocked licensed shop and a public telephone. Campers and caravanners have a choice of hard or grass pitches, some with electric hook-up points. The park also provides the latest luxury static caravans for hire; these have all modern amenities, hot and cold water, mains drainage, shower, colour television, cooker and fridge.

Glen Dochart Caravan Park

The park is ideally situated for salmon and trout fishing on the River Dochart or Loch Lubhair. Permits and fishing tackle are available from the park shop. There are a number of walks from the park to suit everyone, from the casual rambler to the ardent hill walker. It was whilst we were here that we took a particularly lovely walk to Balquhidder, where we visited Rob Roy's grave.

There is an abundance of wildlife, and deer roam the surrounding hills; eagles and other rare birds have also been spotted.

Bryan and Margaret Donaldson, who run the site, also point out to their visitors that there is a licensed hotel only a short walk from the park, where refreshments, bar snacks and meals can be easily obtained.

The Donaldsons have worked very hard to achieve and maintain this pleasant and friendly park in its glorious setting, and they will be pleased to offer advice on the many activities and places of interest in the surrounding area.

The small village of Crianlarich is a peaceful and remote place, and if you have ever wanted to sample life on a working estate or even live in a mansion house, then we recommend that you come to **Lochdochart Estate**, some four miles from Crianlarich.

Here you will be able to live in the north wing of the mansion house, which is fully self contained and sleeps up to nine guests. The wing has three bedrooms, a bathroom, living room and large kitchen diner. All modern facilities are available, with colour television, coal fire, dishwasher, an automatic washing machine, and heaters in all the bedrooms. The house is full of character, and two of the bedrooms even have antique brass beds.

Adjacent to loch and river, the house is set in a secluded and beautiful position amidst hills and woods. The estate itself has been run by the Christie family since 1906, when it was primarily a sporting estate extending to over ten thousand acres. Now, although smaller, it has been developed into a farming and forestry enterprise with one thousand and eight hundred black-faced sheep, and seventy-five pedigree Galloway hill cattle.

The family are willing to introduce interested visitors to the animals, and if you are lucky enough to be here at the right time you can watch shearing and dipping taking place.

The surrounding countryside is full of unspoilt natural beauty, and the range of activities for the visitor is endless, including canoeing, hill walking, climbing, fishing and pony trekking, which can be arranged. The Christies' son, Peter, is a qualified canoeing instructor, and is willing to take visitors out Canadian canoeing for a small extra charge, with a visit to the ruined castle on the island in the loch. He will also take guests walking amongst the hills, lochs and mountains to see the unspoilt natural habitat for birds and deer. Alternatively, if you are feeling really adventurous, you could perhaps try a 'wilderness' expedition, which is also run by Peter.

All in all a stay with the Christies is an adventure in its own right, and is most certainly a magical combination for a holiday with a difference.

Crianlarich is on the famous West Highland Way walking route from Glasgow to Fort William, and as such makes an ideal base for those wishing to explore the beautiful West Highlands of Scotland.

We made a point of stopping here in order to pay a visit to the **Rod and Reel Lounge Bar and Restaurant**, which is very much a family concern and is run by Bill and Elspeth Paulin with their two daughters and sons-in-law.

The restaurant specialises in local fresh produce and excels in the choice and preparation of game and fish. Steven Gibson, who is the chef here, has created an interesting menu, putting a great deal of care and thought into the preparation of the dishes. All in all we are sure you will agree that he has created a good 'value for money' menu to satisfy most tastes. Guests might like to have a drink from the well-stocked bar while making their choice from either the full table d'hote or a la carte menu.

Elspeth and Bill Paulin, along with their family, extend a warm welcome to all those visiting the area who are hill walking, climbing, skiing or just having a relaxing holiday in the Highlands. What could be more relaxing than such a welcome in this lovely restaurant?

Rod and Reel Lounge Bar Restaurant

A few miles to the north of Crianlarich is the small village of **Tyndrum** and if you are looking for a place in which to stay and base yourself, you could not match the inviting welcome that we received at the **Invervey Hotel**.

Handily situated near to the A82, which passes right by the hotel, the views are hugely enjoyable. Indeed the surrounding area was aptly described, in 1876, by Queen Victoria as being set in a "wild, rugged, picturesque glen surrounded by high rugged mountains".

Take the great Queen's recommendation and stop at Invervey, as here there will be no shortage of activities and interesting things to do. We discovered that local activities include nature trails, golf, walks around rivers or mountains and, of course, fishing.

There are 21 bedrooms in the hotel, nine of which are en suite. The hotel has ground floor rooms that are ideal for the disabled.

The large and comfortable lounge, like the rest of the hotel, is restful and welcoming and we noticed that the rooms are all thoughtfully double glazed for extra warmth, with of course central heating.

We thoroughly enjoyed our stay here and particularly felt comfortable in the lovely bars and dining room, with its panoramic views. We noticed the numerous beautiful pictures that adorn the hotel and were interested to discover that many of them had been painted by local artists.

We wondered how the village had acquired the interesting name of Tyndrum, and were fascinated to discover that the name itself comes from the phrase, 'tigh an droma', which translates as 'the house on the ridge'.

Our hosts, John and Barbara Riley informed us that there is an operational gold mine across the hillside. Visitors though will be hard pressed to choose from the splendid variety of activities in the surrounding area since the familiar landmarks of Loch Lomond, Glencoe, Ben Nevis and the Trossachs are all within easy reach.

Whatever your intentions, we are sure you will enjoy the warmth and hospitality of the hotel and its excellent traditional feel and welcome.

Invervey Hotel

If we had not followed the A85 all the way from Lochearnhead we could have turned right after five miles towards Loch Tay on the A827. So often, we were faced with the dilemma of where to go next, faced as you will be in this delightful countryside with the abundance of sights to see. At **Killin** however, we found a quiet village which lies close to the enchanting Falls of Dochart. Nearby, are the ruins of **Finlairg Castle**, which was a Campbell seat associated with the notorious Black Duncan, whose beheading pit can still be seen here.

The towering form of **Ben Lawers**, some three thousand nine hundred and eighty four feet above sea level, provides an impressive sight from here. Ben Lawers has long held a reputation as a botanical paradise and, if you have the energy to climb to its summit, there are magnificent views stretching from the east coast to the west. The National Trust has issued a guide book to the flora and fauna of Lawers which we found informative, but be warned as there is a sign warning against the removal of any plants.

It is in Killin that you will come across the **The Famous Capercaillie Restaurant**. It will become quickly clear that this is an ideal place to take in some of the stunning local scenery, as the Falls of Dochart and surrounding mountains are easily visible.

This unusually named restaurant really is full of character being of

Danish design and built in Danish pine. The interior is all pine and has a wonderful, comfortable feel. The restaurant is attractively decorated, with silk flowers on all the tables.

The food is described as Traditional Scottish Fayre, but you have only to look at some of the magnificent names of the dishes on the menu to realise that this is an understatement; the specialities really are something to be savoured. Why not start your meal off with home made pate or hot prawns in nutmeg? Main course dishes have such scintillating titles as Entrecote Steak Gerrand (Entrecote steak sauted in onions, peppers, flamed in whisky, poached in red wine and horseradish, tomato and cream sauce) or how about The Tipsy Fillet, thick slices of fillet steak sauted in shallots, mushrooms, with a hint of tarragon flamed in brandy and finished in a red wine and cream sauce. It sounds delicious doesn't it ?

Capercaillie Restaurant

The Restaurant also offers Bed and Breakfast accommodation, with six rooms available, three of which are en-suite. Facilities for the disabled are excellent as three of the rooms are on the ground floor level. There is also a self catering chalet available to hire.

The grounds are secluded and attractive, containing a patio area and pond. As the surrounding area is so beautiful there is much to see and do during your visit, with many good walks nearby. Horse riding and fishing are also available. Boat hire can be arranged through the Restaurant for either pleasure boating or fishing on Loch Tay

From Killin, we drove down to rejoin the A85 which then runs eastwards along the northern bank of Loch Earn, and into the small town of **Comrie**. **St Fillans** on the east side of the loch is a centre for watersports and sailing. It was here that we were told a gruesome tale about the MacGregors who, at Ardvorlich on the south side, reputedly beheaded a forester of the king's against whom they had a grievance, and presented his head on a plate, with a crust of bread between his teeth, to his sister.

Comrie is a small pretty little village and we paid an interesting visit to the **Museum of Scottish Tartans** in Drummond Street, which houses an amazing range of examples, numbering over one thousand three hundred, and provided us with an intriguing insight into their production with demonstrations of weaving.

Nearby **Crieff** is a charming place, popular with visitors and we enjoyed spending a few hours looking around the town. While you are here, you must make sure to visit **The Second Thoughts Craft Shop**. It is a delight to come across a real Aladdin's Cave, and that is what we found here, in Galvelmore Street, Crieff.

To get into the shop we walked through a stone built archway. Once inside we immediately noticed that it is an imaginatively converted stable, filled with an impressive variety of gifts and crafts, many hand made in Scotland. Things on show include wooden toys, cards, costume jewellery, basketware, pot pourri, dried flowers and many other fascinating objects; the list is endless.

The character of the place has been carefully maintained by Irene Petrie, whose ideas and drive have gone a long way towards creating the atmosphere of the shop. Visitors are encouraged to browse, and there are even facilities to occupy the children outside whilst you do this.

We noticed a lovely collection of lamps hanging from the beams, and although they are not for sale, they fit in beautifully with the surroundings and are part of a private collection belonging to Irene's mother. You may also notice in and around the shop part of a collection of horse-drawn farm implements, lending the 'Second Thoughts' great atmosphere and character.

The Second Thoughts Craft Shop

Be sure to stop off at this delightful craft shop, as it really is an experience not to be missed. Irene is particularly friendly, and was glad to welcome us in to browse around spending a happy hour here.

After stopping for some time to wander around this pleasant town, we took ourselves off to No 1, West High Street where we found **Harts Restaurant and Coffee Pot**.

This super little place is bound to have something to suit your palate, especially if you are looking for a splendid high tea with all the trimmings. We enjoyed some aromatic Earl Grey served with deliciously warmed scones, jam and cream.

If you are looking for something more substantial, you will not be stuck for choice as the Restaurant and Coffee Pot, as it is known, has a tempting selection of starters and main courses, all of which are very reasonably priced.

Most of the ingredients are locally produced and freshly prepared to order, and the majority of the tempting home-baked food is available throughout the day. You may also choose some of the delicious house wine to accompany your meal. If you prefer not to drink and drive there are non or low alcohol drinks available. To round off your meal, there is a fine selection of quality coffee available.

Whatever your needs, you will be delighted with the impressive range of food and snacks available from this enterprising little business, where Olive and Bryson Hart will be ready to welcome you.

Harts Restaurant & Coffee Pot

Often, to find the best places in a town, it's a wise idea to follow the locals, and if you've ever wondered what the locals of Crieff do at the weekend, then you can discover this by popping in to **The Meadow Inn**. It is one of those lucky places which combines the best of three worlds: an excellent bar, lovely restaurant and eight double rooms, three of which are en-suite.

There is ample parking at the rear of the inn, and children are welcomed here. The building itself dates from 1900 and the bars and restaurants are extremely comfortable and spacious. There is very often live entertainment on Friday and Saturday nights, which is very popular with the locals.

Mrs Stevens, the proprietor of the Meadow Inn, informed us that there will be the added attraction of a beer garden in the near future, which is always a great bonus during the summer months. You are sure to receive a warm welcome at this friendly local inn, so do make sure that you make a point of stopping here to say hello.

The Meadow Inn

Aberfeldy will always be associated with a new era in the Highlands that began with the formation of the Black Watch. It was on this spot on the Tay in 1739, that the first of these regiments was incorporated into the British army, which was an attempt to bring into line and control the warring factions and clans of the Highlands.

The name Black Watch came about as the tartans worn by the men were darker in contrast with the red coats of the regular army. This area has strong connections with General Wade, and to investigate this further, we moved a mile and a half from Aberfeldy. Just three quarters of a mile along the A827, we were lucky enough to find **Weem Hotel**. This lovely 17th century hotel stands in the picturesque Tay Valley and is run by Terry Wise and Judith Hardaker, who refer to themselves as "the chalk and cheese of a highly successful team!" Whatever their secret, it surely is the right combination as the hotel is a charming place, full of warmth and character.

There are fourteen rooms here, all of which are en-suite, with either bath or shower rooms, television, radio, video and telephone. There really is a magical atmosphere, and Terry and Judith have obviously worked hard since 1986 when they arrived, and began the long job restoring the atmosphere of the hotel as it once was, though this time with all creature benefits and modern comforts. We were fascinated by the wonderful 17th century shutters, and by the 18th century working fireplace with its roaring log fire in the dining room, where the head chef ensures that there is always an excellent choice from the menu.

The history of the hotel is no less fascinating. Part of the building dates back to the 16th century, and it was originally known as the Weem Inn. At the time it offered the guest a rather less comfortable alternative which, depending on your ability to pay, might have ranged from a heap of heather or straw to a straw mattress, with a blanket and pillow being extra.

It was also the watering place of the Clan Menzies, with their ancestral home next door, who came here to drink the home-made whisky and ales. A famous resident of the hotel was the afore mentioned General Wade, who stayed here whilst he was directing the building of the Aberfeldy Bridge across the Tay. General Wade was sent to Scotland originally to assess what measures were necessary to subdue the rebellious Highlanders, and his reports culminated in his appointment as Commander-in-Chief in Scotland. Whilst in office, he directed the construction of military roads, bringing the north and west of Scotland within easy reach of those south of the border. Wade eventually died in 1748, and has the fourth verse of the National Anthem dedicated to his honour.

The hotel may be used as a base for any number of activities. It has for instance its own stretch of the River Tay for trout and salmon fishing, and there are over twenty-two golf courses to be found within a thirty-five mile radius. Alternatively, you may just decide to tour the local area and soak up the atmosphere and history. There are beautiful lochs nearby, and other pastimes may include skiing, pony trekking, mountaineering, orienteering, stalking or shooting. Wildlife is plentiful in the valley, and includes deer, buzzards, eagles, osprey and even the occassional wild cat.

The Weem Hotel

Whatever you want to do, even if it is just to relax in these beautiful surroundings, Terry and Judith promise to try and cater for your every whim and fancy. This must surely be an offer you cannot refuse. You'll have difficulty finding a hotel as warm and welcoming as the Weem.

Passing back through Aberfeldy we joined the A9 from where it is but a short distance to the town of **Pitlochry**.

We are now in one of the most beautiful areas in the British Isles, and we were not surprised to learn that the town is a popular centre for visitors, with its magnificent scenery and wide range of entertainments.

Dunkeld is some 12 miles to the south of Pitlochry and one would not suspect from the appearance of this charming little town that it possessed such a turbulent history. In fact, Dunkeld became the religious centre of Scotland in the 9th century, and before that was the ancient capital of Caledonia (the name itself means 'fort of the Caledonians').

This small town was the home of kings and the site of at least one bloody battle in the 17th century when, after the battle of Killicrankie, a raw regiment of Cameronians were ordered to hold the town against the Jacobites. As the rebellious Army advanced, they did great damage to the town, causing the Cameronians to retreat to the cathedral and Dunkeld House. Here, running out of ammunition, they were forced to rip the lead from the mansion's roof in desperation. Somehow they succeeded in driving the Jacobites off and even pursued them, singing hymns as they went.

Prior to this, however, we were amazed to learn that the Vikings had attempted to attack the town. They managed to do this by bringing with them a number of small horses aboard their ships, which enabled them to invade further inland than was previously possible. On at least one occasion, they were successful, and managed to capture and devastate Dunkeld.

Today Dunkeld is a little more tolerant of her visitors and this very attractive town can offer some of the best facilities for crafts. In a building that once was the City Hall is a unique business **The Highland Horn and Deerskin Centre** owned by Jeremy Law and his wife. They make and sell a range of things in deerskin and horn that cannot be obtained anywhere else in the world.

The City Hall is a hive of activity. In addition to themselves, the Law's have a staff of eight people who are intensely proud of the goods they produce and then sell in the retail shop.

It was not until after 1980 that a shop was created in the building, we thought this to be a well laid out room. The beautifully designed and made garments are displayed on highly polished wooden tables, which enhance the colour of the deerskin.

The traditional skill of the Highland leatherwork is displayed at its best in the handcrafted deerskin bags. Everyone is made in the workshop and when we examined the inside of the bags we found they were all lined with finest sueded calfskin.

If ever a slipper fitted like a glove, you will find it is true of the Deerskin bootees. They are made of soft, durable deerskin uppers with elasticated ankle gussets. They are truly featherlight

One of the most useful purses we have ever bought is the unique two-way zip purse. Measuring just 6"x 2½", it will easily hold up to £8 in change on one side, and on the other there is an identical zip pocket which holds notes.

We purchased a Horn handled walking stick, which was well made and well balanced, the range included all sorts of things. There were Shoe Horns, Pate Knives made entirely from real cowhorn, Staghorn handles on quality Sheffield steel knives, even an Orange Peeler.

Highland Horn & Deer Skin Centre

We are quite sure you will be tempted to buy something while you are there but it is good to remember that the centre has a mail order service, which could well help solve the problem of Christmas presents.

Next time we are in the Highlands we will certainly go back, and be quite sure that the Laws and their staff will give us a warm welcome in the best of Scottish traditions.

Close to the picturesque River Tay, we visited the cathedral, set in some really lovely grounds. Further along the Tay, we came across one of Thomas Telford's finest bridges, built in 1809. A riverside path leads from here downstream to the famous Birnam Oak, which is the sole remainder of Macbeth's Birnam Beeches. We followed the signposts from the A9 Perth to Inverness Road, and seven miles south of Pitlochry, deep in the countryside, we came across the **Dowally Craft Centre and Restaurant**.

It is well worth taking the trouble to stop here, for inside you will find a fascinating range of pottery, which is made on the premises, as well as other crafts and some interesting gifts. This purpose-built craft centre is one of Scotland's largest and is open from 10.00am to 6.00pm, with extended hours in the summer. Apart from the crafts and gifts, there is a new 'shop within a shop', which stocks a wide range of fashionable clothing.

There is ample car parking space and even a picnic area inside the grounds. Alternatively you may decide to adjourn to the stylish, timber lined restaurant attached to the centre, as here you will be able to sit down to either a snack or a full meal. The restaurant caters for a wide range of tastes, and includes vegetarian food in its choice.

Dowally Craft Centre & Restaurant

Further up the River Tay is **Ballinluig**. This is where Rob Roy escaped his captors by breaking out of jail in 1717. It is now a friendly little village with a lovely inn, ideal for a stop and refreshment.

The Ballinluig Inn is some two hundred years old, and proved well worth a visit during our tour of this scenic area. We noticed at once that there is a strong local trade here, and we could well understand why. As we enjoyed a drink in the Stable Bar, we discovered from hosts Sonia, Bryan and Terry that the inn was originally a farmhouse and stables. The Stable Bar still retains much of its old world charm, with exposed beams and rough plastered walls, and is a popular place for holidaymakers, hill walkers and fishermen. The atmosphere is friendly and relaxed, and we enjoyed a drink here.

The restaurant, which has forty covers, continues the comfortable old world theme, and we had difficulty making a choice from the chef's specialities and the mouth-watering range of starters. We began our meal with deep fried mushrooms stuffed with Brie and coated in seasoned breadcrumbs, and to follow we treated ourselves to one of the chef's specialities, poached Tay salmon steaks in white wine, served with a rich butter and egg sauce. Our meal was of excellent quality and very reasonably priced. Apart from the restaurant, you may have a bar meal served in the Stable Bar; they really do have an excellent choice here.

There is ample parking outside, and if you would like to stay on a while to explore this lovely area, the inn has eight en-suite bedrooms, all of which are very comfortably furnished. Children are most welcome, and you will find the Ballinluig Inn to be a comfortable and relaxing base for touring around either Pitlochry or Perth.

The Ballinluig Inn

Pitlochry has been described as the "jewel in Perthshire's crown", and it certainly is set amidst some magnificent scenery with plenty of first class accommodation and a wide range of activities.

There are two distilleries here that we were keen to find out more about, one being reputedly the smallest distillery in the world. This you will find at **Eradour** and it has been making whisky since 1825. It wasn't until 1986 that the proprietors decided that the old place was worthy of greater recognition, and set up the visitor centre selling a new brand of ten year old Highland malt. Come along to see the production process and take away a sample of this fascinating place.

The other distillery is the **Blair Atholl Distillery**, owned and managed by Arthur Bell & Sons plc. This is production at the other end of the scale and there is a tour to help you understand the distillery process. There is also a shop here with a wide range of single malts and blended whiskies for sale. Afterwards why not relax over a cup of coffee.

Finding somewhere to stay in a town with so much to offer can sometimes be a problem, so in Pitlochry you should be sure to make the most of your visit by stopping at the **Airdaniar Hotel**, on Atholl Road. Here in the heart of Highland Perthshire you will be welcomed warmly by the Mathiesons to their hotel, which we are sure you will agree is beautifully situated and enjoys delightful views of this romantic countryside.

The hotel has nine bedrooms, all en-suite, and include colour televisions, direct dial telephones and tea and coffee making facilities. With baby listening devices available as well, this is sure to appeal to both families with young children and couples.

A real treat is that the hotel is a member of the 'Taste of Scotland' scheme and is justly famous for the range and quality of its menus and dishes, which are complemented by a comprehensive wine list. We were very impressed with the standard of both restaurant and bar meals.

When we enquired further about the 'Taste of Scotland', we were told that it is dedicated to promoting the high standards of hospitality and cuisine based on the best fresh produce from Scotland. Those establishments who belong to the scheme have to meet a very high standard indeed, and membership says a lot for the Mathiesons and the Airdaniar Hotel.

The hotel itself is a charming Victorian villa, which is situated in its own grounds and gardens and retains much of the character of the period.

If you are tempted by an excellent choice of menus for both lunch and dinner then why not pay a visit to the **Luggie Restaurant and Carvery** which you will find in Rie-Achan Road in Pitlochry. This restaurant runs as a self-service coffee shop in the day and is renowned for its cold table at lunchtime.

In the evening the excellent carvery takes over. There is a wide range of food here and the place has an in house bakery supplying them with a mouth-watering selection of breads and pastries. We were also glad to find that vegetarian meals are always available. We were impressed with the cosy feeling of the restaurant and enjoyed the old fashioned charm of the beamed ceilings and solid stone which is combined tastefully with the best of modern well planned facilities. Be sure to pay a visit to either the hotel or restaurant, as they are places of great character.

The Airdanair Hotel

One of Pitlochry's major attractions is the **Salmon Ladder**, at the Fish Pass on Loch Faskally. Here there is an observation chamber for visitors to watch the salmon by-passing the dam by a series of 34 connecting pools. We are sure you will agree this is quite a feat, and the fish can be seen gathering their strength for a final push up into Loch Faskally.

Two miles from Pitlochry on the B8019 to Killiecrankie, you will come across the **Faskally Caravan Park**, which is an excellent stop for either bringing your own caravan or tent, or perhaps booking into one of the well-equipped permanent caravans on the site. The position of the park could not be better, as it is based on a number of sheltered fields which lie above the River Garry, and we were struck by the wonderful views of the surrounding countryside beyond.

There is plenty of room here, as the site covers some twenty-three acres. The static caravans have all been well equipped with fully fitted kitchens, colour televisions, fitted bedrooms and showers. There are even gas fires in case the weather proves to be a bit chilly, should you come here earlier or later on in the season.

The services on the site are geared towards catering for all the campers, with excellent facilities for relaxation including a bar, restaurant, showers, shop, launderette, children's playground and an indoor games area. In fact Mr Hay's customers often return year after year to take advantage of this haven, and we think you will agree that this is quite understandable, given the super setting and plentiful amenities.

Faskally Caravan Park

Discerning visitors who appreciate an elegant home in peaceful surroundings will enjoy staying at **Druimuan House**, near Killiekrankie, which is open from March to November. The house has six guest bedrooms, and four of these are en-suite. The building dates from 1863 and is most interesting to look at, with its small turrets and wing extension of 1907. Those who stay in this lovely house will be treated to the spectacular views of the surround-

237

ing countryside.

The pass of Killiekrankie was one of Queen Victoria's favourite spots, and is famous for the battle of 1689 when the Jacobites overwhelmed the English troops of King William. Iain and Jane Macdonald-Smith, who run the house, tell us that the battle was reputedly fought over and around the property. 'Soldiers Leap' is only half a mile away, this is where later in the ensuing struggle by the 'Kings over the Water' to reclaim their throne, Bonnie Prince Charlie once fought, and forced his soldiers to leap across the river.

In the grounds of the house, Iain and Jane also let two self-catering flats and a cottage. All units come provided with everything you might possibly require for your stay, including a colour television. Linen can also be supplied for a small extra charge. Apart from the magnificent views, both the flats and cottage make an ideal base for touring the Highlands.

Pitlochry is nearby, and the surrounding area offers fishing, golf, bird watching and superb opportunities for walking. There are also some lovely woods and rivers, set against dramatic mountain scenery. The Highland Games, which are held every September, are a fascinating attraction. Make sure you get a chance to go to the twice weekly 'Highland Nights' which are held in the summer by the Tay. This is an experience not to be missed. Details can be obtained from the excellent Tourist Information Centre here.

The **Pitlochry Festival Theatre** is set on the banks of the River Tummell and offers entertainment throughout the summer which is of a very high standard. It makes sense to have a look at the programme and book ahead if possible. **Blair Castle** is also easily reached, being only three miles away.

Our stay at Druimuan House, as we are sure it will be for you, be it here, or in the flats or the cottage, was a very wise choice, making an excellent base in this lovely area.

Druimuan House

Blair Atholl has Blair Castle which is a white turretted baronial mansion and the seat of the Duke of Atholl, chief of Clan Murray. It has had amongst its famous visitors Mary Queen of Scots and Queen Victoria. It is said that the castle was renowned for its generosity in the entertainment of its visitors, and there is an account of Mary's visit in 1564 when two thousand clansmen were employed to drive the game from the surrounding area. The final bag included 360 deer and five wolves. This gave Blair a reputation as one of the finest hunting chateaux in Europe.

The castle today has many fascinating collections of furniture, portraits, china, arms, armour, etc. Another interesting point is that this stronghold was the last one in Britain to be besieged, and also that the last Duke is the only British subject allowed to maintain a private army. There is much to do and see in this fascinating castle.

If, like us, you were taken with the magnificent Blair Castle and enjoy the peaceful feeling in this lovely village, then you may have noticed on your travels the charming St Andrews Crescent where The Firs, a guest house in an enviable position, can be found.

This friendly house is run by Kirstie and Geoff Crerar, who have been working hard upgrading the accommodation progressively since they moved back into the area in 1986. The property has four letting bedrooms, all with their own washbasin and two with showers, and there are plans afoot for en-suite facilities by 1990. There is ample car parking space here and the house is set in its own spacious grounds. Blair Atholl is also handy for the main London to Inverness Intercity railway. If you have young children, you will be delighted to know that high chairs, toys and even disposable nappies are provided.

The Firs

Kirstie and Geoff have put a lot of forethought and hard work into The Firs, and the results are enviable. We were delighted to be welcomed in the evening, after our day exploring the area, to a delicious home cooked, three course meal that was extremely satisfying.

Blair Atholl is a very quiet village, though Kirstie and Geoff point out that there is much to do if you are feeling especially active, and the village is also an ideal base for touring, being only a couple of miles from the A9, bringing most of Scotland within easy reach. Be assured that a warm welcome awaits you in this Highland home from home.

It must seem to you that our lives consist of going from one hotel, guest house or pub to another. This is almost true but not quite. In Scotland to even begin to describe the scenery to you would make us wax poetic and poets we are not. Therefore, we have tried to take you along the routes from which you will get the best views and so inevitably we need to find watering holes to house and feed us.

Just four miles from Blair Atholl you will find the most hospitable **Bruar Falls Hotel**, which is a comfortable, family run hotel. There are a total of seven letting rooms here, all of which are conveniently situated on the ground floor, with colour televisions and tea and coffee making facilities. Families are well catered for, with a cot and family room available. We loved the real log fire in the restaurant, by which we were able to relax and unwind whilst making our choice from the generous menu.

Our meal was accompanied by a selection from the extensive wine list, and we soon felt at home. Children's meals are available at half price, which is always a nice touch. As the name suggests, Bruar Falls is close to the renowned beauty spot where visitors can see a real triple waterfall! The Spencers and the Robertsons, who run the hotel, told us that the building is over two hundred years old, and was used as a billet for Highlanders during the '45 rebellion and also has a history as a coaching inn.

Whether you just want to relax and enjoy the sights or travel further into the Highlands and major cities, or perhaps spend some time taking part in local sports, you will find the Bruar Falls Hotel small and friendly and an ideal stop.

The Bruar Falls Hotel

Here we left the A9 and drove down towards **Loch Rannoch**, where we wanted to take advantage of the peace and quiet and simply walk a little. This is an ideal spot and we wandered into the village of **Kinloch Rannoch** where a friend had recommended that we look for Cuilmore Cottage, a coveted and unpretentious little restaurant and guest house.

Cuilmore Cottage lies only one hundred yards from the shore of Loch Rannoch on the edge of the village of Kinloch Rannoch, and is one of those rare places that once discovered are always remembered and treasured. This 18th century stone croft is quite simply a delight, and you will certainly not forget your visit, whether it is to stay in one of the three large bedrooms or simply to stop and sample the delights of the cuisine that includes Cuilmore in the 'Taste of Scotland' recommendation.

As a guest, you will be treated to the delicous home-made fare that makes up the filling breakfast of free range eggs, muffins, wholemeal rolls and wonderful home-made jams and marmalades. In these surroundings guests are invited to explore the splendid scenery, and to make complimentary use of the cottage's sailing dinghy, canoe and mountain bikes. Both useful local knowledge and advice on a variety of activities is offered by hosts, Jens and Anita Steffen.

Dinner in the intimate restaurant is enhanced by the small numbers allowed here, and really is an experience not to be missed. Guests are encouraged to discuss the menu beforehand, and to provide their own wine to complement the wonderful selection. Jens and Anita will do their best to meet your own requirements truly taking advantage of the best of the freshly grown and caught local produce.

Whatever your plans or requirements, we are quite sure that you will enjoy your stay at Cuilmore Cottage, and will want to return one day.

Cuilmore Cottage

Seven miles west of Kinloch Rannoch on the B846 stands **Talladh-a-**

Bheithe Lodge. This imposing stone built house started life as a hunting lodge for one of the large, local country estates, and stands in its own grounds enjoying magnificent views over Loch Rannoch. The Lodge is now a guest house and restaurant, providing some ideal accommodation in which to enjoy the scenic grandeur of the surrounding Perthshire countryside.

Talladh a Bheithe has the most beautiful landscaped gardens amid seven acres of parkland, and provides a peaceful ambience for visitors, with efficient but discreet service and excellent food. Sitting just ten miles from Rannoch Station, the Lodge is easily accessible for those seeing Scotland by rail. Drivers can find it on the North Lochside Road.

Accommodation is available in single and double rooms, most with ensuite bathrooms and all with washhand basins. There is an excellent family suite too, with double bedrooms and full ensuite facilities.

Talladh a Bheithe

The house is beautifully decorated and furnished. All rooms have Adam fireplaces, adding a touch of elegance to the surroundings. Visitors will enjoy a hearty breakfast and you may also decide to sample some of the delicious lunches, afternoon teas and evening meals which are increasingly popular with non residents.

Without a doubt this area is one of outstanding natural beauty. A veritable paradise for walkers, anglers, yachtsmen, cyclists and nature lovers who all come to Talladh a Bheithe Lodge to enjoy the peace and tranquillity it provides.

The Douglas Window, Stirling Castle

Tayside to Fife

Caledonian Equestrian Centre

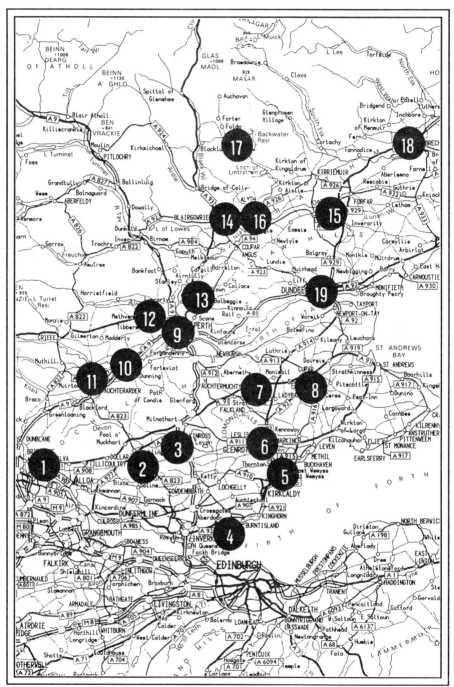

Please turn to Reference Section for further information.

CHAPTER TWELVE

Tayside to Fife

We have already paid a visit to Stirling in the previous chapter, and yet it is here that we start our final journey to the east of Central Scotland.

We start our voyage in an appropriate place, **Alloa**. This strange name comes from the Celtic and means 'swift ford'. Its origin no doubt refers to the magnificent sweep of the Firth of Forth which stretches out beneath the town. Alloa has an interesting story in connection with the sea which we were enthralled to discover.

Before the river silted up it had formed part of Scotland's naval dockyard in the 16th century. Here in 1511, James IV launched the great flagship of the Royal Scottish Navy, the 'Great Michael'. There was an astounding amount of work that went into the production of this ship. It reputedly had sides that were 10ft thick, and had taken up the entire resources of the woods in Fife to produce. She was a truly international vessel, with shipwrights from France, gunners from Holland, ironmongers from Spain and tinsmiths from Cornwall all being employed in her production. With 300 guns she was far ahead of other ships of the time, and was to be the pride of the King and Navy.

Unfortunately, after two years of being docked for want of a better purpose, she was finally taken out and entrusted to the command of a less than capable courtier, the Earl of Arran, who had never actually been to sea. Alas, the king realised only too late that the wrong man had been given the job, and by the time an experienced captain had been sent to replace the incompetent Earl, not a trace of the Great Michael could be found. It is to this day a mystery as to what happened to this extravagant and costly ship. There is a rumour that a wrecked hull, found years later at the port of Brest in France, was indeed all that was left of the Great Michael.

Four miles from Stirling on the A91 at **Blairlogie** is the **Blairlogie House Hotel**, owned and run by Mr and Mrs Collie. This glorious Victorian country house has been a hotel for the last thirteen years, and you may notice that the rooms have been named after the previous owners.

The hotel is set in eleven acres of its own grounds containing lovely lawns and even a small waterfall which, together with the panoramic backdrop of the Ochil Hills, gives a wonderful feeling of space and peace to the house.

There are seven en-suite bedrooms, complete with tea and coffee making facilities, colour television and direct dial telephone. All the bedrooms are comfortably furnished, some with antiques

Before dinner you might like to have a drink in the elegant bar, where lunches are also served. The dining room is truly the jewel of the hotel, attractively decorated in yellow and blue and set off with two magnificent fireplaces. We have never found anything to beat the comfort of a real log fire, and one is lit here most evenings. There is an extensive wine list from which to choose something to accompany your meal chosen from the sumptuous dinner menu.

There are a wealth of activities available to guests, and we particularly enjoyed a game of croquet on the lawns. For the sporting person there are both fishing and shooting nearby, as well as ice-skating and swimming, depending on the season.

Blairlogie House Hotel

Blairlogie House is close to Stirling yet also within easy reach of Glasgow and Edinburgh. This proximity, combined with the best of county life and good friendly service, has put the hotel firmly on our list of places to which to return.

Take the north road out from Alloa, through Tillicoultry and on towards **Dollar**. Dollar was the scene in 877 AD of the defeat of the 'Scots' in battle by the Danes. **The Dollar Academy** is a fine building here well worth a look, being a good example of Classical Georgian style built by Sir William Playfair in 1819. Sir William Playfair also designed the Academy and National Gallery in Edinburgh.

In Glen above Dollar sits **Castle Campbell**, commanding long views over the plains of the Firth. Built at the end of the 15th century, it was burned by Cromwell although the ruin is quite impressive. We were told that the castle was once known as 'Castle Gloom' as it is set amongst the glens of 'Care' and 'Sorrow' and by the waters of 'Grief'. One wonders how they came by their names.

Just past Dollar is **Rumbling Bridge**, where the River Devon falls through a ravine spanned by three bridges. A footpath from the north side gives good access to the spectacular gorges and falls, one of which is known as the Devil's Mill. Another, Cauldron Linn, is a mile downstream, with Vicar's Bridge, a beauty spot, a mile beyond this.

We stopped at the Powmill Farm Milk Bar on the A977, which is a fascinating place, and was actually the first milk bar in Scotland. Here there is plenty to satisfy a healthy appetite, with a range of food being served, from snacks to full meals at the food and salad bar. The salads are certainly inviting, and we were also tempted by the delicious aroma of home baking arising from the kitchen. In fact the **Powmill Farm Milk Bar** comes highly commended in the Egon Ronay guide.

Whilst you are here, let the children play in the large grass area while you look around the garden centre or the gift shop. The garden centre also houses a kitchen showroom, which has kitchens from Scotland's leading specialist, 'Crannog', who are renowned for their real wood kitchens.

Powmill Farm Milk Bar

The A977 took us across to **Kinross** on the west side of Loch Leven. In the town you will see an interesting tolbooth that dates back to the 16th century and that was restored in 1771 by Robert Adam.

Kinross House has a fine Renaissance exterior and was built for Daniel Defoe between 1685 and 1690. The gardens of the house are most interesting and are open from May to September.

There is also a museum in the town that gave us an interesting insight into the history of the town and the loch with its famous castle.

We took the chance to visit **The Grouse and Claret Restaurant**. The name of this lovely place comes as no surprise as it is set in the beautiful surroundings of the Heatheryford Country Centre.

To get to the country centre and restaurant simply leave the M90 at Junction 6, where you will find the entrance opposite the Granada service station. The Grouse and Claret Restaurant offers a wide ranging and mouthwatering menu specialising in trout, shellfish and tempting game dishes to cater for all tastes, together with a delicious variety of desserts, and an interesting wine menu. The idyllic setting overlooks its own trout ponds with the Lomond Hills to the east and the Ochill Hills to the west.

This really is a special place with a peaceful atmosphere, serving delightful food and wine. The decor is charming and the old sandstone buildings are filled with unusual antique furniture, old rugs and lovely pictures. There are many fine examples of local craft work, some of which are for sale. Our hosts were keen to point out that the function room can cater for parties of up to 70 guests, and also boasts special musical evenings and concerts to suit a wide range of tastes. The conservatory overlooks the waters and is an ideal place in which to make the most of the stunning sunsets.

The delicious home made food is set off nicely by the charming surroundings, whilst outside in the large grounds there is much of interest to be seen with wildfowl, ducks and poultry around and even ducks to be fed. The atmosphere of the place is warm, inviting and friendly; we were made to feel especially welcome. If you would like to stay a while to enjoy the comforts and delights of the Grouse and Claret and its surroundings then there are 5 bedrooms available, three of which are suitable for the disabled.

The **Heatheryford Country Centre** has become a centre for not only fishermen, but also artists and naturalists. It offers a splendid opportunity for you to become proficient in the art of fly-fishing as lessons are available. Being only half an hour from Edinburgh and within easy reach of many of Scotland's major towns and cities, the centre and its excellent restaurant, the Grouse and Claret, make an ideal place for a visit whether its simply for lunch or dinner or a memorable stay for a day or so.

The Grouse & Claret Restaurant

Kinross means more to us since we watched the excellent series 'Resuce' on ITV. Did you see it? It showed the R.A.F Helicopter Rescue service at work and one of the squadrons is based at Kinross. What incredibly brave men they are. It was quite nerve wracking watching them on television but when you are face to face with the terrain that they have to cover, it brings a realism to their actions that no television screen can possibly do.

Loch Leven was of course where Mary Queen of Scots was kept prisoner during 1567, until her daring escape eleven months later in 1568. Her story has been told before in this book, although you may now take the opportunity to visit the island and castle by ferry from Kinross. Mary was held in the small round tower which is separate from the main keep.

If the island looks large today it is as well to remember that the water level was much higher then, so the island would have been far smaller. The original size of the island was probably in keeping with the boundary walls of the castle.

We were fascinated to be told that Kinross was once a tiny county in its own right, though it has now been swallowed in the Tayside region.

Visitors to the loch and Kinross should ensure that they pay a visit to **Todd and Duncan Ltd**, at **Loch Leven Mills**. Open Monday to Saturday from 9.00am to 5.30pm all year round, the Loch Leven Mill shop has the largest selection of cashmere, camelhair and lambswool sweaters produced by Scotland's leading knitters.

Todd & Duncan Ltd

Todd and Duncan Ltd was established in 1867 and is today the largest spinner of Cashmere yarns in the world. Part of Dawson International, they supply yarns to all knitters in Scotland, and their own group of Ballantyne, Pringle, Braemar, McGeorge, Barrie and Glenmac are world famous for their quality.

There are often many bargains and special offers to be had here, and the mill shop is a stockist of Daks Simpson suits, skirts and blouses. Browsing can be fun and there is a wide selection of gift items including rugs, scarves and ties, all of which make ideal presents.

Why not refresh yourself after looking around, in the coffee lounge that offers a delicious range of home-baked snacks?

Kinross itself has much to offer, and we paid an interesting visit to the local history museum in the High Street. Other places of interest are the butterfly farm in Kinross and Vane Farm Bird Sanctuary. The Loch Leven National Nature Reserve is the most important area for freshwater breeding and migratory wildfowl in Britain. In the winter months the loch is a favourite breeding ground for wild geese, ducks and other wild fowl.

Travel down to the south of the loch and you will have the chance to observe and even partake in one of the most exhilirating of all activities, gliding. At Portmoak Airfield in **Scotlandwell** visitors are welcome to view the gliding, and if inclined, to be taken for a trial instructional flight.

From Kinross it is possible to join the M90 which will take you south to **Dunfermlinein** no time at all. This ancient town was the seat of many Scottish Kings and Queens and in fact was once itself the capital of Scotland. The palace now lies in ruins beside **Dunfermline Abbey,** which contains many royal graves including most notably that of Robert the Bruce who died in 1327.

We were fascinated to discover that during restoration work on the abbey in 1818, workmen who were excavating came across a vault containing a stone coffin, in which was a skeleton wrapped in thin lead. Some of the teeth were still in the head and there were shreds of gold cloth still clinging to the bones. Any doubt that this was the body of Robert the Bruce was removed when it was noticed that the breastbone was sawn away so that his heart could be removed by Sir James Douglas.

You might recall in a previous chapter how Sir James was pledged to take the heart of the king for burial in the Holy Land. Before the new tomb was ready the king lay in state and many hundreds of people came to pay their respects.

Dunfermline boasts a list of interesting buildings and some lovely parks. One of the town's most famous sons was Andrew Carnegie who went to America and became a self-made millionaire in the iron and steel industry. The cottage where he was born in 1835 is now a museum, and the town contains many fine buildings housing galleries and museums donated by Carnegie. We spent a pleasant time wandering around the lovely gardens, and the visitor will find a wide choice of tea rooms and cafes in which to take refreshment.

From Dunfermline, travel a few miles to the east on the A92 to the small town of **Aberdour**, which is famous for its 'silver sands' and its attractive position between dramatic cliffs. It was here that an amorous young Frenchman propositioned the young Queen of Scots, and was beheaded for his unwelcome attentions.

In the high street at Aberdour you will find an excellent place to stay in the

Aberdour Hotel. The hotel was formerly a coaching inn in the 16th century, where horses could be changed en route from Dunfermline to Kinghorn.

Aberdour Hotel

The village itself is steeped in history. The quaint harbour is still here and there is also a 12th century church and castle. Minutes away from the hotel are excellent beaches and a golf course. Even the local station has won awards and been featured on BBC TV.

Only twelve miles from Edinburgh and eight miles from Dunfermline, there are a wide range of activities available to the visitor. There are many local walks worth taking, and both boat hire and fishing are readily available.

The hotel has seven bedrooms, with tea and coffee making facilities and all rooms have central heating and continental quilts. There is the added luxury of a laundry and ironing service available. The furnishings are comfortable and the attractive use of natural light oak is a pleasure to see.

The atmosphere is warm and friendly throughout the hotel and the dining room can cater for up to thirty two people. We were enchanted by the dried flower arrangements and the use of old Singer treadle sewing machine tables in the dining room.

The lounge bar makes a lovely retreat with its open log and coal fire, and we were impressed by the menu which boasts an interesting mix of traditional, oriental and sea food dishes. Vegetarians are also well catered for here.

Mike Taddei, the landlord, told us that his own Adiary honey is available throughout the year, whilst his own chickens provide fresh eggs daily for breakfast. There is ample space for children to play in the courtyard area and they also have their own menu. The bar is well stocked with a selection of beers and wines.

We love to hear stories of ghost and legends and we were told that the hotel is supposedly haunted by one of the former kitchen maids. She has been spotted on occasions walking between the kitchen and ladies toilet dressed in an old fashioned kitchen gown and hat. We suspect that she is as reluctant to leave this lovely hotel as we were.

The hotel is unsurprisingly recommended by the Good Beer, Bed and Breakfast Guide and also the European Good Food Guide. We would certainly add our recommendation to that impressive list.

Staying within the coast road, we made our way up through the lively resort of Buntisland and onto **Kirkcaldy**. This thriving town once developed through the linen trade into the manufacture of linoleum. The latter was apparently discovered when a local family had the idea of making more durable cloth that would be suitable for the covering of floors. It was originally made from cork imported from Spain, and whale oil. This combination at one time gave the town a rather unique smell.

There is a wealth of interesting buildings throughout the town, including **Raith**, probably built by MacDuff and Balwearie, which has strong connections with the renowned wizard, Michael Scott, whose practices and proficiency in alchemy and astrology earned him a fearful reputation. He even has a mention in the eighth Circle of Dante's 'Inferno'.

Adam Smith, the economist, was born here, and it was here that he retired to write his famous book 'The Wealth of Nations' which appeared in 1776. We also learned that the last two duels to be fought in Scotland, in 1822 and 1826, took place in Kirkcaldy.

Kirkcaldy is also known as "the long town", and if you take the time to walk down its four mile long main street you will find out why it was so named. There are libraries, museums and galleries throughout, which make interesting viewing. We were delighted to be able to walk and unwind in Ravendcraig and Beveridge Park with their excellent facilities for bowling, tennis and boating. There are many good picnic areas and plenty of activities for the young ones.

Dysart village lies just to the north of Kirkcaldy, and is worth a visit to stop and walk around the delightful harbour with its rows of pantiled fishing houses now restored by the National Trust. The name 'Dysart' itself actually means 'desert' or 'hermitage', and it was in the 6th century that St Serf settled at Culross and established a retreat at Dysart. St Serf is credited with the conversion of Fife to christianity and he reputedly kept a pet robin. His life abounds with rumour and legend; one source claims that he was the son of a Caanite king and an Arab princess, while another says that he was pope for seven years.

Dysart once did a brisk trade with the Continent in salt, though by the end of the 18th century, nailmaking had become its principal industry, with over twelve million nails produced each year.

Also dating from the 18th century is the **Old Rectory Inn,** which is the perfect place to stop and refresh yourself while making the most of this interesting and relaxing coastal area. We found the food here interesting and varied. Where else could one find an inn that can offer not only English and Scottish food, but also French, Italian and Spanish dishes? The bar will cater for all tastes and we were presented with a choice of over 40 wines. The building has an interesting history and we noticed that the inn comes with an Egon Ronay recommendation.

Old Rectory Inn

We made a point of stopping off here and enjoyed our lunch in the bar. They even provide an opportunity to dine in style in the evening in their sumptuous and comfortable dining room. Do try and pay a visit to this delightful inn.

Turning inland we took the A92 up towards **Glenrothes** which has become the centre for a rapidly expanding electronics industry. At nearby **Leslie** the elegant and comfortable **Rescobie Hotel** is in a secluded position, set in two acres of grounds on the outskirts of the village.

This charming small hotel is given its distinctive character by the fact that it is run like a country house. On arrival we were welcomed by one of the owners. Friendly waitresses in tartan skirts were summoned by the press of a bell, and we were given a front door key to allow us to come and go at will.

We found the fittings and furnishings were in keeping with the family atmosphere: old mahogany nestles in corners, and antique maps rub shoulders with sporting prints and Cornish oils and watercolours. In the summer we were told golf holds sway, and conversation in the lounge revolves around St Andrews and Gleneagles. In winter, when the nights draw in and the log fires are lit, the talk is of walking or shooting.

Ideal for a peaceful stay or break, the Rescobie Hotel has eight bedrooms, all with private shower or bathroom; we certainly appreciated the direct-dial telephone and colour TV. A full breakfast is included in the room price and is available from 7.00 am. We selected our lunches and dinners from a choice of a la carte, table d'hote and vegetarian menus, and our meals were served in the main dining room, a lovely room in red and gold, although there is also a smaller room which doubles as a twelve seat conference room.

It is little wonder that the Rescobie Hotel is commended by the Scottish Tourist Board, and we too recommend that you make a point of stopping at this delightful country house hotel.

The Rescobie Hotel

From Leslie we rejoined the northern route to **Falkland**, where there is a splended palace and gardens set in this delightful small town. The buildings, in Renaissance style, date from 1501-41 and were the favourite seat of James V who died here in 1542, and of his daughter Mary Queen of Scots.

There is a rather grisly story that Robert the Second died here after being imprisoned and forced by starvation to eat his own flesh. A woman in an adjoining cell, who is said to have fed him for a while from her own breasts, was put to death for her trouble.

When James VI was here he was forced to listen to the preachings of John Knox the reformist. Legend has it that the King kept interrupting the preacher until he was reminded in no uncertain terms that the King was merely "God's silly Vassal".

Apart from being a fine palace with some exemplary architecture of the period, the gardens contain the original royal tennis court, the oldest in Britain, built in 1539.

In the town with that most delightful name,Auchtermuchty we came across two very enterprising ladies. Both Miss Anne Miller and her mother are the hard working force behind the **Alante Coffee and Crafts Shop** which you will find at 42 High Street.

Alante Coffee & Crafts Shop

Once you have had a good look around this charming place, you may feel in need of refreshment. You need look no further, as the coffee shop here can offer you its home-baked specialities, and a delightful range of handmade chocolates, all of which are baked and prepared on the premises by the Millers. We stopped for lunch, which was delicious, but you may choose to have afternoon tea, morning coffee or even breakfast here. The menu varies daily, and there is a good vegetarian selection too. Children are welcome, and special portions are available for them.

Be sure to pay a visit to this lovely place. You will find much here of interest, and the Millers will be ready to welcome you.

We will always associate Auchtermuchty with John Junor, who used to write such an entertaining and sometimes sniping column in the Sunday Express. He comes from here and frequently referred to the place.

Turning left onto the B936 you will find **Colzie Hill** two miles along the road on the left hand side.

We discovered that there are magnificent views from here; especially north over the Tay to the Grampian Mountains. The surrounding area is alive with activities from walking and riding in the beautiful coastal scenery, to hang gliding for the more adventurous. Cycling is such a peaceful way to see the countryside and we were pleased to find that it is possible to hire cycles in the area to do just this.

The **Colzie Hill Recreation Centre** offers opportunities for clay pigeon shooting, and has over sixty areas available for this and many other activities including, 'off the road' driving to test your skills.

There is a cottage here dating from 1850 which is available for hire to visitors, and has eight bedrooms in all. The comfortable cottage can offer all the usual amenities including video, woodburning stove and even a jacuzzi. We were impressed by the length of the attic lounge which is over thirty feet long and has majestic south-westerly views.

Colzie Hill is also ideal for the more experienced rider as guests to the cottage can keep their horses at the stables.

The shooting lodge itself looks up towards the Grampian mountains and, looking from the veranda, the views are breathtaking. The lounge can cater for any number in your party up to thirty. Meals are available for groups who come to the Hill for a day's activities and a warming menu of game and traditional Scottish Fayre is served.

If you are as curious as we were about the range of the day's activities, then you will be interested to find out that visitors will be able to take part not only in clay pigeon shooting and 'off the road' driving but also, mountain biking, tractor and trailer manouvering, fly casting and even JCB digging!

Colzie Hill is ideal for a day's activities with a difference, and it certainly is the place to pick up and practice a new set of skills.

You may prefer however, to opt for one of the more leisurely half day and day tours by Range Rover. These tours will depart from any St Andrews hotel and take you into the Highlands and back. What an excellent idea and a wonderfully stylish and relaxing way to travel and enjoy the marvellous countryside.

One of the most popular tours is the half day 'Macbeth and the malt' tour, which takes in one hundred and thirty miles and four places associated with the 11th century king. And of course, the trip would not be complete without taking in a full tour of a whisky distillery.

Colzie Hill Recreation Centre

We travelled on the A91 to pay a visit to **Cupar** before making our way across to the historical university town of St Andrews on the coast. Just off the main road, in the handy car park overlooking the spacious public park, is the **Eden House Hotel**, only 5 minutes' walk from the centre of Cupar, and incidentally ideally situated for many famous golf courses. The hotel boasts ten bedrooms complete with tea and coffee making facilities and two bathrooms.

This lovely Victorian house retains its original fireplaces, so charming in winter, and some detailed and interesting cornices. Unwind, as we did, in the comfortable lounge bar and just soak up the atmosphere of this informal, friendly and relaxing hotel.

The main dining room has twenty covers and offers a competitive range of foods for breakfast, lunch, afternoon tea and dinner. The tradtional food was much to our liking, and the bar stocks some good beer and an interesting selection of wines.

There are many places of interest to visit in the locality, brochures on what to see and do are available from the hotel, and of course St Andrews is only nine miles away. We also found the Management and Staff an invaluable source of information.

Eden House Hotel

Near to Cupar on the A91 we came across the **Scottish Deer Centre,** which is a unique opportunity to see, and even feed and touch these noble beasts. The centre makes an ideal day out for all the family, with many attractions and picnic areas. There are super facilities for the young ones, with adventure playgrounds both indoors and outside.

Reaching **St Andrews,** we were struck by the charm and gentility of the town which houses the oldest of the Scottish universities, being established by Papal decree in 1411. The calm of the town today gives no hint of the violent and bloody struggles that took place here during the Reformation.

One particular churchman, Cardinal David Beaton, was particularly relentless in the punishment of considered heretics, watching more than one victim burning at the stake. He in turn was murdered by the Reformers, who were joined by John Knox and occupied the castle, until the French attacked in 1547 forcing a surrender. Knox was taken away and subjected to the life of a galley slave for eighteen months. He swore to return to St Andrews for vengeance upon the places of worship, and indeed came back to Scotland eventually in 1559 to incite his followers to destroy the cathedral. We have never understood so many of these unchristian and senseless deeds purportrated by supposed men of God.

Today there is a far more peaceful air in the town, and the place attracts holiday makers and visitors to its stretches of safe, sandy beaches with delightful dunes and wonderfully clear waters. And, of course, there is the golf with St Andrews, home to possibly the most famous golf course in the world at the Royal and Ancient Golf Course founded in 1754. A visit to this historic place is a must, even if you are not a player.

The A94 takes you on a splendid journey across the Firth of Tay, on a magnificent bridge into the bustling city of Dundee. The bridge is a replacement for the first Tay bridge that was tragically swept away on 28th December 1879 taking with it a train that was carrying seventy-five passengers.

The panoramic views as you enter the city establishes Dundee as one of the most beautiful city settings anywhere in the world, set against the majestic backdrop of the Sidlaw Hills and fronted by the Tay.

In the Victoria Docks we were able to see Captain Scott's famous ship, Discovery, and also the frigate Unicorn which is now a floating museum. This famous frigate was built in 1824 and was in use until 1968, making it the oldest ship afloat in Britain.

Captain Scott's Ship, 'Discovery', Victoria Docks

One of Dundee's most famous sons was the self-styled poet, William McGonagall, whose unique approach to theatre and verse was to make him renowned, if not for the skill of his work then for its infectious delivery. At one literary occasion he was made a presentation of a large sausage, rather than be offended by this dubious award, he later wrote to thank the bequeathers, declaring that it was the best he had ever tasted.

From Dundee we took the A85 which led us eastwards towards **Perth**, the 'fair city' as it is sometimes known. Apparently the site even impressed the Romans, who compared the Tay to the Tiber. Perth too has had its share of fallen bridges due to repeated flooding, though as a port it eventually lost out in importance to Dundee. The proximity of Perth to **Scone Palace** ensured the town royal visitors, and indeed it was at one time pronounced capital of Scotland before Stirling, and eventually, Edinburgh received that honour. Perth has always had its fair share of prosperity, notwithstanding nine floods, seven sieges and five plagues. In the city you will come across the Fairmaid's House.

The actual house on this site has origins which go back to the 13th century, although **The Fair Maid's House** is probably best associated with Sir Walter Scott's novel, 'The Fair Maid of Perth'.

It is really quite fitting that the building is used today as a centre for Scottish crafts, and we were most impressed by the wealth of choice available to us. This exclusively Scottish range comes from leading designers in the field. There is so much to see here, including silver jewellery, pottery, designer knitwear, horn, wood, weaving and much more, all displayed in this historic house with its famous literary associations.

The Four Maids House

Visitors keen to know more about the history of the house and the site may like to ask Mrs McDonald, as she will be happy to answer any questions. The shop will be of tremendous interest to anyone who appreciates the art and skill involved in producing hand made goods of this quality. We were delighted to discover that upstairs there is a doll workshop, where Sheena Macleod creates her handmade 19th century character dolls of fishermen, crofters, knitters and spinners.

In Scott's tale 'The Fair Maid of Perth' he relays the true story of a gladiatorial contest that took place in 1396 in Perth. King Robert III forced the warring clans of Chattan and Kay to fight out their differences in the ring. Thirty men from each clan took part, and they fought to the death until there was only one Kay and eleven badly wounded Chattans left alive. The legend is that the surviving Kay escaped by diving into the Tay. This tale seems even more barbaric by the fact that an enclosure was provided and local nobles invited to watch as an audience.

It was a pleasure for us to stay at **The Dunallan Guest House** at 10 Pitcullen Crescent in Perth, where our hosts Jim and Cathy Brown were two of the most obliging people that we had come across in our travels.

Dunallan Guest House

The guest house itself was built around 1890 and has six rooms, three of which are en-suite. One of these is a family room, and the Browns welcome children whom they are pleased to cater for, and there is a cot for babies. In fact Jim and Cathy are even willing to babysit.

The house is nicely decorated and comfortably furnished. It is also extremely handy for the city centre of Perth, being only ten minutes' walk away. Evening meals are provided, and the cooking is wholesome, traditional and extremely delicious. Vegetables are always freshly grown, and if you are lucky enough to be here when rhubarb crumble is served, you will find that the rhubarb comes ripe from their garden. The Browns regret that no dogs are allowed.

Whether your staying in Perth to make the most of the local attractions or planning to use it as a base for excursions, Dunallan Guest House is an ideal, friendly place in which to stay. Jim is a mine of useful information when it comes to local knowledge and will be glad to direct you accordingly. Both Jim and Cathy do everything in their power to ensure that your stay with them is as happy and as comfortable as possible.

Dunallan Guest House is a member of the Scottish Tourist Board's classification and grading scheme, and has attained the standard represented by two crowns and commended. Inspection is thorough and carried out annually.

The city seems to be an elegant mix of Georgian and Victorian architecture, and if you look closely in the centre, you will be able to spot as we did the remaining 18th century shop fronts and odd medieval corners. Having wandered around enjoying the sights we were in need of quenching a well earned thirst. We made our way to **The White Horse Inn** in North William Street, where we were warmly greeted by Jim and Brenda Calderwood.

This historical Inn was built in 1820, and became a stopping and changing point for stagecoaches en route from Aberdeen to Edinburgh, and finally London. Such journeys must have been tiresome and uncomfortable for the traveller, especially if you were one of the twelve on the outside of the coach. The sight of the White Horse Inn must indeed have been a welcome one. The name of this hostelry stems from a former owner who would always place at least one white horse in the team of four.

The White Horse Inn

Today the Inn can offer the best in service and hospitality in keeping with its fine traditions. Visitors will find ample accommodation, with nineteen bedrooms, seven of which are en-suite. The atmosphere of the place is cosy and relaxing and guests will be able to enjoy the same homely feeling in either the public or the lounge bar, where there is a wide selection of drinks. Bar meals are available in the Coachman's Lounge. At weekends this is a popular place with locals and visitors alike as live entertainment is a regular feature.

Guests staying at the Inn will also be able to take advantage of a 10% discount offered in the Horseshoe Steakhouse Restaurant, this has an excellent value for money selection of local and traditional dishes, with a superb choice of steaks from which to indulge.

The White Horse Inn extends a welcome to all, whether you are merely passing through, or are intending to make the most of Perths many attractions.

If you have ever wondered where the warming spirits served in these friendly pubs come from, you will find the answer in Perth's case to be not too far, as there are two whisky distilleries in the city as well as a manufacturer of port.

Dewar's Whisky blending and bottling plant have guided tours twice daily, and you will get a fascinating insight into the process from blending to despatch. Alternatively, there are eighteen acres of delightful gardens surrounding the headquarters of **Arthur Bell Distillers** which are free for visitors to enjoy. The connection to the name does not end there, as you may have noticed the Bell Sports Centre in Hay Street which provides a whole range of facilities for the enthusiast.

Coach House Restaurant

The Perth Museum and Art Gallery makes a fascinating visit, and of course do try to visit the beautifully restored Repertory Theatre in the High Street.

No-one coming to enjoy the beautiful environs of Perth should leave without paying a visit to the **Coach House Restaurant**. It is a perfect spot for lunch or dinner, and especially for that 'special' meal after the theatre. You will find the Coach House in North Port, close to the museum.

The magnificent 17th century building gives charm and character to this modern Scottish restaurant. The awards and recommendations for the establishment are endless, and Simon and Brenda Burns are credited with running a smooth ship. Lunch here is made up of five courses, and is served between 12.00pm and 2.00pm, whereas dinner comprises a grand total of seven courses and is served from 7.00pm to 10.00pm in addition to after the theatre. The restaurant is often visited by both local and visiting celebrities, which says a lot for its reputation and standing both inside and outside of the community.

A warm welcome is extended to all, and especially to well- behaved children. Just give Simon and Brenda a little advance warning and they will be happy to cater for your needs.

Follow the A9 out of Perth travelling south east and you will be able to take the B9141 to the small village of **Dunning**. Here we came across **Duncrub Holidays**. They really have it all worked out for the guests who hire their superb range of self-catering properties near the village of Dunning, which lies ten miles west of Perth.

There are a choice of four properties available. Dalreoch House, which is a traditional farmhouse dating from 1760, comes set in its own acre with attractive garden and well-stocked trout pond. A comfortable and inviting home, it has two twin bedrooms available and evening meals can also be arranged.

Coachman House is converted from an old stable block, and has three twin bedded rooms and a double bedroom, while Gean Tree Cottage and Oak Tree Cottage are slightly smaller, though maintaining the standards of excellence and comfort set in all the properties.

All the accommodation comes with everything needed for your stay, and there are no 'hidden extras'. The beauty and tranquillity of the settings are magical, and yet major touring and sports centres are not far away.

Duncrub Holidays

Golfers will be especially well rewarded here, as there is a nine hole course on the doorstep, and the famous courses at Gleneagles are only seven miles away. And, of course, it only takes an hour to get to St Andrews itself. Walking is readily available, as is fishing or even sailing and windsurfing.

There are certainly no shortage of things to do and see in this part of the country. Nearby there are also, tennis and badminton courts for the use of guests.

The houses are set amidst this beautiful countryside with commanding views of the Ochils to the south, and the Grampians and Trossachs to the north and west. With all this and the top standard of accommodation it would be hard to think of a reason for not coming here.

At nearby **Auchterarder** we stopped to browse in the wealth of delightful antique shops, and dream about all the superb antiques we could buy if only we could win the football pools!

We always love to see an interesting building, and the **Collearn House Hotel** is no exception. Peacefully set in the village of Auchterarder, off the A9, this hotel has to be seen to be believed. Built in 1870, the hotel is an outstanding example of Victorian eccentricity, and has been lovingly restored to its former glory by the present owners. It now combines all the splendour of the bygone age with the best of modern amenities.

A closer inspection reveals the most delightful details, with beautiful wood panelling and carving everywhere, and the windows containing some of the most amazing stained glass.

Collearn House

The hotel has eight en-suite bedrooms and each has tea and coffee making facilities, colour television and its own telephone. The rooms are all luxuriously furnished in the style of the hotel. Guests and non-residents may choose to visit the bar, which is relaxing and friendly, before eating in the restaurant which has a wonderful selection of the best of Scottish and traditional cooking. It is no surprise that the restaurant comes with four crowns commended, as the menu is one of the most thoughtful that we have come across. The only difficulty you'll be likely to face is the choice.

We can highly recommend the friendly service in this family run hotel, and can assure you that a visit to the Collearn House Hotel will really be one of the highlights of your trip.

What a nice village is **Blackford** . We discovered it as we drove along the A9. If you go across the humpbacked bridge and into Stirling Street you will find **The Blackford Inn,** which is an ideal place to stop awhile and take some refreshment, whether it just be for a drink, or for a more filling meal in the excellent restaurant.

The charm and appeal of the Inn are immediately obvious to the visitor, as the place maintains its two hundred and fifty year old atmosphere, with its low beamed ceilings and a warming log fire. The Inn is extremely popular with the locals, who are a friendly bunch and made us feel quickly at home.

The Inn was taken over in October 1989 by Jim Kean and Janey Brown who introduced a locally renowned chef, David Payne. The splendid restaurant is decorated with a charming selection of local pictures and golfing prints, the latter being no surprise as they are a reminder of the many famous courses within easy reach. It is possible to enjoy a wide range of food here, from a simple sandwich to a selection of innovative and mouthwatering dishes, using fresh local produce. To accompany your meal you might like to try one of the many wines from around the world that are offered. The Inn is also well known for its fine selection of malt whiskies, and of course has a good selection of beers.

Jim Kean told us "our philosophy here is that you can come and get a meal as good as any you'd find in a top class restaurant but for a more reasonable price, and in a more informal atmosphere". The Inn's motto is 'The wee Inn with the big welcome', this we certainly found to be true.

Our visit to the Blackford Inn gave us a wonderful insight into the renowned warmth and hospitality of the area, and left us with some lovely memories and many new friends. You would be well advised, if intending to go for a meal, to book in advance, especially at weekends.

From Auchterader it is possible to leave the main roads and travel up towards the A85 via some small and quiet routes, taking you through very pleasant countryside. Once we reached the A85 we visited **Methven** where Robert the Bruce was defeated by the English in 1306. Methven Castle is also here which, although not open to

Blackford Inn

267

the public, was where James IV's widow, Margaret Tudor, died in 1541.

Close to the north of Methven, off the A85 Perth to Crieff road, we came across the delightful **Cloag Farm Cottages**, owned and run by David and Moira Smythe. They have three cottages that they let out on a weekly basis.

The farm cottages are exemplary in the provision of self-catering accommodation. All three cottages are in a row, commanding wonderful views over the Ochils and into Fife. Each cottage comes complete with a living room, kitchen, bathroom and two bedrooms, both of which sleep two.

They are uniquely situated on this working farm, offering the perfect retreat, and yet are within easy striking distance of all Scotland's major centres, with superb walking country literally only minutes away.

The Smythes have taken a great deal of trouble to ensure that their guests have every conceivable need. There are open fires in the lounges, and all the cottages have full central heating. A detailed list of all accessories is available from the Smythes upon request. Well-behaved pets are welcomed, and David and Moyra will even go so far as to provide groceries in advance if needed.

The nearby village of Methven is within walking distance and only two minutes away by car. The village has a post office, shops, two pubs and a garage. Perth itself is only seven miles away. The cottages at Cloag Farm are ideal for families or anyone who wishes to get away from it all, and yet have places like Edinburgh or St Andrews within easy reach.

Cloag Farm

Between Methven and Perth an interesting stop is **Huntingtower Castle**, formerly known as Ruthven Castle. This splendid place is a 15th century mansion that was the scene of the raid of Ruthven in 1583, when James VI found himself captive at the hands of his nobles who demanded the removal of certain royal favourites. The king tried to escape (he was 16 at the time) but found his way barred and was kept virtual prisoner for ten months, being forced to sign proclamations declaring himself a free agent. The nobles managed to hold on to some power for a few months, though the Earl of Gowrie (Lord Ruthven), who had originally invited the king to his hunting seat and capture, was eventually beheaded in 1585.

James waited a full eighteen years to take revenge on the remainder of the family, and the earl's grandson and his brother were killed in mysterious circumstances, their dead bodies tried for treason and their estates forfeited to the Crown. The name of Ruthven was abolished by an Act of Parliament, and the castle's name changed to Huntingtower. The castle has some fine painted ceilings that are well worth a look at.

The A94 runs north east from Perth through mostly farming country. The B953 leads off the main road at **Balbeggie**, six miles north towards the hills which include Dunsinane, made famous by Shakespeare in 'Macbeth'. There is an old ruin on the hill where Macbeth was slain, according to Shakespeare.

Here at Balbeggie we came across the **Caledonian Equestrian Centre** at Pitskelly Farm. Owned by Mr and Mrs Bruce, the centre is well established in covering all aspects of equestrian activities.

The Caledonian Equestrian Centre

If you have never thought about horse riding until now, it is something really worth considering. We have some friends who have taken it up late in life, and who have proved to us beyond doubt that it is never too late to learn and enjoy this wonderful experience.

Expert tuition is available from fully qualified staff, who will be glad to help beginners of all ages. Young ones inevitably, are often keen to have a go, and the centre will cater for them from the age of six. Of course the centre does not only care for beginners: even highly experienced riders will find their 'match' here.

Riding is one of those activities highly suitable for the disabled, and we were pleased to learn that the centre gives regular disabled group riding sessions.

Within easy reach of Perth, the Caledonian Equestrian Centre is a perfect place for the whole family to visit.

As the A94 reaches **Coupar Angus**, keep an eye out for the jail tower which was built in 1762. There are also the remains of a 12th century abbey here.

Nearby, **Blairgowrie** is well sited close to a series of small lochs. The small town is situated in the heart of fruit growing and farming countryside. Did you know that Blairgowrie is Gaelic for 'field of goats'? The altitude and soil seem to combine to give just the right growing conditions for what are described as the raspberries to match anything grown in Dregon. These raspberries are largely picked for the jam factories of Dundee.

We found in a quiet part of Blairgowrie, **Mullion House**, which is a beautifully restored Victorian country house dating from 1850 and set in its own one and a half acre grounds. Mullion House offers five letting bedrooms, four of which are en-suite with either private bathroom or shower.

The house is beautifully decorated throughout and has the most glorious ornate ceiling in the drawing room. There are open fires, which give the place a delicious feeling of warmth, and you will enjoy the traditional dining room.

Mullion House

We found the service at Mullion House to be excellent, and the food was especially good. We feasted on a delicious meal starting with a hearty home-made soup, followed by Roast Saddle Venison for our main course. To round off our fayre, there was an excellent choice of three or four home-made desserts. The food at Mullion House is a speciality, and local homegrown vegetables are used whenever possible. After a comfortable night's sleep we were glad to come down to a full traditional Scottish breakfast, giving us an excellent start to the day.

There is a first class recreational centre in Blairgowrie with many facilities including a swimming pool, games hall, gymnasium and sunroom. There are also excellent walks, in the vicinity, one favourite of ours going from Wellmeadow alongside the lovely wooded west bank of the River Ericht, and past a rocky gorge.

Another delightful country house which we discovered is the Kinloch House. A highly individual and most attractive country house hotel sitting three miles west of Blairgowrie. You will find it on the A 293 Dunkeld road here in the heart of the beautiful Perthshire countryside.

Built in 1840, Kinloch House is a substantial stone building which was modernised in 1911 when the magnificent oak panelled hall, staircase and gallery were added. Later, the owners embarked upon a programme of restoration designed to retain the character of the house, whilst providing all the facilities today's clients have come to expect of a modern hotel. Today therefore, Kinloch House is among the best hotels in Scotland and is recognised as such by all the major hotel guides.

The house is beautifully decorated, filled with antique furniture and many fine paintings. There is a comfortable resident's lounge and conservatory.

The cocktail bar is both a focal point and a meeting place, where virtually any request for a drink can be met from its well stocked gantry. Malt whisky connoisseurs alone have a choice of over 132 tipples!

The dining room offers the very best in Scottish fayre. Chef, Bill McNicoll produces a menu which changes daily, and offers an extensive choice of dishes prepared from the finest raw materials in the world - Scottish of course! Regular appearances on the menu include Scottish beef and lamb, shellfish and fish, salmon and game, venison and wildfowl. All food is skilfully prepared, and here you will find that dinner is regarded as the signature to what has hopefully been an enjoyable day.

There are twenty one guest rooms, including four downstairs in the new east wing, and two suites. Most have a southerly aspect and all have private facilities. Each room is traditionally furnished and some have four poster or half tester beds.

Leisure pursuits available to those who stay at Kinloch House are many and varied. The area is well served with golf courses, with around forty of them within an hour's drive including of course, St Andrews, as well as Rosemount and Carnoustie. Salmon fishing on the Tay as well as trout fishing on the local lochs is a popular pastime. Shooting on local estates is the preoccupation during the winter months and if something a touch more leisurely is your forte, then there are many excellent walks to be enjoyed in the surrounding countryside.

We can promise that, whatever your interest, a warm welcome will be found at Kinloch House.

Kinloch House

We had heard much about the rapidly developing skiing centres in Scotland, especially from our son-in-law who seems to us to have tried them all! Yet, we were unprepared for the excellent standards and facilities available to those who take advantage of the **Altamount Chalets** near Blairgowrie at any time of year.

There are eighteen one, two or three bedroomed Scandinavian style chalets set beautifully in two and a half acres of landscaped parkland, only five minutes' walk from the centre of Blairgowrie.

The chalets are totally self-catering, and the only things that guests are asked to provide are their towels and tea towels. Open throughout the year, the chalets can take advantage of an enormous range of activities available in the locality.

Altamount Chalets

Spring time brings the valley into true beauty, and the wildlife reserve at Loch of the Lowes welcomes many migratory visitors, including ospreys. Summer is packed with events, including Highland games and sheepdog trials. Then of course there is the legendary fruit picking that is available in the autumn months. The autumnal colours are quite unforgettable in the heather-clad hills, and in the winter Blairgowrie comes alive as sports enthusiasts come up for skiing at Glenshee. Apart from skiing, visitors may go pony trekking, touring, walking, fishing or play golf, tennis and squash.

There is certainly no shortage of activities, as we are sure you will agree, and we can think of no better place to stay whilst you are here than in one of the attractive **Altamount Chalets**. There are special skiing holiday packages here, which we thought were especially enticing.

All the chalets are warm, insulated and come complete with colour television. Bookings are also taken for weekend or short breaks during the spring, autumn and winter.

The road out of Blairgowrie took us through Rattray towards the small town of Alyth. Here we found a charming folk museum which has interesting displays of life in the local community and in the surrounding countryside.

Close by is **Glamis Castle**, mentioned by Shakespeare in 'Macbeth'. The 'Lord of Glamis' was the second of the titles which the witches foretold for Macbeth. There have been many famous visitors to this castle, including James V, and his daughter Mary Queen of Scots. Sir Walter Scott was another visitor here, and we also learned that it was the childhood home of Queen Elizabeth, the Queen Mother, whose father was the fourteenth Earl of Strathmore. The buildings, with their turrets and parapets are striking, and the castle is well worth a visit.

We came to Alyth after visiting Glamis Castle, and came across an excellent place for refreshment in **The Stables Inn,** in Mill Street. Whether you visit the castle or not, do be sure to make a stop here. You will be welcomed in this family run and friendly establishment, by Helen, Gavin and Chris.

The inn is popular with locals, and you won't find a stronger recommendation for a place than that. Inside the Stables Inn is warm and comfortable, with the lovely fireplace adding to the welcoming atmosphere.

The well-stocked wine cabinet will cater for most tastes and make the perfect accompaniment to some of the excellent bar food. If you prefer, you may like to eat in the restaurant which has a fine choice of Scottish fare and a tempting selection of home cooking and baking. Children are welcome in the restaurant.

The small town of Alyth is very attractive, with its burn flowing through it alongside the main street. A chat to Chris, Gavin or Helen will point you in the right direction for local sightseeing. Perhaps they, or their friendly customers, will tell you about some of the excellent country walks nearby. The town is handy for both Perth and Dundee, and is within easy commuting distance of either. If you would like to stay in the area for a while then Chris will be happy to arrange local accommodation for you. It is well worth dropping in for a visit to the friendly crowd at the Stables Inn.

The Stables Inn

Those of you who would like to take advantage of the glorious mountain scenery would be well advised to pay a visit to **The Glenisla Hotel** just outside Alyth.

It is always delightful to come across a place that is fully bound up with the history of the local area, this pleasure was confirmed when we found this super hotel set in the heart of the Kirkton Of Glenisla.

The scenery alone would be enough to justify the highest praise, flanked with sweeping hillsides and the River Isla running along the floor of the valley.

The hotel itself has six bedrooms, all en-suite with Colour TV and tea and coffee making facilities. Visitors will be able to take advantage of a separate bar in the old part of the hotel, complete with log fires and oak beams. The cosy residents lounge also has a log fire, and can boast the most marvellous views of the hillside. Although the hotel has been refurbished, many of the original features have been retained. We were delighted with their own colour schemes and the general standard of decor, and furniture which is comfortable and pretty, lending a cosy and friendly air to this historic farm house and country inn.

The restaurant maintains the high standards set by the hotel, and comes complete with large fireplace and original woodwork, with grand shutters opening out onto the lovely countryside. There is particular emphasis on local produce on the menu and the accent is definitely on quality. A fine selection of wines have been chosen to please even discerning palates, to accompany your meal.

The Glenisla Hotel has a history stretching back over four hundred years, and there is a comprehensive guide sheet available that tells of the many characters and stories associated with the Hotel and the community. One that we found especially intriguing was that during the refurbishment of the hotel, wall paintings were discovered and that these paintings are currently under analysis by the University of Dundee. Part of these paintings have been preserved behind glass and may be seen by the hotel guests. One of the subjects depicted is a rowan tree, which we were told was believed to be necessary in order to ward off witches!

The Glenisla Hotel

Within easy reach of the hotel are a wealth of activities which can be arranged for you including golf, hang gliding, riding, walking, fishing, cycling, clay pigeon shooting and rough shooting. Of course it would not do to forget to mention that you are only twenty minutes away from the ski slopes!

Our journey through Southern and Central Scotland is now drawing to a close, and our final excursion took us to the west through Forfar on the A94 and into the small town of Brechin. You will notice the distinctive local red sandstone that has been used to build much of this characterful town.

Brechin is perhaps best known for the small cathedral which today serves as a parish church. We noticed that the cathedral has a round tower, which is an unusual feature. In fact, there are only two such towers in Scotland. This tower has an Irish influence, and was built between AD990 and 1012 as a refuge for the clergy in times of invasion by the Northmen.

You may also notice that the door is some six feet above ground level! This makes it somewhat difficult to gain entry. The cathedral itself is actually eighty-six feet high, if you don't count the roof cap which was added last at a later date. The carvings inside also point to an Irish influence, and one that

275

we found fascinating was of the crucifixion, showing the legs of Christ uncrossed, in the Irish tradition.

Also built in the local sandstone is the **Northern Hotel,** which is a category B listed building dating from 1836. The hotel was formerly a coaching inn, and today still caters for travellers with seventeen well furnished en-suite bedrooms, all with their own tea and coffee making facilities, telephone, and colour television.

There are three bars in the hotel which are open to non-residents, one of which houses a pool table. The hotel also runs the grand restaurant here that dates from late 1800. It has beautiful cornicing and carvings coming down from the ceiling. The carvery has a speciality of Scottish roasts, and visitors may also choose from the a la carte menu.

Just nine miles from the sea, the hotel is in a good position for you to take advantage of the coast and the surrounding countryside. As well as Montrose on the coast, Aberdeen, Dundee and Perth are all within travelling distance.

There are many historic sites and buildings in the area, and **Brechin Museum** gives a penetrating insight into local history. Visitors staying at the Northern Hotel will also be well placed to take advantage of a wealth of sports available locally in the lovely countryside, including shooting, fishing, walking and golfing.

Northern Hotel

Now at our journey's end, we hope that you have enjoyed as we have the characters, stories and magic that makes this land so invigorating and enjoyable to visit. We have certainly learned much to interest us, and without doubt shall one day return again to the many friends we have made here and to the places we have learned to love and respect. We know that there are a multitude of places that we have omitted to write about but hopefully in the second edition of this book we will make amends for this.

Sundial - Glamis Castle

Reference Guide

to

Hotels, Guest Houses, Inns, Public Houses,

Self-catering Accommodation, Farm Accommodation,

Caravan and Camping Parks, Restaurants,

Riding Schools and Places of Interest

Details in this section are for guidance only.
For more information please contact the individual establishments
who will be only to pleased to help.

Berwickshire and East Lothian

Inns & Public Houses

Name Address	Map Ref.	Tel No.	Open	Hours	Accom.	Licensed	Children	Disabled	Rest'ant	Refresh-ments	Credit Cards	Pets	Entrance fee	Page
Canty's Brig Berwick-Upon-Tweed	2	0289 86255	All Year	Varied		*	*		*	*				4
The Castle Inn Hotel Greenlaw Berwickshire	5	03616 217	All Year	Varied	*	*	*		*	*	*			7
The Craw Inn Auchencrow Berwickshire	7	08907 61253	All Year	Varied		*	*	*	*	*	*			9
The Spirit Level School Road Coldingham	8	08907 71387	All Year	Varied	*	*	*		*	*				11

Hotels & Guest Houses

Name Address	Map Ref.	Tel No.	Open	Hours	Accom.	Licensed	Children	Disabled	Rest'ant	Refresh-ments	Credit Cards	Pets	Entrance fee	Page
The Queens Hotel Main Street Gullane, East Lothian	11	0620 842275	All Year		*	*	*		*	*	*			14

Restaurant

Name Address	Map Ref.	Tel No.	Open	Hours	Accom.	Licensed	Children	Disabled	Rest'ant	Refreshments	Credit Cards	Pets	Entrance fee	Page
Waterside Bistro Nungate Haddington	12	0620 825674	All Year	Varied		*	*		*	*	*			16

Places of Interest

Name Address	Map Ref.	Tel No.	Open	Hours	Accom.	Licensed	Children	Disabled	Rest'ant	Refreshments	Credit Cards	Pets	Entrance fee	Page
Berwick Barracks Off Church Street Berwick upon Tweed	1	0289 304493	Apr-Sep	Daily 10-6pm Tue-Sun 10-4pm										4
Coldstream Museum Market Square Coldstream	4	0890 2486	Whit-Sep	Mon, Fri Sun 2-5 Sat10-1				*						6
Daniel Smith Kilt Maker High Street Dunbar	10	0368 63992	All Year	Varied			*	*			*			13
Jim Clark Memorial Room Newton Street Duns	6	0361 82600 ext 36	Mar-Sep	Mon-Sat 10-1, 2-5 Sun 2-5pm			*	*						8
John Muir Country Park Dunbar	10				TELEPHONE FOR DETAILS									13
Manderston House Duns	6	0361 83450	Mid May-Sep	Thur-Sun Bank Hol Mon, May & Aug						*				9

Places of Interest

Name Address	Map Ref.	Tel No.	Open	Hours	Accom.	Licensed	Children	Disabled	Rest'ant	Refresh-ments	Credit Cards	Pets	Entrance fee	Page
Norham Castle Norham	3	028982 329	Apr-Sep	Daily 10-6 Tue-Sun 10-4pm										5
St Abbs Head Nature Reserve StAbbs	9	08907 71443	Apr-Jul	Varied					*					12

Roxburghshire

Inns & Public Houses

Name Address	Map Ref.	Tel No.	Open	Hours	Accom.	Licensed	Children	Disabled	Rest'ant	Refresh-ments	Credit Cards	Pets	Entrance fee	Page
Horse & Hounds Inn Bonchester	9	045086 645	All Year	Varied	*	*	*	*	*	*	*			38

Hotels & Guest Houses

Name Address	Map Ref.	Tel No.	Open	Hours	Accom.	Licensed	Children	Disabled	Rest'ant	Refresh-ments	Credit Cards	Pets	Entrance fee	Page
Hopehill House Off Mayfield Drive Hawick	5	0450 75042	All Year		*				*	*				30
Liddesdale Hotel Newcastleton Roxburghshire	10	03873 75255	All Year		*	*	*		*	*	*			39
Mansfield House Hotel Hawick	5	0450 73988	All Year		*	*			*	*	*			32
Spreadeagle Hotel 20 High Street Jedburgh	8	0835 62870	All Year		*	*			*	*				36
Sunlaws Hotel Heiton Kelso	2	05735 331	All Year		*	*	*	*	*	*	*			24

Caravan Park

Name Address	Map Ref.	Tel No.	Open	Hours	Accom.	Licensed	Children	Disabled	Rest'ant	Refresh-ments	Credit Cards	Pets	Entrance fee	Page
Bonchester Caravan Park, Bonchester Bridge, Hawick	9	0450 86676	Apr-Oct		*		*			*				37

Restaurants

Name Address	Map Ref.	Tel No.	Open	Hours	Accom.	Licensed	Children	Disabled	Rest'ant	Refresh-ments	Credit Cards	Pets	Entrance fee	Page
Copshaw Kitchens, North Heritage Street, Newcastleton	10	03873 75250	All Year	Wed-Mon		*	*	*	*	*	*			39
Dames Bistro, Hawick	5	0450 78441	All Year	9-5pm			*	*	*	*				31
The Old Smiddy, Melrose	4	089682 3171	All Year	9.30am-11pm		*	*		*	*				27

Places of Interest

Name Address	Map Ref.	Tel No.	Open	Hours	Accom.	Licensed	Children	Disabled	Rest'ant	Refresh-ments	Credit Cards	Pets	Entrance fee	Page
Abbotsford House, Abbotsford, Melrose	3	0896 2043	3rd Mon Mar-Oct	10-5pm Sun 2-5			*	*	*	*				26
Floors Castle, Roxburghshire	1	057383 23333	May-Sep	12.30-5pm		*	*	*	*	*				23

Places of Interest

Name Address	Map Ref.	Tel No.	Open	Hours	Accom.	Licensed	Children	Disabled	Rest'ant	Refresh-ments	Credit Cards	Pets	Entrance fee	Page
Kelso Abbey Bridge Street Kelso	1	031 244 3101	Apr-Sep Oct-Mar	9.30-7 Sun 2-7 9.30-4 Sun 2-4										21
Melrose Abbey Melrose	4	031 244 3101	Apr-Jul Oct-Mar	9.30-7 Sun 2-7 9.30-4 Sun 2-4			*	*						27
Melrose Station Crafts Palmer Place Melrose	4	089682 2546	All Year	10am-6pm		*	*	*	*	*	*			28
Scottish Academy of Flaconry Hawick	5	045086 666	TELEPHONE FOR DETAILS											33
Tom Scot Knitwear Denholm Hawick	6	0450 87531	All Year	10-12 noon 2-4.30pm			*	*			*			34
The Woodland Centre Jedburgh Roxburghshire	7	08353 306	Mar-Oct				*	*		*				35

Peeblesshire and Selkirkshire

Inns & Public Houses

Name Address	Map Ref.	Tel No.	Open	Hours	Accom.	Licensed	Children	Disabled	Rest'ant	Refresh-ments	Credit Cards	Pets	Entrance fee	Page
The Bridge Inn Galashiels Selkirkshire	4	0896 2397	All Year	Varied		*		*		*				50
Countryside Inn Kirnlaw Peebles	10	0721 20100	All Year	Varied	*	*	*		*	*				57
Tibbie Shiels St Mary's Loch Selkirk	1	0750 42234	All Year	Varied	*	*	*	*	*	*	*			45

Hotels & Guest Houses

Name Address	Map Ref.	Tel No.	Open	Hours	Accom.	Licensed	Children	Disabled	Rest'ant	Refresh-ments	Credit Cards	Pets	Entrance fee	Page
Caddon View Guest House Pirn Road Inner Leithen	6	0896 830208	Closed mid Jan to mid Feb		*		*	*		*				52
The Clovenford Hotel Clovenfords Galashiels	5	089685 203	All Year		*	*	*	*	*	*				51
Glen House Inner Leithen Peebleshire	7	0896 830210	All Year		*	*	*	*	*	*	*			54

Hotels & Guest Houses

Name Address	Map Ref.	Tel No.	Open	Hours	Accom.	Licensed	Children	Disabled	Rest'ant	Refreshments	Credit Cards	Pets	Entrance fee	Page
Philipburn House Selkirk	3	0750 20747	All Year	Varied	*	*	*	*	*	*	*			48
Tweed Bridge House Chambers Terrace Peebles	11	0721 20590	All Year	Varied	*	*	*		*	*	*			58

Caravan and Camping Parks

Name Address	Map Ref.	Tel No.	Open	Hours	Accom.	Licensed	Children	Disabled	Rest'ant	Refreshments	Credit Cards	Pets	Entrance fee	Page
Crossburn Caravan & Camping Park Edinburgh Road, Peebles	9	0721 20501	Apr-Oct		*		*			*	*			56

Restaurants

Name Address	Map Ref.	Tel No.	Open	Hours	Accom.	Licensed	Children	Disabled	Rest'ant	Refreshments	Credit Cards	Pets	Entrance fee	Page
Court House Coffee Shop Market Place Selkirk	3	0750 22058	All Year	9am-6pm		*	*		*	*				47

Places of Interest

Name / Address	Map Ref.	Tel No.	Open	Hours	Accom.	Licensed	Children	Disabled	Rest'ant	Refresh-ments	Credit Cards	Pets	Entrance fee	Page
Bowhill House, Nr Selkirk	2	0750 20732	House July, Grounds Apr-Aug	1-4.30 Sun 2-6 12-5, 12-5, Sun 2-6, cl Fri			*	*		*				46
Halliwells House, Halliwells Close, Market Place, Selkirk	3	0750 20096	Apr-Dec	Varied			*	*						48
Kailzie Gardens, Nr Peebles	8	0721 20007	End Mar-Oct	11-5.30			*	*						55
Neidpath Castle, Peebles	9	08757 021 or 0721 20333	Apr-Sep	11-5 Sun 1-5			*							59
Robert Smailes Printing Works, Innerleithen, Tweedale	6		Mid Summer-Oct	10-1 2-5 Sun 2-5										52
Selkirk Glass, Linglie Mill, Riverside Ind Est, Selkirk	3	0750 20954	All Year	Varied				*		*				48
Traquair House, Innerleithen	6	0896 030323	TELEPHONE FOR DETAILS						*	*				53
Waverney Mills Woollen Museum, Galashiels	4		TELEPHONE FOR DETAILS											50

Mid and West Lothian

Inns & Public Houses

Name Address	Map Ref.	Tel No.	Open	Hours	Accom.	Licensed	Children	Disabled	Rest'ant	Refreshments	Credit Cards	Pets	Entrance fee	Page
The Original Rosslyn Inn Main Street Roslin	6	031440 2734	All Year	Varied	*	*	*		*	*				74
The Railway Tavern Penicuik	7	0968 76802	All Year	Varied		*	*			*				75
The Sheep Heid Inn The Causeway Duddingston	2	031661 1020	All Year	Varied		*	*	*	*	*	*			67
The Sun Inn Lothian Brdige Dalkeith	4	031663 2456	All Year	Varied	*	*	*		*	*	*			72

Hotels & GuestHouses

Name Address	Map Ref.	Tel No.	Open	Hours	Accom.	Licensed	Children	Disabled	Rest'ant	Refreshments	Credit Cards	Pets	Entrance fee	Page
Hamilton Lodge Portobello	6	031669 0676	All Year		*	*	*	*	*	*				71
Houston House Uphall West Lothian	5	0506 853831	All Year		*	*	*	*	*	*	*			76

Places of Interest

Name / Address	Map Ref.	Tel No.	Open	Hours	Accom.	Licensed	Children	Disabled	Rest'ant	Refresh-ments	Credit Cards	Pets	Entrance fee	Page
Cannongate Tolbooth, Cannongate, Royal Mile, Edinburgh	1	031 225 242 Ext 6678				TELEPHONE FOR DETAILS								70
Dalkeith Country Park, Dalkeith, Nr Edinburgh	4	031 663 5684	End Mar-Oct	11-6pm			*	*						72
Edinburgh Castle, Castlehill, Edinburgh	1	031 244 3101	All Year	Varied										63
Lasswade Cottage, Lasswade	5					TELEPHONE FOR DETAILS								73
Palace Of Holyrood House, Edinburgh	1	031 556 7371	All Year	Varied										63
Rosslyn Chapel, Rosslyn	6	031 440 2159	Apr-Oct	10-5pm Sun 12-4.45										74
Royal Scottish Academy, Princess Streeet, Edinburgh	1	031 667 6671	All Year	Mon-Sat 10-9pm Sun 2-5pm				*						69

Lanarkshire and Renfrewshire

Inns & Public Houses

Name Address	Map Ref.	Tel No.	Open	Hours	Accom.	Licensed	Children	Disabled	Rest'ant	Refresh-ments	Credit Cards	Pets	Entrance fee	Page
Horsemill Inn & Woodyet Farm Denny	7	0324 822241	All Year	Varied		*	*	*	*	*	*			91

Restaurants

Name Address	Map Ref.	Tel No.	Open	Hours	Accom.	Licensed	Children	Disabled	Rest'ant	Refresh-ments	Credit Cards	Pets	Entrance fee	Page
La Nuit South Street Armadale, West Lothian	5	0501 30115	All Year	Varied		*	*		*	*				88

Places of Interest

Name Address	Map Ref.	Tel No.	Open	Hours	Accom.	Licensed	Children	Disabled	Rest'ant	Refresh-ments	Credit Cards	Pets	Entrance fee	Page
Biggar Gasworks Museum Biggar	2	031 225 7534	Jul-4 Sep	2-5pm Sun11-5pm										83
Calderglen Country Park Strathaven Road East Kilbride	4	03552 36644	All Year	10-dusk										85
Craignethan Castle Crossford	3	031 244 3101	Apr-Sep Oct-Mar	9.30-7 Sun 2-7 9.30-4 Sun 2-4			*							85

Places of Interest

Name / Address	Map Ref.	Tel No.	Open	Hours	Accom.	Licensed	Children	Disabled	Rest'ant	Refresh-ments	Credit Cards	Pets	Entrance fee	Page
Gladstone Museum North bach Road Biggar	2	0899 21050	Mar-Oct	10-12.30 Sun 2-5										83
Muiravonside Country Park Falkirk	6	0506 845311	All Year				*	*		*				89
Museum of Scottish Lead Mining Ind Goldscaur Road, Wanlockhead	1	065974 374	Mar-Sep	11-4pm										81
The White Hart Gallery High Street Biggar	3	0899 20214	All Year	Varied			*	*						83

Dumfriesshire

Inns & Public Houses

Name Address	Map Ref.	Tel No.	Open	Hours	Accom.	Licensed	Children	Disabled	Rest'ant	Refresh-ments	Credit Cards	Pets	Entrance fee	Page
The Station Inn Kirkpatrick Fleming	4	04618 627	All Year	Varied		*	*			*				98

Hotels & Guest Houses

Name Address	Map Ref.	Tel No.	Open	Hours	Accom.	Licensed	Children	Disabled	Rest'ant	Refresh-ments	Credit Cards	Pets	Entrance fee	Page
Auchen Castle Hotel Beattock Moffat Dumfries	7	06833 407	All Year		*	*	*		*	*	*			104
Barjarg Country Hotel Auldgirth Dumfriesshire	10	0848 31545	All Year		*	*	12+		*	*	*			109
The George Hotel Moniaive Dumfries	11	08482 203	All Year		*	*	*		*	*				110
Holm Park Holiday Centre Moffat	6	0683 20998	Apr-Dec	All Day	*	*	*	*	*	*	*			103
Lockerbie House Hotel & Restaurant Lockerbie, Dumfriesshire	5	05762 2610	All Year		*	*	*		*	*	*			100

Hotels & Guest Houses

Name Address	Map Ref.	Tel No.	Open	Hours	Accom.	Licensed	Children	Disabled	Rest'ant	Refresh-ments	Credit Cards	Pets	Entrance fee	Page
Northfield House Annan Dumfriesshire	2	04612 2851	Closed Jan		*			*		*				96

Caravan & Camping Parks

Name Address	Map Ref.	Tel No.	Open	Hours	Accom.	Licensed	Children	Disabled	Rest'ant	Refresh-ments	Credit Cards	Pets	Entrance fee	Page
Holm Park Holiday Centre Moffat	6	0683 20998	Apr-Dec	All Day	*	*	*			*	*			103
Queensberry Bay Caravan Park Annan Dumfriesshire	3	046 17205	Mar-Oct		*	*	*	*		*				97

Riding Centres

Name Address	Map Ref.	Tel No.	Open	Hours	Accom.	Licensed	Children	Disabled	Rest'ant	Refresh-ments	Credit Cards	Pets	Entrance fee	Page
Holm Park Holiday Centre Moffat	6	0683 20998	Apr-Dec	All Day	*		*	*			*			103

Places of Interest

Name / Address	Map Ref.	Tel No.	Open	Hours	Accom.	Licensed	Children	Disabled	Rest'ant	Refresh-ments	Credit Cards	Pets	Entrance fee	Page
Caerlaverlock Castle Nr Dumfries	9	031 244 3101	Apr-Sep Oct-Mar	9.30-7 Sun 2-7 9.30-4 Sun 2-4										107
Dramlanrig Castle Thornhill Sanquhar	12	0848 30248	T E L E P H O N E F O R D E T A I L S				*	*		*				112
Moffat Fishery Hammerlands Moffat	6	0683 21068	All Year	Varied				*		*			*	102
Moffat Museum Moffat	6	0683 20868	Easter week Whit-Oct	10.30-1 2.30-5			*							102
Old Blacksmiths Shop Visitors Centre Gretna Green	1	0461 38363 38224	All Year	Varied				*		*				95
Robert Burns Centre Old Town Mill Dumfries	8	0387 64808	Apr-Sep Oct-Mar	10-8 Sun 2-5 Tue-Sat 10-1, 2-5			*	*		*				106

Kircudbrightshire and Wigtownshire

Inns & Public Houses

Name Address	Map Ref.	Tel No.	Open	Hours	Accom.	Licensed	Children	Disabled	Rest'ant	Refresh-ments	Credit Cards	Pets	Entrance fee	Page
The Anvil Inn Kirkgunzeon Dumfries	4	038776 666	All Year	Varied		*	*			*				123
The Downshire Arms Stranraer	20	0776 2402	All Year	Varied	*	*	*		*	*				146
The Star Hotel Twynholm Kirkcudbrightshire	6	055 76279	All Year	Varied		*	*	*	*	*	*			130

Hotels & Guest Houses

Name Address	Map Ref.	Tel No.	Open	Hours	Accom.	Licensed	Children	Disabled	Rest'ant	Refresh-ments	Credit Cards	Pets	Entrance fee	Page
The Bank of Fleet High Street Gatehouse of Fleet, Castle Douglas	8	05574 302	All Year		*	*	*		*	*				131
Cairngill House Hotel Sandyhills Dalbeattie	3	038778 687	All Year		*	*	*		*	*				122
Castlewigg Hotel Nr Whithorn Wigtownshire	13	09885 213	All Year		*	*	*	*	*	*	*			138

Hotels & Guest Houses

Name Address	Map Ref.	Tel No.	Open	Hours	Accom.	Licensed	Children	Disabled	Rest'ant	Refresh-ments	Credit Cards	Pets	Entrance fee	Page
Corsemalzie Hotel Port William Newton Stewart Wigtownshire	12	0988 86254	All Year		*	*	*		*	*	*			136
The Eagle Hotel Port William Wigtownshire	12	09887 280	All Year		*	*	*		*	*	*			139
Hill of Burns Hotel Hill Street Creetown, Wigtownshire	11	067182 487	All Year		*	*	*		*	*				134
Knocknassie House Hotel Kirkclom Wigtownshire	19	0776 854217	All Year		*	*	*		*	*				145
Lochnaw Castle Leswalt By Stranraer Wigtownshire	18	077687 87227	All Year		*	*	*	*	*	*				143
Long Acre Manor Hotel Ernespie Road Castle Douglas	5	0556 3576	All Year		*	*	*		*	*				125
Mabie House Hotel Mabie Dumfries	1	0387 63188	All Year		*	*	*	*	*	*	*			118
Tigh-na-Mara Sandhead Wigtownshire	15	077683 210	All Year		*	*	*		*	*				141

Hotels & Guest Houses

Name Address	Map Ref.	Tel No.	Open	Hours	Accom.	Licensed	Children	Disabled	Rest'ant	Refresh-ments	Credit Cards	Pets	Entrance fee	Page
Woodburn House Haugh of Urr Castle Douglas	4	055 666217	All Year		*		*			*				124

Self Catering Accommodation

Barend Holiday Centre Sandyhills Dalbeattie	3	038778 663	All Year		*	*	*	*	*	*				121

Farmhouse Accommodation

Barncrosh Farm Castle Douglas	6	055668 216	All Year		*		*	*	*	*				127

Farmhouse Accommodation

Creebridge Caravan Park Newton Stewart Wigtownshire	10	0671 2432	Mar-Oct		*		*	*		*				133

Restaurants

Name Address	Map Ref.	Tel No.	Open	Hours	Accom.	Licensed	Children	Disabled	Rest'ant	Refresh-ments	Credit Cards	Pets	Entrance fee	Page
The Alexandra Restaurant Stranraer	20	0776 2149	All Year	9am-9pm			*	*	*	*	*			147
Rendezvous Restaurant King Street Castle Douglas	5	0556 2969	All Year	Tues-Sun		*	*	*	*	*				126

Places of Interest

Name Address	Map Ref.	Tel No.	Open	Hours	Accom.	Licensed	Children	Disabled	Rest'ant	Refresh-ments	Credit Cards	Pets	Entrance fee	Page
Arbigland Gardens Kirkbean	2	038 788 283	May-Sep	Tue, Thur Sun 2-6pm			*	*		*				
Ardwell House Ardwell	17	077686 227	Mar-Oct	1-6pm										143
Galloway Deer Museum Nr New Galloway	9	06442 285	Apr-Sep	10-6pm			*	*						133
Castle Kennedy Nr Stranraer	20	0776 2024	Apr-Sep	10-5pm			*	*		*				147
Glenluce Abbey Glenluce	14	031244 3101	Apr-Sep Oct-Mar	9.30-7 Sun 2-7 9.30-4 Sun 2-4				*						140

Places of Interest

Name Address	Map Ref.	Tel No.	Open	Hours	Accom.	Licensed	Children	Disabled	Rest'ant	Refresh- ments	Credit Cards	Pets	Entrance fee	Page
Lochnaw Castle Leswalt By Stranraer	18	077687 227	All Year	Varied	*	*	*		*	*				144
Logan Botanical Gardens Nr Port Logan	16	077686 231	Apr-Sep	10-5pm										142
MacLellan's Castle Kirkcudbrightshire	7	031 244 3111	All Year	Varied										129
Shambellie House Museum of Costume New Abbey	1	031 225 7534	May-Sep	Varied										118
Sweetheart Abbey New Abbey	1		Apr-Sep Oct-Mar	9.30-7 Sun 2-7 9.30-4 Sun 2-4				*						117
Threave Gardens Nr Castle Douglas	5	0556 2575	All Year	9.30- Sunset										126

Ayrshire

Inns & Public Houses

Name Address	Map Ref.	Tel No.	Open	Hours	Accom.	Licensed	Children	Disabled	Rest'ant	Refresh-ments	Credit Cards	Pets	Entrance fee	Page
The Market Inn Castlehill Road Ayr	11	0292 262411	All Year	11am-11pm		*	*	*	*	*				164
The Stair Inn Bymauchline	10	0292 591562	All Year	12 noon 12pm	*	*	*	*		*	*			163

Hotels & Guest Houses

Name Address	Map Ref.	Tel No.	Open	Hours	Accom.	Licensed	Children	Disabled	Rest'ant	Refresh-ments	Credit Cards	Pets	Entrance fee	Page
Anchorage Hotel Temple Hill Troon	12	0292 317448	All Year		*	*	*	*	*	*	*			167
Culzean Castle Culzean	4	06556 274	Apr-Oct		*	*	*	*	*	*	*			155
Elderslie Hotel Broomfields Largs	15	0475 686460	All Year		*	*	*	*	*	*	*			174
Kirkton Jean's Kirkoswald Ayrshire	6	06556 220	All Year		*	*	*	*	*	*	*			159

Hotels & Guest Houses

Name Address	Map Ref.	Tel No.	Open	Hours	Accom.	Licensed	Children	Disabled	Rest'ant	Refresh-ments	Credit Cards	Pets	Entrance fee	Page
Kings Arms Hotel Barr South Ayrshire	1	046586 230	All Year		*	*	*		*	*				152
Southfield Hotel Girvan Ayrshire	3	0465 4222	All Year		*	*	*		*	*	*			154
Sorn Hotel Main Street Sorn	8	08907 71387	All Year		*	*	*		*	*	*			161

Caravan & Camping Parks

Name Address	Map Ref.	Tel No.	Open	Hours	Accom.	Licensed	Children	Disabled	Rest'ant	Refresh-ments	Credit Cards	Pets	Entrance fee	Page
Croft Head Caravan Park Ayr	11	0292 263516	Mar-Oct		*	*	*	*		*				166

Restaurants

Name Address	Map Ref.	Tel No.	Open	Hours	Accom.	Licensed	Children	Disabled	Rest'ant	Refresh-ments	Credit Cards	Pets	Entrance fee	Page
Laigh Milton Mill Gatehead Kilmarnock	13	0563 34230	All Year	Varied	*	*	*	*	*	*	*			168

Places of Interest

Name Address	Map Ref.	Tel No.	Open	Hours	Accom.	Licensed	Children	Disabled	Rest'ant	Refreshments	Credit Cards	Pets	Entrance fee	Page
Ailsa Craig Island in Firth of Forth	2	0465 3219				TELEPHONE FOR DETAILS 065 56 646								151
Burns House Museum Castle Street Mauchline	9	0290 50045	Mar-Oct	Mon-Sat 11-12.30 1.30-5.30 Sun 2-5pm			*	*						162
Cathcartson Visitor Centre Dalmellington	7	0292 550339 550426	Mar-Oct	2-5pm				*						160
Crossraguel Abbey Maybole	17	031 244 3101	All Year	Varied			*	*						159
Dean Castle Country Park Kilmarnock	14	05632 6401	All Year				*	*		*			*	170
Dick Institute Elmbank Avenue Off London Road, Kilmarnock	14	0563 26401	Apr-Sep	Varied			*	*						171
Kelburn Castle Largs	15	0475 568685	Mar-Mid Oct			TELEPHONE FOR DETAILS								175
Land of Burn's Alloway	5	0292 42700	All Year			TELEPHONE FOR DETAILS								157

Places of Interest

Name Address		Tel No.	Open	Hours	Accom.	Licensed	Children	Disabled	Rest'ant	Refresh-ments	Credit Cards	Pets	Entrance fee	Page
Scottish Maritime Museum Laird Forge Gothrie Road, Irvine	16	0294 78283	Mid Apr-Mid Oct											171

The Isles of Arran, Cumbrae and Bute

Hotels & Guest Houses

Name Address	Map Ref.	Tel No.	Open	Hours	Accom.	Licensed	Children	Disabled	Rest'ant	Refreshments	Credit Cards	Pets	Entrance fee	Page
Ardmory House Hotel, Ardbeg, Rothesay, Isle of Bute	4	0700 2346	All Year		*	*	*		*	*	*			182
Argylle Private Hotel, Rothesay, Isle of Bute	4	0700 2424	All Year		*	*	*		*	*				183
Black Rock Guest House, Corrie, Isle of Arran	7	077081 282	Mar-Oct		*		*	*	*	*				191
Lochranza Hotel, Lochranza, Isle of Arran	6	0770 83223	All Year		*	*	*	*	*	*	*			190
Pirates Cove, Brodick, Isle of Arran	5	0770 2438	Mar-Oct		*	*	*		*	*				187

Riding Centre

Name Address	Map Ref.	Tel No.	Open	Hours	Accom.	Licensed	Children	Disabled	Rest'ant	Refreshments	Credit Cards	Pets	Entrance fee	Page
Kingarth Trekking Centre Kilchattan Bay Isle of Bute	4	0700 83627	All Year	10am-5pm			*	*					*	183

Places of Interest

Name Address	Map Ref.	Tel No.	Open	Hours	Accom.	Licensed	Children	Disabled	Rest'ant	Refreshments	Credit Cards	Pets	Entrance fee	Page
Ardencraig Gardens & Museum Rothesay Isle of Bute	2	0700 4225	May-Sep	Mon-Fri 9-4.30 Sat-Sun 1-4.30				*		*				183
Brodick Castle Brodick Isle of Arran	5	0770 2202	Apr-Sep	Varied			*	*		*			*	185
Bute Museum Stuart Street Rothesay	2	0700 3380	All Year	Varied			*	*						182
Isle of Arran Heritage Museum Brodick	5	0770 2636	May-Sep	Mon-Fri 10-1pm 2-5pm			*	*		*				188
Museum of Cumbraes Garrison House, Millport Isle of Cumbraes	1	0475 530741	Jun-Sep	Tue-Sat 10-4.30			*	*						181
Rothesay Castle Rothesay	3	031 244 3101	All Year	Varied										183

Strathclyde

Inns & Public Houses

Name / Address	Map Ref.	Tel No.	Open	Hours	Accom.	Licensed	Children	Disabled	Rest'ant	Refreshments	Credit Cards	Pets	Entrance fee	Page
Whistlefield Inn, Loch Eck, By Dunoon	4	0369 86250	All Year	Varied	*	*	*	*	*	*	*			203

Hotels & Guest Houses

Name / Address	Map Ref.	Tel No.	Open	Hours	Accom.	Licensed	Children	Disabled	Rest'ant	Refreshments	Credit Cards	Pets	Entrance fee	Page
Anchorage Guest House, Balloch, Dumbartonshire	2	0389 53336	All Year		*	*	*	*	*	*				199
Crinan Hotel, Lochgliphead, Argyll	10	054683 261	All Year		*	*	*	*	*	*	*			210
Dunderave Castle, Inveraray, Argyll	8	0499 2009	All Year		*	*	*	*	*	*	*			209
Enmore Hotel, Dunoon, Argyll	6	0369 2230	All Year		*	*	*	*	*	*	*			205
The Glendaruel Hotel, Glendaruel, Argyll	7	036982 274	All Year		*	*	*	*	*	*	*			205

Restaurants

Name Address	Map Ref.	Tel. No.	Open	Hours	Accom.	Licensed	Children	Disabled	Rest'ant	Refreshments	Credit Cards	Pets	Entrance fee	Page
Bouquet Garni & Herbs Wine Bar Lochgoil Head Argyll	3	03013 206	Seasonal	12-3pm 6-11pm		*			*	*	*			202

Places of Interest

Name Address	Map Ref.	Tel. No.	Open	Hours	Accom.	Licensed	Children	Disabled	Rest'ant	Refreshments	Credit Cards	Pets	Entrance fee	Page
Argyll Wildlife Park Dalchenna Inveraray	9		All Year	9.30-7			*			*				201
Auchindrain Museum Nr Inveraray	9	04995 235	Apr-Sep	Varied			*	*						209
Carrick Castle Lochgoilhead	3	0698 66111 Ext 2245	All Year	Varied			*	*						202
Dumbarton Castle Dumbarton	1	031 244 3101	Apr-Oct Oct-Mar	9.30-7 Sun 2-7 9.30-4 Sun 2-4										199
Strone House Strone Argyll	5	03698 4355	All Year	9-5.30			*	*			*			204
Younger Botanical Gardens Loch Ech Dunoon	4	0369 6261	Apr-Oct	10-6pm				*						204

From Campsie Fells to the Forest of Atholl

Inns & Public Houses

Name Address	Map Ref.	Tel No.	Open	Hours	Accom.	Licensed	Children	Disabled	Rest'ant	Refresh-ments	Credit Cards	Pets	Entrance fee	Page
Ballinluig Inn Ballinluig Perthshire	16	079682 242	All Year	Varied	*	*	*		*	*	*			234
Meadow Inn Burrell Street Crieff, Perthshire	12	0764 3261	All Year	Varied	*	*	*		*	*				230

Hotels & Guest Houses

Name Address	Map Ref.	Tel No.	Open	Hours	Accom.	Licensed	Children	Disabled	Rest'ant	Refresh-ments	Credit Cards	Pets	Entrance fee	Page
Airdanair Hotel Pitlochry Perthshire	15	0796 2266	All Year		*	*	*		*	*	*			235
Arden House Callander Perthshire	5	0877 30235	Feb-Nov		*	*	*		*	*				220
Bruar Falls Hotel Pitlochry Perthshire	18	079683 243	All Year		*	*	*	*	*	*	*			240
Gilmore Cottage Guest House Kinloch Rannoch Perthshire	19	08822 2218	All Year		*		*		*	*				241

Hotels & Guest Houses

Name / Address	Map Ref.	Tel No.	Open	Hours	Accom.	Licensed	Children	Disabled	Rest'ant	Refreshments	Credit Cards	Pets	Entrance fee	Page
Cross Keys Hotel, Kippen, Stirlingshire	2	078687 293	All Year		*	*	*	*	*	*	*			216
Druimuan House, Killiecrankie, Perthshire	17	0796 3214	Apr-Nov		*		*		*	*				238
Firs Guest House, St Andrews Crescent, Blairatholl	18	0796 81256	Feb-Nov		*	*	*	*	*	*				239
Invervey Hotel, Tyndrum, Crianlarich, Perthshire	9	08384 219	All Year		*	*	*	*	*	*	*			225
Talladh-a-Bheithe Lodge, Loch Rannoch, Pitlochry	19	08823 203	Apr-Nov		*	*	*	*	*	*				242
Topps Farm Guest House, Denny, Stirlingshire	1	0324 822471	All Year		*	*	*		*	*				215
Weem Hotel, Aberfeldy, Perthshire	13	0887 20381	All Year		*	*	*	*	*	*				231

Self Catering Accommodation

Name Address	Map Ref.	Tel No.	Open	Hours	Accom.	Licensed	Children	Disabled	Rest'ant	Refreshments	Credit Cards	Pets	Entrance fee	Page
W J & C S R Christie Ltd Loch Dochart Estate Crianlarich	8	08383 274	All Year		*		*	*						224
The Steading Balquhidder Lochearnhad	7	08774 218	All Year		*		*	*						222

Caravan & Camping Sites

Name Address	Map Ref.	Tel No.	Open	Hours	Accom.	Licensed	Children	Disabled	Rest'ant	Refreshments	Credit Cards	Pets	Entrance fee	Page
Faskally Caravan Park Pitlochry Perthshire	17	08823 2007	All Year		*	*	*	*	*	*				237
Glendochart Caravan Park Luib Crianlarich Perthshire	8	05672 637	Mar-Oct		*	*	*	*	*	*				223
Immervoulin Caravan Park Strathyre Perthshire	6	08774 285	Apr-Oct		*		*	*		*				221

Restaurants

Name Address	Map Ref.	Tel No.	Open	Hours	Accom.	Licensed	Children	Disabled	Rest'ant	Refreshments	Credit Cards	Pets	Entrance fee	Page
Rod and Reel Crianlarich Perthshire	8	08383 271	All Year	Varied		*	*		*	*	*			224

Restaurants

Name Address	Map Ref	Tel No.	Open	Hours	Accom.	Licensed	Children	Disabled	Rest'ant	Refresh-ments	Credit Cards	Pets	Entrance fee	Page
Harts Restaurant & Coffee Pot, High Street, Crieff, Perthshire	12	0294 78283	Mid Apr-Mid Oct	Varied		*	*	*	*	*	*			229
The Famous Capercaillie Restaurant, Dochart Falls, Killin, Perthshire	11	05672 355	All Year	Varied		*	*	*	*	*	*			226

Places of Interest

Name Address	Map Ref	Tel No.	Open	Hours	Accom.	Licensed	Children	Disabled	Rest'ant	Refresh-ments	Credit Cards	Pets	Entrance fee	Page
Ben Lawers, Killin	10	05672 397	Mar-Sep	Varied			*	*						226
Blair Castle, Blair Atholl	18	079681	Apr-	10-6			*	*		*				238
Doune Motor Museum, Doune, Nr Stirling	4	0786 841203	Apr-Oct	10-5			*	*		*				220
Dowally Craft Centre & Restaurant, By Pitlochry, Perthshire	15	03502 604	All Year	10am-6pm		*		*	*					233
Edradour Distillery, Pitlochry	15	0796 3524			TELEPHONE FOR DETAILS									235

Places of Interest

Name Address	Map Ref	Tel No.	Open	Hours	Accom.	Licensed	Children	Disabled	Rest'ant	Refresh-ments	Credit Cards	Pets	Entrance fee	Page
Highland Horn & Deerskin Centre Dunkeld Perthshire	14	03502 569	All Year	9am-5.30pm			*	*			*			232
Second Thoughts Craft Shop The Stable Galvelmore Street, Crieff	12	0764 4480	All Year	10am-6pm			*	*						228
Stirling Castle Stirling	3	031 244 3101	All Year	Varied			*	*						216

Tayside to Fife

Inns & Public Houses

Name Address	Map Ref.	Tel No.	Open	Hours	Accom.	Licensed	Children	Disabled	Rest'ant	Refresh-ments	Credit Cards	Pets	Entrance fee	Page
The Blackford Inn, Blackford, Perthshire	14	076402 336	All Year	Varied	*	*	*		*	*				267
The Old Rectory Inn, Dysart, Kirkaldy, Fife	5	0592 51211	All Year	Varied		*	*		*	*	*			255
Stables Inn, Alyth, Perthshire	16	08283 2236	All Year	Varied		*	*		*	*				274
White Horse Inn, North William Street, Perth	9	0738 28479	All Year	Varied	*	*	*	*	*	*	*			263

Hotels & Guest Houses

Name Address	Map Ref.	Tel No.	Open	Hours	Accom.	Licensed	Children	Disabled	Rest'ant	Refresh-ments	Credit Cards	Pets	Entrance fee	Page
Aberdour Hotel, High Street, Aberdour	4	0383 860325	All Year		*	*	*		*	*	*			253
Blair Logie Hotel, Blair Logie, Stirling	1	0259 61441	All Year		*	*	*		*	*	*			247

Hotels & Guest Houses

Name Address	Map Ref.	Tel No.	Open	Hours	Accom.	Licensed	Children	Disabled	Rest'ant	Refresh-ments	Credit Cards	Pets	Entrance fee	Page
Collearn Hotel Auchterader	11	0764 63553	All Year		*	*	*		*	*	*			266
Dunallan Guest House Pitcullen Crescent Perth	9	0738 22551	All Year		*		*		*	*				262
Eden House Hotel Cupar Fife	8	0334 52510	All Year		*	*	*		*	*	*			259
Glenislar Hotel Glenislar Nr Blair Gowrie Angus	17	057582 223	All Year		*	*	*	*	*	*	*			275
Kinloch House Hotel Blair Gowrie Perthshire	14	025084 237	All Year		*	*	*	*	*	*	*			271
Mullion House Coupar Angus Road Rosemount, Blair Gowrie	14	0250 2825	All Year		*	*	15+			*				270
Northern Hotel Clerk Street Brechin, Angus	18	03562 2156 5505	All Year		*	*	*		*	*	*			276
Rescobie Hotel Valley Drive Leslie, Fife	6	0592 742143	All Year		*	*	*	*.	*	*	*			255

315

Self Catering Accommodation

Name Address	Map Ref.	Tel No.	Open	Hours	Accom.	Licensed	Children	Disabled	Rest'ant	Refreshments	Credit Cards	Pets	Entrance fee	Page
Altamount Chalets Blair Gowrie Perthshire	14	0250 3324	All Year		*		*	*						272
Cloag Farm Cottages Cloag Farm Methven, Perthshire	12	073884 239	All Year		*		*	*						268
Duncrub Holidays Dalreoch Dunning, Perth	10	076484 368	All Year		*		*	*						265

Restaurants

Name Address	Map Ref.	Tel No.	Open	Hours	Accom.	Licensed	Children	Disabled	Rest'ant	Refreshments	Credit Cards	Pets	Entrance fee	Page
Alanti Restaurant Auchtermuchty Fife	7	0337 28561	All Year	Varied			*	*	*	*				257
The Coach House Restaurant North Port Perth	9	0738 27950	All Year	Varied		*	*	*	*	*	*			264
Powmill Farm Milk Bar Powmill Kinross	2	05774 376	All Year	Varied		*	*	*	*	*				249
The Grouse & Claret Restaurant Heatheryford Kinross	3	05776 64212	All Year	Varied		*	*	*	*	*	*			249

316

Riding Centres

Name Address	Map Ref.	Tel No.	Open	Hours	Accom.	Licensed	Children	Disabled	Rest'ant	Refresh-ments	Credit Cards	Pets	Entrance fee	Page
Caledonian Equestrian Centre Pitskelly Balbeggie	13	08214 426	All Year		*		*	*		*				269

Places of Interest

Name Address	Map Ref.	Tel No.	Open	Hours	Accom.	Licensed	Children	Disabled	Rest'ant	Refresh-ments	Credit Cards	Pets	Entrance fee	Page
Colzie Hill Recreation Auchtermuchty Fife	7	0337	All Year	Varied			14+			*			*	257
Fairmaids House North Port Perth	9	0738 25976	All Year	10am-5pm			*	*		*	*			261
Glamis Castle Glamis	15	030784 242	Mid Apr-Mid Oct	12-5.30pm			*			*				273
Lochleven Mill Shop Lochleven Mills Kinross	3	0577 63521	All Year	9am-5.30pm			*	*		*	*			251
Perth Art Gallery & Museum George Street Perth	9	0738 32488	All Year	Mon-Sat 10-1pm 2-5pm				*						264
Royal Research Ship Victory Victoria Docks Dundee	19	0382 201175	Apr May Sept	Varied			*							260

317

Places of Interest

Name Address	Map Ref.	Tel No.	Open	Hours	Accom.	Licensed	Children	Disabled	Rest'ant	Refresh-ments	Credit Cards	Pets	Entrance fee	Page
Scottish Deer Centre Nr Cupar	8	033781 391	May-Oct Oct-May	10-6pm 10-4pm			*			*				259

A - Z Index

to

Cities, Towns, Villages and Hamlets

Index

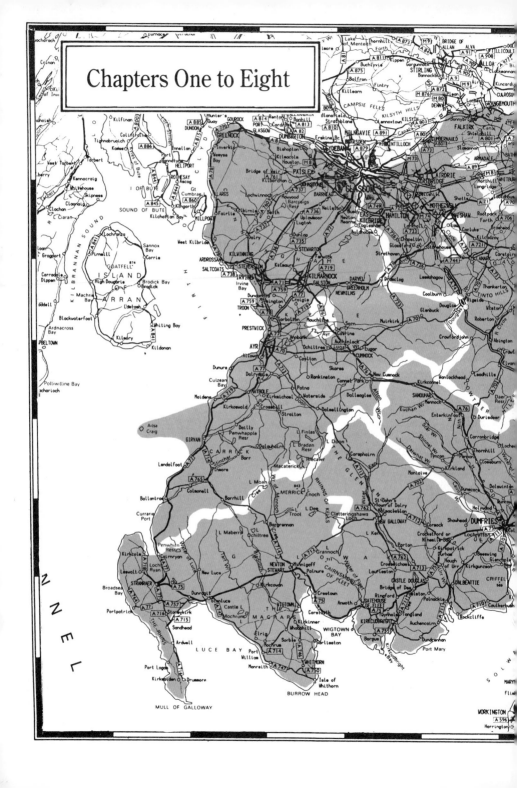

Chapters One to Eight

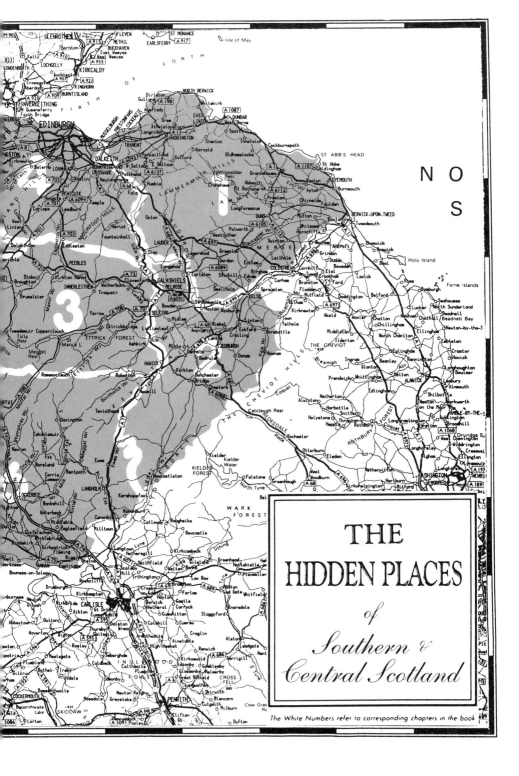

THE

HIDDEN PLACES

of

Southern &

Central Scotland

The White Numbers refer to corresponding chapters in the book

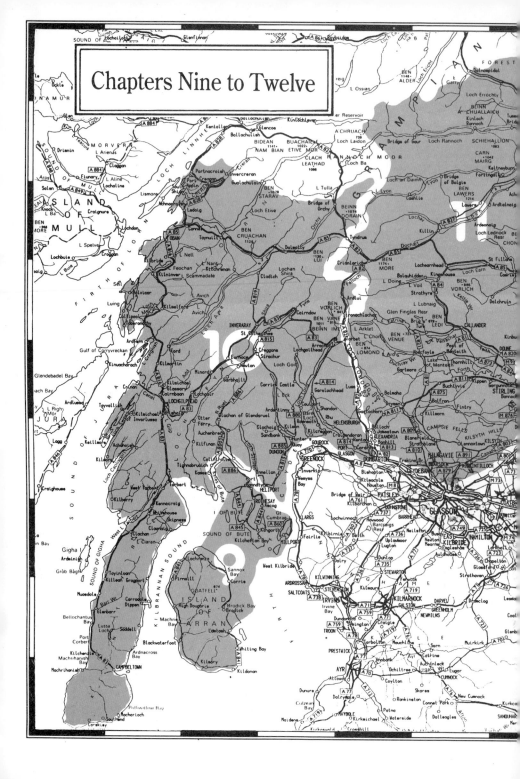

Chapters Nine to Twelve

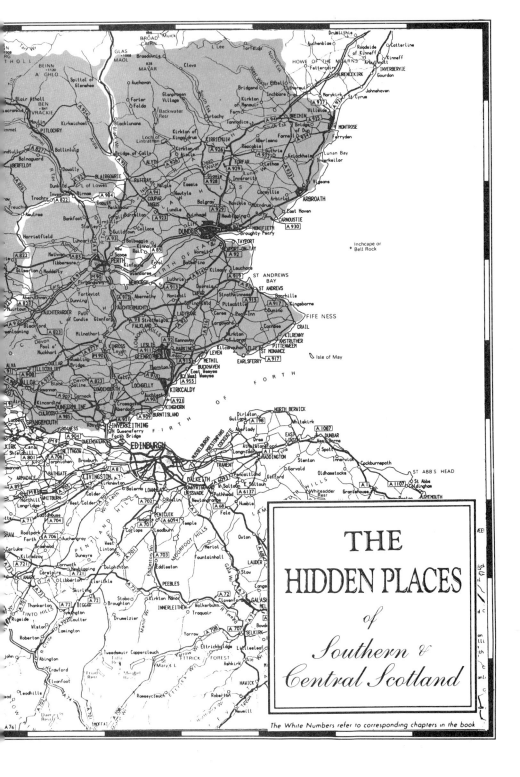

THE
HIDDEN PLACES
of
Southern &
Central Scotland

The White Numbers refer to corresponding chapters in the book

THE
HIDDEN PLACES

If you would like to have any of the titles currently available in this series, please complete this coupon and send to:

M & M Publishing
Hammerain House
Hookstone Avenue
Harrogate
HG2 8ER

Somerset, Avon and Dorset	☐ £ 5.90 inc. p&p
Norfolk & Suffolk	☐ £ 5.90 inc. p&p
Yorkshire South, East & West	☐ £ 5.90 inc. p&p
Devon and Cornwall	☐ £ 5.90 inc. p&p
North Yorkshire	☐ £ 5.90 inc. p&p
Cumbria	☐ £ 5.90 inc. p&p
Southern and Central Scotland	☐ £ 5.90 inc. p&p
Sussex	☐ £ 5.90 inc. p&p
Hampshire and the Isle of Wight	☐ £ 5.90 inc. p&p
Set of any Five	☐£ 25.90 inc. p&p

Please tick to receive further information about future titles ☐

NAME ....

ADDRESS ....

....

TEL. No. (Daytime) ....

Please make cheques/postal orders payable to:
M & M Publishing Ltd.
Access/Visa/Barclaycard (please delete) Card No.

Expiry date ....

Signature ....

M&M
Publishing Limited

Dear Reader,

We have enjoyed compiling this book. Constantly have we been amazed at the places we have visited. It brought home to us how little we knew of this county of ours. We hope you too have found the book pleasurable and informative.

It would be very helpful to hear from you, the reader, of any interesting places that we have not mentioned and that will add to the enjoyment of the next edition. We will be happy to repay this kindness, by sending you a complimentary copy of any one of the books in this series you may care to choose.

Joy David.

Please write to:

Joy David,
M & M Publishing Ltd.
Dolphin House, Sutton Harbour, Plymouth PL4 0DW.

Notes

You may like to use this page to make your own notes.

Notes

You may like to use this page to make your own notes.

Notes

You may like to use this page to make your own notes.

Notes

You may like to use this page to make your own notes.

Notes

You may like to use this page to make your own notes.

Notes

You may like to use this page to make your own notes.

Notes

You may like to use this page to make your own notes.